The Roman Empire unc

£8.99
(22)
HIST

The First Tourist

Travels in search of Saint Helena

Jonathan Hibbs

© Jonathan Hibbs 2005

Reproductions of coins in the plate section by kind permission
of the Rheinisches Landesmuseum Trier

ISBN 0-9551149-0-x
ISBN 978-0-9551149-0-8

Published by Jonathan Hibbs
Typeset by Regent Typesetting
Printed by in Great Britain by Antony Rowe Ltd
Chippenham, Wilts

To my father
Derek Melbourne Hibbs
1924–2004

Preface

FOR MORE THAN 1,500 years she was a household name. Her story was the received wisdom of popular history, as much a part of everyday life in the Christian world as the Gospel truth itself.

From the Pope to the humblest peasant, everyone in Christendom knew how Helena, elderly mother of the Roman emperor Constantine, had travelled to the Holy Land and miraculously discovered the cross on which Jesus was crucified.

Today the claim, and the grotesque cult of relics that it spawned, is acutely embarrasing to the modern Roman Catholic Church. A legend that was once such common currency that many ordinary people in this country actually believed Helena was British, is now almost forgotten.

Yet thousands of tourists still travel to the Middle East to visit the historic sites in Bethlehem and Jerusalem that tradition says Helena identified as the places where Jesus was born and died.

Having encountered the tale on one such trip in the winter of 1992/3, I began to investigate the rise and fall of this enigmatic Roman empress. With the intention of following in the footsteps of Helena's own pilgrimage in the year 327, I set out to uncover the facts behind the fiction that grew up around her memory.

Who was this mysterious woman who became the role model for a religion? Was she a pioneering feminist in her own right, the inventor of archaeology and populariser of foreign travel? Or the unwitting pawn of her royal son and the early church fathers, who manipulated her simple beliefs for higher political and theological purposes?

The First Tourist was conceived as a title for a contemporary travelogue, starting at the parish of Holy Cross in the Lancashire town of St Helens, and ending in the Church of the Holy Sepulchre at Jerusalem. Most of the visits to the locations in the story took place between 1995 and 2000, not necessarily in the order in which they appear in the text, and I wrote about some of them at the time for my then employer, *The Daily Telegraph*.

As I started writing, I also kept on reading, and the project swiftly became an historical detective inquiry. Every published work I consulted threw up a host of other references, and I spent many happy hours in the British Library tracking them down. Almost by accident, I discovered my light-hearted examination of an old and discredited tradition was about to throw a new and unexpected light on the continuing controversy about the origins of Christianity. So the final product describes a personal journey into a fascinating past, at the expense of a few detours down the lesser-known byways of revealed religion.

As a book, therefore, *The First Tourist* may well fall between several stools. The tone may be too irreverent for readers of a devout disposition. The personal touch may be too intrusive for academics to take the research seriously. And some of the findings may be too remote or irrelevant for a popular audience.

The work has been a long time in gestation – a hobby-horse reined in by the demands of a career in journalism and public relations – and I take all responsibility for its shortcomings. However, I would like to thank all those whose enthusiasm, generosity and scholarship contributed to its birth.

Unlike some authors, I cannot rehearse a long list of librarians, editors and researchers who were aware they were taking part in a significant literary event. Nevertheless, I have endeavoured to record in the footnotes all those many published sources from whom I gleaned information, captured images and borrowed ideas.

In particular I would like to thank my mother, Mary, for reading an early version of the manuscript and making many valuable suggestions about its content. I would also like to express my gratitude to Lesley Exton, who brought her formidable forensic skills to bear on the task of proof-reading and sub-editing, and forged a raw text into a recognisable book.

Finally, I would like to record how indebted I am to my partner, Vicki Chapman, not only for her forbearance of my obsession with another woman, but also for accompanying me throughout this journey of discovery. Vicki gave me the faith to keep going in the face of distractions and disappointments. With characteristic determination, she ultimately ensured that this project came to fruition. I am more grateful to her than words can articulate.

Contents

PROLOGUE

Bethlehem

'If any want to become my followers, let them deny themselves and take up their cross and follow me.'

Gospel according to St Mark[1]

PEACE ON EARTH was in short supply that Christmas Day, and there was precious little goodwill between the two priests squaring up for a confrontation over one of the most sacred sites of Christendom. For one God-awful moment, I thought the black-bearded Orthodox monk and the brown-robed Franciscan friar were going to come to blows – on the spot in Bethlehem where Jesus Christ is said to have been born.

They were yelling and gesticulating furiously at each other in an irreverent spat about who had the right of way. Admittedly, conditions were particularly cramped in the narrow confines of the Grotto of the Nativity. Two narrow, twisting staircases led down to the tiny underground crypt, and the angry clerics could not agree which was the entrance and which was the exit.

It was the friar's fault. He had spotted the queue of tourists, amongst whom I was patiently waiting, and promptly took his party of Italian pilgrims down the other side. By the time I squeezed into the crush beneath the Basilica, the Italians were singing hymns, praising the Lord, and sorely testing the patience of the Greeks already inside and trying to get out. As tempers frayed, I caught a brief glimpse of a hole in the ground, marked by a silver starburst, underneath an altar table so low that suppliants were forced to kneel and humbly prostrate themselves even to read the legend: *Hic De Virgine Maria Iesus Christus Natus Est.*

There was just enough elbow room to snatch a photograph across the sea of bobbing heads, whose owners were crossing themselves before a life-size model of the nativity scene in an alcove. Beyond the crowds was the entrance to an ancient complex of underground workings where groups of clergy had set up altars in the tombs and cells of saints and hermits for a whole series of underground religious services. I wriggled free, thinking blasphemous thoughts about whether hell was being incarcerated in a cave with several self-satisfied Christian tour groups wearing crosses on their kiss-me-quick-style hats. It was more like the January sales than Christmas.

The three great Christian denominations – Roman Catholic, Greek Orthodox, and Armenian Orthodox – jealously guard their custodianship of the holy places. While the world agonises over the continuing struggle for territorial supremacy on the West Bank between Arab and Jew, locals still recall the vicious fist fight that broke out in 1984 between rival Greek and Armenian caretakers for the right to clean the Bethlehem shrine. Yet that was as nothing compared with the April day in 1873 when an armed mob of brigands invaded the grotto of the Nativity, attacked and wounded eight attendant Franciscans, and set about sacking the crib. As the furious Latins blamed Greek perfidy, the Turkish authorities were forced to post an armed guard to maintain order.[2]

Nevertheless, the minor incident I witnessed put into perspective the sombre seasonal message delivered by Monseigneur Michel Sabbah, the Latin Patriarch of Jerusalem, from the pulpit of the neighbouring St Catherine's Cathedral earlier that Christmas morning. Warning about the dangers of religious fundamentalism and 'increased aggression' in the name of God, he said: 'We are still in need of a saviour here in our land. Peace and justice have not yet been restored.'[3]

The Basilica of the Nativity claims to be the oldest functioning church in the world, but little now remains of the building erected in 327 on the orders of Constantine the Great under the supervision of his mother, Helena, who was visiting Palestine at the time. It was spared the Persian invasion of 614, which obliterated most Christian shrines in the Holy Land – reputedly because the rampaging general Shahrbaraz was stopped sharply in his tracks when he saw a mosaic over the door. This portrayed the three Wise Men of the East, and the heathen warrior was quite disarmed by the sight of them dressed in the characteristic oriental robes of his native land. Yet with the alternating decay and restoration of intervening centuries, fragments of patterned paving are all that survive from the original structure. They are now visible beneath huge trap doors in the marble Crusader flagstones, under the shadow of giant reddish brown limestone columns installed by the Emperor Justinian in the sixth-century reconstruction which forms the basis of the dark, cavernous hall that dominates Manger Square today.

Outside, hundreds of tourists milled around a mangy, windswept coach park surrounded by plastic hoardings advertising El Grotte Crafts, Il Bambino Arts, the Good Shepherd Store and the Tachi Restaurant. The post office was open to frank late Christmas cards with a special stamp, a valuable service for souvenir hunters that only contributed to the somewhat unspiritual atmosphere. I sought refuge in an Arab cafe and over breakfast of *fuul* beans and black tea reflected on how Biblical tours had become such big business 2,000 years after the birth of Jesus. In this cynical mood, I could not help thinking, how did they *know* this was the place where it all started?

✝

EARLY CHRISTIAN WRITERS attested that the spot was identified and venerated as early as the second century. The scriptural scholar Origen, travelling 'in a search for the footsteps of Christ' about a hundred years later, was proudly taken to the site by local people. 'If anyone wants further proof to convince them that Jesus was born in Bethlehem, besides the prophecy of Micah and the story recorded in the Gospels by Jesus' disciples, he may observe that, in agreement with the story in the Gospels about his birth, the cave at Bethlehem is shown where he was born and the manger where he was wrapped in swaddling clothes,' he wrote.[4] Unfortunately, none of the Gospels mentioned anything about a cave.

In modern, multi-cultural Britain we are so familiar with the Christmas story, set out each Yuletide in the service of nine lessons and carols, that either through faith or disinterest few people bother to question its credibility. Perhaps because society is now so tolerant of religious diversity, the traditional tale is allowed to stand unchecked while believers and doubters just disagree over its divine implications. I was astonished to discover just how slender was the evidence that Jesus hailed from Bethlehem, and how persuasive the case that it was a legend that grew up after his death.[5]

Despite a good God-fearing upbringing – or maybe because of it – I didn't realise, for example, that neither Mark, probably the earliest Gospel account, nor John, the latest and most theologically-inclined, mentioned the birth of Jesus at all. Or that the record of the other two Gospel writers was inconsistent, and at variance with contemporary sources like the Jewish historian Josephus.

'Jesus was born in Bethlehem in the land of Judea in the days of Herod the King,' asserted Matthew.[6] Wise men from the east, following a star, alerted the great independent Jewish ruler to the prospect of a rival, forcing the holy family to flee into Egypt to escape the slaughter of the first-born.

Luke disagreed not only with all these dramatic details, but more importantly the date. The birth happened at the time Quirinius was governor of Syria, he said, when 'it came to pass in those days there went out a decree from Caesar Augustus that all the world should be taxed.'[7] Quirinius was indeed in charge of the region in AD 6, when the province of Judea first came under Roman rule, but this was almost a decade after the death of King Herod in 4 BC. Since both events can be independently verified, at least one of these Gospel authors must be misguided.

Alarm bells ring throughout Matthew's opening chapters for another reason. He appears over-anxious to make his brief account conform to Jewish tradition, showing how Jesus' birth and baptism fulfilled the archaic prophecies of the Hebrew scriptures. The wise men were dispatched to Bethlehem to investigate only because they reminded Herod about the Messianic prediction of Micah. 'For thus it is written by the prophet,' they warned, that out of the little town in the land of Judah 'shall come forth a governor which shall be shepherd of my people Israel.'[8]

Luke maintained that Joseph hailed from Nazareth, in Galilee, the province where Jesus was brought up and began his mission. However, he claimed Joseph had to register for the tax in Bethlehem because he was descended from the House of David. This is improbable because Galilee was independent from Roman control in the period when Luke himself set his story, and not bound by the census ordered when direct rule was imposed on Judea. There was no point in Joseph and his heavily pregnant wife travelling to a different province in order to register for a property tax, especially since they clearly owned nothing in the locality because they had to lodge at an inn once they were there.

Perhaps we should not be surprised at such confusion. The Gospel authors were neither contemporaries of Jesus, nor even historians in the modern sense, but evangelists recounting an oral tradition about mysterious concepts which had already passed through several generations before they were first put down on parchment. Matthew wrote in Hebrew for the rump of the first church congregation which remained in Palestine after the martyrdom of its leader, the disciple James, in AD 62. This group, anxious to stress its roots in Judaism to avoid persecution, operated not unlike one of the pious Jewish sects which proliferated at the time, calling on sinners to repent and be baptised and give money to charity, but retaining an essentially conservative outlook.

On the other hand, Luke was writing towards the end of the first century, and with a different purpose, to convert a Gentile audience to a new revealed religion as part of St Paul's mission to the wider Greek-speaking world. By the time he set out his version, the legend of the birth was already well established among true believers. Maybe he bent the facts he knew to fit the story? Even those who might have claimed to be eyewitnesses would not have remembered Jesus until the deeds of his adult life made him famous in death. It was the drama of the resurrection, the belief that a man had come back from the dead as the Son of God, which galvanised these men and women to spread the faith and in the process recall the teachings of the humble preacher from Galilee. Bethlehem had, after all, been renowned for centuries amongst Jews as the undisputed birthplace of the great King David. Why not the 'son of David' too?

Catholic apologists have resorted to all sorts of intellectual ingenuities to get round the historical problems posed by the Gospel texts. Father Jerome Murphy-O'Connor, a leading authority on the archaeology of the Holy Land, argued that Mary and Joseph were all along natives of Bethlehem and only moved to Nazareth later because of the atmosphere of insecurity prevailing in their homeland to which Matthew referred. He also skated over the absence of any Gospel reference to a cave by reworking Luke's Greek for 'no room at the inn' to mean that Mary laid Jesus in a manger because they had 'no space in the room.' Many houses in the area are apparently still built in front of caves, he noted, unwilling to let go of the tradition of centuries. On this basis the good father postulated the birth taking place in a back area of the house belonging to Joseph's parents which was normally used for sheltering animals in bad weather.[9]

✝

IT WAS CERTAINLY cold and wet that Christmas Day I spent in Bethlehem, but to get away from the crowds I followed a signpost for the Shepherds' Fields. On the way I passed a church called the Milk Grotto, built over another cave where it is said the holy family hid while fleeing from Herod on their way to Egypt. Devout women come here to pray for fertility, attracted by the fairy-tale which attributes the white colour of the rocks to splashes of Mary's milk which fell from her breast while she nursed the baby Jesus. The cellar was shut to inspection, but nevertheless I was struck by how readily another element in the legend had found a convenient corroboration in geography, reinforcing the original belief that Jesus' birth had taken place just a stone's throw away. Mind you, Matthew, who carried the story of the wise men's warning and the flight to Egypt, made no mention of the shepherds watching their flocks by night; it was left to Luke to tell of the good tidings brought by the angel, that a saviour had been born in the city of David.

The village of Beit Sahur, the house of the shepherds, is nowadays more of a suburb on the eastern edge of Bethlehem. The ruins of a chapel mark the first public proclamation of the holy birth, watched over by a posse of shaggy-eared goats grazing in a barbed wire enclosure. A friendly Greek priest emerged from a modern house of God nearby and got the keys to the site. Although this Orthodox church would not celebrate Christmas for another 11 days, because it still relied on the old calendar, he acknowledged that December 25th was a 'special day' for us.[10] Lifting a set of trapdoors in the floor, he proudly displayed the perfectly preserved mosaic that had been laid in the fourth century after the site was first identified. It became the crypt of a later church, yet at 12 feet below the present ground level offered a graphic illustration of how the landscape had changed in two millennia. Walking back alongside the dry stone walls of an olive grove to the bus stop for Jerusalem, I passed an alternative sign for the Shepherds' Fields, pointing two kilometres away in a different direction. On this, too, the Greek Orthodox priests and the Roman Catholic friars could not agree.

✝

THAT BRIEF VISIT to the environs of Bethlehem sowed an idea in my mind that offered a solution to the puzzle that had plagued me all day. 'Another find from Helena, the patron saint of Christian marketing,' I noted caustically in my diary. I cannot now recall whether the Greek priest said something that alerted me, whether there was an inscription at the ruin, or whether it was just another throwaway line in the guidebook. Yet I was becoming increasingly conscious of how the name Helena kept cropping up as the authority for these holy places. Because she was responsible for the construction of the Basilica of the Nativity, it was generally assumed locally that she had sought out both the refuge of the holy family and the shepherds' fields too. In the course of my visit to the Middle East, such assumptions were peddled as the small change of conversation around every tourist trap, incessantly invoked by the self-appointed guides, unemployed busybodies and proselytising bores which the presence of gullible foreigners always seems to attract. Incredibly, this one woman appeared to hold the key to the entire archaeology of Palestine. Almost as influential as the Virgin Mary, nearly as mysterious as Mary Magdalene, her ghost haunted all the sacred sites where modern pilgrims paid homage to the Bible story.

All I knew for sure at the outset of this quest was that Helena was the mother of Constantine the Great, the emperor who ended the persecution of Christianity in Rome. Three hundred years after the life and death of Jesus, at an advanced age, she embarked on an expedition to the Holy Land. Some local sources implied that she had been instrumental in converting her son to the faith in the first place; yet all attributed to her a decisive moment in ecclesiastical history. For if the disciple Peter was the rock on which the early church was founded, Helena went out and sought the very stones the early fathers had trodden. Then she persuaded Constantine to sanctify her discoveries by building basilicas upon the remains, turning neglected sites into magnificent sights commemorating the birth, death and ascension of Christ.

As my inquiries proceeded, it became clear that the ball Helena started rolling soon engulfed her in a growing myth. Having apparently located the place of the crucifixion, at the spot in Jerusalem on which Constantine then built the Holy Sepulchre, it was soon said that she had unearthed the remains of the True Cross on which Jesus died as well. Having supervised the construction of another church on the Mount of Olives to mark where the resurrected Jesus last appeared to the disciples on earth, it was but a small step to claiming that Helena founded two other chapels nearby as well: the Eleona, where Jesus wept over the fate of Jerusalem and foretold the second coming, and the Paternoster, from where he preached the Lord's Prayer. Modern research has established the existence of fourth-century foundations in all these places, though the Byzantine remains are obscured by Crusader foundations – or in one case a mosque, because Islam also believes Jesus ascended into heaven.

Nevertheless, her personal example directly inspired the first wave of mass pilgrimage to the region. Christians throughout the ages have been seized with a natural urge to see the places that bore witness to the facts of the Bible story with their own eyes. The earliest pilgrim we know about was Melito of Sardis, a second-century bishop who undertook a quest to the land 'where these things were seen and done.'[11] Yet it required a wealthy widow with the authority of the Roman emperor behind her to blaze a popular trail. Helena made it possible by stamping the imperial seal of approval on the identification of religious sites, and beginning the process of constructing Christian monuments which in turn became objects of veneration in their own right. Penitents flocked to pray at the holy places in her footsteps.

Within the next hundred years, an unknown traveller from Bordeaux who left the first written record of the journey was followed by Egeria, a nun from Spain; Silvia of Aquitaine, sister-in-law of the imperial prefect; the elder Melania who founded a monastery on the Mount of Olives; the pious Paula who accompanied the early church father St Jerome; and Fabiola, a rich widow from Rome. Jerome, the translator of the Greek Bible into the Latin Vulgate, gave the movement considerable impetus. He presided over a fashionable circle of highborn Christian women at Rome, many of whom followed him to Palestine. By the beginning of the fifth century the place was packed with monasteries and hospices to cater for the flood of visitors.

Yet if imitation is the sincerest form of flattery, no more fitting tribute was paid to Helena's influence than that her expedition was echoed more than a century later by another imperial mother, this time Eudocia, wife of Theodosius II, the emperor of the East. Her purpose was to give thanks for the marriage of her daughter Eudoxia to Valentinius III, emperor of the West, and she emulated Helena by making generous donations to many churches en route. Eudocia acquired a reputation for piety that paralleled Helena's, and after she settled in the Holy Land her hobby becoming the gathering of relics that subsequently laid the foundation for the great Byzantine collection in Constantinople.

✝

THESE FIRST TRAVELLERS were christened *peregrini*, literally 'foreigners' in Latin, whose wanderings were etymologically compared to the roaming of wild animals. They aimed to re-enact the suffering of Jesus through undertaking long, arduous and even dangerous journeys. Their intention was to bear witness in a symbolic emulation of the martyrs who had seen the risen Christ. They sought salvation for their restless souls, and in the personal search for holiness travelled eastwards towards Jerusalem, not only the location of the Bible story but the venue for the Last Judgement and the direction from which was anticipated the Second Coming. Nor could they keep still: as Jerome wrote of Paula's visits: 'So great was the passion and enthusiasm she exhibited for each that she could never have torn herself away from one had she not been eager to visit the next.'[12]

The Arab conquest of the seventh century and the destruction wreaked in the name of Islam fuelled Christian fervour even further. During the Dark Ages, Helena was credited with founding almost all the churches in Palestine, marking not just the major events of the New Testament but a couple of the Old to boot. 'This blessed and holy empress Helena gave orders that churches should be founded in the places where for our salvation our Lord Jesus Christ went about and wrought his glorious wonders,' said one anonymous admirer who listed her achievements in an eighth-century travel guide.[13]

Attributed to Helena's zeal were monuments in the garden of Gethsemane and at the tomb of the Virgin Mary, by the tomb of Lazarus at Bethany, and near the cave of John the Baptist by the Jordan; she built upon the locations of the healing at Capernaeum, the miracle of the loaves and fishes, and the marriage at

Cana in Galilee; found the houses of both Mary Magdalene and Peter's mother-in-law at Tiberias, the place of the transfiguration on Mount Tabor, even the precise spot at Nazareth where the Archangel Gabriel appeared to the Virgin Mary in a vision.[14] Then, apparently, the restless pilgrim returned to Jerusalem and revisited Mount Sion to consecrate the room where the disciples held the Last Supper and the apostles were visited by the Holy Spirit at Pentecost, not to mention the house of Caiaphas the high priest where Jesus was taken after his arrest and denied by Peter.

Finally, this over-enthusiastic author observed, 'Now that these venerable and holy churches of our God had been brought into existence in the places where it had been directed that they should be founded by the great-hearted and truly Christ-loving Helena, blessed mother of the holy great emperor Constantine, she immediately offered faithful hymns to God who himself had travelled in these places.'

Helena left a legacy that so captured the mediaeval imagination that the armies of Christendom embarked on a series of ruinous Crusades to preserve the purity of the holy places. The Christian kings of Europe sought to protect a pilgrim trail that by the 11th century had become a mass movement – and if necessary take precious relics back to Europe for safe keeping. Although the chief relics of Christ and his passion were long venerated at Jerusalem, there was an increasing trade in fragments of the True Cross and other minor relics from the East, brought back by devout pilgrims, enterprising merchants or even as gifts from visiting potentates.

Indeed mediaeval pilgrimages became such big business that they were indistinguishable from crusades, since the visitors from the West were increasingly forced to travel in large armed bands for their own security. After the Caliph of Egypt, al-Hakim bi-Amr Allah, captured Jerusalem in 1009 and razed the Holy Sepulchre to the ground, the Frankish knights put the symbol of the cross on their surcoats and shields and set out to liberate Christ's tomb once again from the darkness brought by the infidel, in a conscious evocation of Helena's original discovery.

Pope Urban II preached the first crusade in 1095, promising the remission of sins for those who 'took the cross' and even threatening excommunication if they turned back before reaching Jerusalem. Of course, the motives of many of those who accepted the challenge, sewing two strips of red material to the shoulders of their garments in a token of their commitment to the church, were probably a lot less lofty. Nevertheless, the chronicles of the crusades record the psychological role played by the official relic of the True Cross as the war standard of the Kings of Jerusalem. Portions were distributed to the barons of Outremer in order to bless their armies in excursions against the infidel, and Amalric I himself wore a fragment around his neck, while the main trophy itself was carried into battle by the Patriarch of the Holy City and held aloft before the troops like a talisman demonstrating that God was on their side.[15]

Unfortunately, the True Cross was captured by one of Saladin's generals in 1187, when the Christian forces were routed at the Horns of Hattin. According to Arab chroniclers, the great Muslim warrior revered the relic himself, took pride in showing it to visiting Christian embassies, and eventually restored it to the care of the remaining priests in occupied Jerusalem. Although Richard the Lionheart repeatedly failed to regain possession of the relic, it became an important bargaining counter in diplomatic negotiations and was a major ingredient in the peace treaty which was finally signed in 1221 to bring the Fifth Crusade to an end. When the time came to surrender the relic, however, it could not be found. The last crusaders sailed home empty-handed, although local traditions survived suggesting that various bishops had managed to save fragments from the infidel by hiding them, and in one case even burying them on the battlefield at the Horns of Hattin.

Despite the failure of the Crusades, and the loss of the True Cross, the custody of the Holy Places remained a vexed theme of European diplomacy throughout the Renaissance, as rival religious denominations sought to exploit the weakness of successive Ottoman rulers to claim primacy over the sanctuaries for themselves. The age-old dispute even provided the pretext for the first modern military conflict, the Crimean War of 1854–6. Then Britain and France joined forces to bolster Turkey, the so-called 'sick man of Europe', against Russian territorial claims – advanced by St Petersburg in the guise of protecting the interests of the Orthodox church in Jerusalem and Bethlehem.

Admiration for Helena's early archaeological efforts also helped spur those 19th-century adventurers and excavators who debouched on the Holy Land seeking scientific proof of the Bible.[16] The establishment of the Palestine Exploration Fund in 1865 added digging to the conviction popularised by the French scholar Ernest Renan that seeing was believing. 'The striking agreement of the texts and the places, the marvellous harmony of the Gospel Ideal with the countryside which served as its frame were for me a revelation,' he wrote in his best-selling *Life of Jesus* after a personal visit to the Holy Land. 'I had before my eyes a fifth Gospel, tattered but still legible.'[17]

Today the thriving tourist industry of the state of Israel remains duly grateful for Helena's legacy, a debt that even extends into territory captured during the 1967 Six-Day War. Recently Roberta Harris, honorary secretary of the Anglo-Israeli Archaeology Society, credited Helena with travelling further afield. In her book *Exploring the World of the Bible Lands* she maintained that Helena also founded the monastic community of St Katharine's, at the foot of Mount Sinai in modern Egypt. Although the claim is repeated in some guidebooks, there is no evidence that Helena came this far, aside from the ruins of a fourth-century chapel and a tradition that the site – allegedly the location of the burning bush that Moses saw in the Old

Testament – was occupied by hermits in early Christian times.[18] Nevertheless, the notion that Helena was active here as well as in Palestine offers a striking contemporary illustration of the continuing power of the myth generated in her name over the centuries.

†

ON MY RETURN to Jerusalem I visited the Garden Tomb, a rural sanctuary on the edge of the Old City which for more than a century some Protestants have regarded as a more preferable site for Jesus' passion than Constantine's church. This captivating oasis of greenery is like a little corner of England in a foreign land, right down to the National Trust-style gift shop at the turnstile entrance, along a quiet side street in the extended Arab quarter to the north of the walls. Such a pleasing atmosphere, all too reminiscent of home, has a powerful effect on Western visitors, appealing to their natural preference for understatement and rational argument, in sharp contrast to the gaudiness of the Holy Sepulchre and the other Catholic sites so steeped in tradition. On that Boxing Day it entranced me, too, as a refuge from the hustle and bustle of the city, where one could stroll among the trees and shrubs, pausing at one of the many wooden benches conveniently placed along the winding network of paths for contemplation or prayer.

Tagging on to a party of American pilgrims, I learned that the garden owed its popularity to the Victorian war hero General Charles Gordon, who indulged his hobby for amateur Biblical studies while on leave in Jerusalem in 1883, two years before his famous victory at Khartoum. He was struck by the death's head appearance of a rocky knoll overlooking an old quarry known locally as Beit-ha-Sekilah, or 'the place of stoning.' The soldier's letters back home and an appeal in *The Times* helped raise funds to purchase the site, swiftly christened Skull Hill. Suspicions that this could be the 'place of the skull' where Jesus was crucified were fuelled by excavations which uncovered an ancient Jewish sepulchre, hewn out of the rock in the Herodian period of the first century AD, and capable of being sealed by a great stone.

An early Christian anchor symbol was found near the doorway, and a pair of red crosses painted on the wall dating from Byzantine times, confirming that the site had been venerated by earlier generations of Christians. For the physical layout of the double chamber inside corresponded tantalisingly with the few references to the tomb of Jesus in the Gospels, including an extra recess at the foot of the grave which suggested it had once accommodated a bigger body than the person for whom it was originally constructed.

'You must make up your own mind,' said Ken, the volunteer guide, concluding his talk after an inspection of the remaining feature of the site, a huge underground water cistern that indicated the area was a rich man's garden in Jewish times. But in case we had not got the point he went on: 'The most important thing to us is that when we found the tomb it was empty, and I thank the Lord for that.' Right on cue, the American pilgrims all chorused: 'A-men.'

If they were right, and this was indeed the family vault in which the wealthy Joseph of Arimathea laid Jesus after taking him down from the cross, then it would deal a fatal blow to the whole Helena story – exploding the central Catholic claim on which it hinged, that the Holy Sepulchre marked the site of the crucifixion and burial of Jesus. On the way out I bumped by chance into the chaplain, the Rev Derek Cook, and mentioned the Helena phenomenon I had encountered at the other Biblical sites, provoking an unexpected anti-papist outburst.

'Hah! I'm glad this place was not discovered sixteen hundred years ago, otherwise *they* would have built a church on top and destroyed the natural setting that gives us inspiration,' he exclaimed, launching into an impromptu lecture on the relative merits of the Protestant and Catholic traditions. In the jaundiced view of the Rev Cook, the rival archaeological arguments came down to a simple supposition.

'If you were the Bishop of Jerusalem and the mother of the Emperor turned up demanding to know where Jesus was crucified, I suspect you could direct her to a suitable spot fairly quickly.'

The chaplain's cynicism about Helena in Jerusalem chimed with what I had instinctively felt about Helena in Bethlehem. If the Gospel writers were so vague themselves about the circumstances of Jesus' birth and death, how did *she* know any better almost three centuries later? Was she prodigious, ubiquitous, or just bogus? Long after leaving the Middle East these questions kept intriguing me, and so I found myself embarking on what was to become my own pilgrimage in Helena's footsteps. It was to take me on a series of journeys round Britain, across Europe, and eventually back to Jerusalem again. Not only did this involve burrowing through the half-forgotten texts that purported to chart Helena's life and times, but it also entailed visiting many of the places that became associated with her story through the ages. Above all, it became a search for the personality of the woman behind the fantastic legend she inspired: an attempt to disentangle the truth about the first tourist from the travellers' tales that had grown up around her.

CHAPTER I

St Helens

I do not believe these fragments of wood were the very cross, but I am bound to add that there is nothing to prove the contrary.

William Cowper Prime[1]

'IT'S NAMED AFTER the church, I believe. I have lived here all my life but I'm not really sure, now you ask.'

The woman behind the desk in the information office at the shopping centre where I had parked the car seemed surprised anyone would willingly visit St Helens, let alone inquire into the etymological origins of this quiet, northern provincial town.

'There's not much to see round here,' she smiled. 'But I suppose we're best known for the saints.'

I paused at the door, wondering if my quest was to be fulfilled before it had begun. She was oblivious to my inner excitement.

'You've heard of The Saints? They're always top of the Rugby League.'

I ventured out into the town centre, clutching a copy of the official guide which proclaimed that St Helens was so called after an ancient chapel of the same name, which in the 14th century was situated in the vicinity of the parish church.[2]

Its modern successor appeared more like a factory than a house of God. A solid shed of dirty reddish-brown brick dominated the pedestrianised precinct, its walls stained with a mixture of soot and mould. Through the grimy windows, not only leaded but barred, were glimpses of a fiery orange glow, as if a devilish crucible was being stoked inside. Above, an assembly-line of pigeons perched on the pitched roof, at the eastern end of which a square tower shot abruptly into the air like an enormous chimney stack, an impression hardly dispelled by the set of louvered ventilation shutters near the top of its otherwise bare sides. Clouds of black smoke belching forth would have completed the image of a dark, satanic mill.

Not so long ago, after the discovery of coal and the development of canals had transformed Lancashire into an engine of the Industrial Revolution, the parish church would have fairly hummed with evangelical fervour. Its congregation was renowned for having the most popular working men's Bible Class in the country, and its clergy led frequent missions to the suburbs of the burgeoning borough. A yellowing newspaper cutting in the library recorded how an estimated 5,000 people flocked to 14 separate services one Sunday in 1894 to mark the refurbishment of the church interior, in keeping with its growing municipal status. The faithful heard the Rev J W Willink preach about the tremendous changes wrought within only a few generations on the settlement that had developed around the old chapel.

'How different was that hamlet to the proud county borough of the present day, with great buildings and many churches, with close on 80,000 inhabitants, and a name that is known far and wide throughout the world,' he exclaimed at Evensong.

Today, however, this memorial to the mass production of civic religiosity brooded silently over the rustle of mid-week shoppers preoccupied with the commercial gods of a more secular age.

No sound from it disturbed the banjo busker gently strumming for spare cash from the steady procession of punters between Marks & Spencer and Woolworths. My spur-of-the-moment visit was just too late for the memorial service to the Life and Work of Sir Alastair Pilkington, FRS, scion of the renowned glass-making family whose enterprise and endeavours had brought prosperity to the town since the early 19th century. A glance at the noticeboard outside the Parish Church of St Helen showed that I would also miss that week's summer organ recital, and would be leaving town before the next instalment of the slide show on the travels of St Paul. But a printed sign propped against the soft red sandstone facade of the main west door beckoned. 'Why not come inside? This church is open for prayer.'

All blasphemous thoughts were banished amid the cool, calm air trapped between strong stone pillars, whitewashed plaster walls and a high wooden ceiling panelled like the bottom of an upturned boat. A crowned king in mediaeval robes looked down from the stained glass window over the altar, his hands spread open as if inviting the vitrine woman at his right hand to speak her secret to a casual visitor gazing up from below. Yet there was nothing to connect any of this classic neo-Gothic construction to the ancient chapel, save perhaps a Latin inscription carved in gilt letters atop the pair of wooden hymn boards either side of the aisle. The legend 'S.Helena' blazed down at me with such intensity that I had to sit down and gather my thoughts.

✠

IT'S A FAIR bet that most people asked about St Helena will, if they recognise the name at all, think of an island in the South Atlantic. One deemed so remote from civilisation that Napoleon was exiled there after he met his Waterloo. Indeed, uninhabited until a Portuguese mariner on his way home from the Indies first set foot there in 1502. He sighted this tropical volcanic outcrop in mid-ocean on May 21st, the feast-day of one of the most popular contemporary saints according to the Eastern Church calendar.[3] What could be more natural than to honour her with the new addition to the atlas?

Her name was thus imprinted on the map of the globe roughly mid-way between St Helena Bay, a feature of the South African Cape, and equatorial Brazil, which being a good Catholic country contains at least three settlements celebrating the memory of the same holy lady. For the record, she is also linked with a town in California, a mountain in Washington State, an island in Lake Michigan, and a sound off the coast of Carolina, not to mention a port in Tasmania and a district of New Zealand. That's not counting the numerous Santa Elena's in the Spanish-speaking world, either, or the other St Helen's (with an heretical apostrophe) on the Isle of Wight. When he had his brainwave on the high seas, captain João da Nova Castella was in good company. Yet nowadays what do we really know about the woman who so readily came to his mind?

✢

MY REVERIE WAS interrupted by a rustling in the pews. The elderly churchwarden shuffling towards me was only too happy to natter away to a casual visitor, oblivious of what had actually brought me to Lancashire. Len Barrett informed me this was the fifth church on the site, the previous version having been completely destroyed by a mysterious fire in 1916. A resident of St Helens for 50 years, Len was also at a loss to explain the name of the parish.

'I have been told, but I can't remember.' He bowed his head, and as if to excuse his memory said he was born in Warrington.

'The church before this was called St Mary's. When this one opened in 1926 it was dedicated to St Helen. With the town being called St Helens I suppose they called the church that, too. But I don't know why the town was called St Helens before that.'

Len was pottering about at the back of the church, where several rows of traditional polished oak pews had recently been removed in favour of a modern structure in varnished teak which would have resembled a doctor's waiting room if vicars held spiritual surgeries.

'When it was first built this church would hold 1,800 people. We are lucky if we get a hundred people on a Sunday now,' he observed. Len retrieved the offering I had left in a basket on the table next to a small pile of parish histories and architectural notes, and advised me to seek further guidance at the Catholic church down the road. Apparently it also bore the appellation of the mysterious St Helen.

✣

DILIGENT ANTIQUARIANS have discovered that St Helens enjoyed a lively ecclesiastical past, but all efforts to link the present Anglican parish church with the original chapel remain conjecture. Potentially the oldest reference point is the nearby parish of Eccleston, now a residential area but once a separate settlement taking its name from the Latin *ecclesia*, a church, and thus implying the existence of a Romano-British place of worship. Celtic influence remained predominant in the region until well after the Roman withdrawal, but the marshlands between the Ribble and the Mersey were eventually overrun by the wild Norsemen of Northumbria and in turn passed under the control of the Kingdom of Mercia. Even the Domesday Book is unhelpful, suggesting a sparse and scattered population in Norman times, and history does not begin until a papal tax assessment in 1292 to fund a crusade. This revealed the existence of a church of Our Lady at Prescot, the 'priest's manor' which was once the most important mediaeval village round about but now is literally just a roundabout on the road to Liverpool; and a church dedicated to St Helen at Sefton, in the suburbs of the big city, too far away for my purposes. It is therefore assumed that the St Helens chapel was not founded until the reign of Richard II, towards the end of the 14th century, when patent rolls first disclosed the existence of a benefice at Hardshaw, in the manor of Windle, near the intersection of the old roads going north from Liverpool to Wigan and west from Warrington to Ormskirk.

Even so, with an ironic twist, the earliest authenticated reference to 'St Elyn's Chapel' was not until after the break with the Church of Rome. In 1552 the arrival of English Protestantism was marked by the issue of a revised Book of Common Prayer. That same year an official inventory of religious goods associated with post-Reformation livings recorded one chalice and a 'little bell' at the said chapel, which was clearly in a pretty poor state. The first endowment to fund a priest was not recorded until six years later, and at the end of the century the incumbent Reader, John Rutter, was excommunicated for performing an illegal marriage following a highly critical Visitation. Not that these events were necessarily an indication of dissolute morals or slackness in the proper observances. There is some evidence that the native population clung tenaciously to Catholicism, and in the shadow of Elizabeth I's penal legislation against Popery, the Old Faith was preserved in Lancashire by missionary priests skulking in the country houses of the landed gentry.

Matters improved after 1613, when members of a prominent local family set up a trust to run a revived 'St Ellen's Chappell' and a free school alongside it, though the original building was demolished to make way for the new foundation. In the religious turmoil of the 17th century this became a meeting place for Protestant dissenters, aided by the fact that it was in private ownership and had escaped episcopal consecration. A certain 'St Ellins Chappell' was described in the Commonwealth Church

Survey of 1650, and its ministers were such ardent puritans that the offspring of one became domestic chaplain to Oliver Cromwell, the Lord Protector. Rival Presbyterians and Anglicans fought over the right to worship at 'St Helin's Chapel' until as late as 1710, when the non-conformists decided to quit and set up their own independent premises, later the Congregational Church of the emerging township. The bishops marked the re-absorption of 'St Hellen's' into the Church of England with another new building, and granted it official status as a 'chapel of ease' to the parent church of Prescot.

The parish of 'St Helens' finally came into its own in 1852, though ironically the church had been known as St Mary's since it was enlarged and effectively rebuilt a fourth time 35 years earlier. By this time an Improvement Commission had been established to impose some order on the rapid growth of the local population around the development of dozens of glass-works, chemical plants and collieries. With the subsequent creation of a borough council, the modern identity of the town of St Helens as a product of social and economic transformation was assured. All this I learned readily from the published sources[4] without once coming across the slightest inkling of any curiosity about the eponymous figure to whom a new shrine had been raised. The curiously inconsistent spelling of the patron saint down the ages did make me wonder, however, whether my Helena had anything to do with the place at all.

✣

'WE DON'T KNOW who she is. It's lost in the mists of time. You will never get to the bottom of that.'

Behind the reception counter at the local history department of the municipal library, Vicky the clerk looked at me with a mixture of interest and incredulity. She probably gets cranks in off the street all the time, I thought. Actually I had been directed from the town hall opposite, an imposing building whose entrance, a pair of studded oak doors under a carved portico flanked by polished granite pillars at the top of a flight of wide stone steps, itself resembled a rather grand church.

The hallway boasted a plaque honouring the closure of the last colliery, another marking the first concert ever conducted by Sir Thomas Beecham, the town's most famous son, and the inevitable roll call of mayors going back to 1868. St Helen was not forgotten, but on that visit none of the staff hanging about the hallway drew my attention to the stained glass window on the main staircase, portraying a tight-lipped young woman weighed down by a crucifix and struggling to gird herself with a buckler conveniently imprinted with the borough coat of arms. Instead, a cheerful caretaker took me back outside and pointed above the Mayor's parlour on the first floor. Nestling apologetically in the apex of the gable, on a pedestal between two miniature polished pink pillars, could just be made out the weathered form of a stone figurine wearing robes, a head-dress, a crown, and a small cross.

'There are five possible Helens,' ventured Vicky, cautiously, as I expounded my mission back at the library. She turned to seek confirmation from a colleague across the reading room. 'Margaret, who do we think St Helen was?'

'The nun?' offered Margaret, hopefully. Vicky emphatically disagreed.

'Some do say she was Helen Burchall, the mother superior of a convent that was built on the site of a well. But we've more or less disproved that. We favour Constantine's mother here. That's the Roman Emperor's mum. After all, there was a Roman settlement at Newton-le-Willows. And the archivist has a theory that it all started with the Knights Templar. We can't prove it, but have a feeling they set it all up.'

Although the archivist was off duty that day, I gathered that some romantic Victorian antiquary had perpetrated the legend of the abbess, despite the complete absence of either any convent or holy well associated with the site. Probably he was confused with the chantry at nearby Windleshaw, known locally as 'the abbey' because it is the town's oldest surviving structure, endowed around 1435 by Sir Thomas Gerard in order that mass might be said for the souls of his family in perpetuity. I never found out about the other three candidates. Poking at random among the papers amassed by the late Frank Pope, a local historian who had taken a particular interest in the derivation of place names, I found a hopeful cross-reference to Ellenglaze in Cornwall and another to Ellan-na-roan in Sutherland but no mention of a person who might have given their name to that ancient chapel.

'I was quite amazed by this when I first came here,' commented the archivist when I telephoned a few days later. 'Nobody was interested. They have blanked it out.' As for her own theory about the Knights Templar owning land in the area during the Middle Ages – well, she threatened to hound me to Kingdom Come if I published her name in connection with such an untested hunch.

'The only way to prove it is by consulting the archives of the hospitallers in the Vatican, or possibly on Malta. That would require major scholarship and a knowledge of mediaeval Latin. But I'm convinced the crux of the matter lies there.'

The crux – an easy cliché no doubt, but one resonant with implications for my tale. Meaning? A difficult matter, a puzzle, the decisive point at issue, yet derived from the Latin word for a cross. One clue buried in the files of the Local History department had intrigued me, a newspaper photograph of a parochial church council meeting from 1952, held at the town hall. Behind the solemn dignitaries was a magnificent mural, depicting a woman of regal bearing in velvet robes, not unlike that contemporaneous Annigoni portrait of the Queen soon after she ascended the throne. Except that this royal vixen was emerging in a blaze of glory from the shadows of an Hellenic temple, her eyes shining through the grainy reproduction, oblivious of the weight of a huge crucifix over the right shoulder. I asked at the town hall again, and was told all the murals in the council chamber were covered up six years before, to make way for pictures of local notables. Though only painted just before the photograph was taken, the plaster was cracking, the colour fading, and so the vision was hidden behind a false wall.

'Some would say that's sacrilege,' grunted the caretaker. In compensation he offered another image of the elusive Helen, this time at the rear of the gigantic bronze Victoria memorial on the roundabout outside. Behind the throne a small blackened knight in full armour raised its sword upturned – in the sign of the cross. If I hadn't known already, it could have been anyone. According to the inscription, the whole edifice was raised by one Col W W Pilkington in 1906. It came as no surprise to discover that the corporate logo of the world's leading producer of sheet glass was a cross, in the flowery form known as *croix fleurie*. That information was only one of the surprises in store further down Corporation Street, when I finally made it to the Roman Catholic Church of St Helen and the Holy Cross.

✢

THREE MASSES a day, confession every morning, benediction twice a week. The work rate advertised by Holy Cross outstripped the Anglican parish church, though it shared some of the external characteristics of its rival, namely a disguise as a warehouse. Conspicuous amid the soot-speckled brick and wire-mesh windows, however, was one small but unmistakable decorative feature carved from a niche above the doorway, a robed figurine wearing long curls under her crown. She had drawn a good four score worshippers that mid-week lunchtime, presided over by a grey-haired man with soft jowls and sad eyes.

'I honestly do not know about her relation to the town,' said

Arthur Willcock, the deacon, as he removed his white cassock and green sash in the vestry afterwards.

'She was the mother of the Emperor Constantine, who was the first Christian emperor of Rome. As far as we are concerned, she is a saint because she was a Christian before her son was. She found what remained of the True Cross, you know.'

He scrutinised me through those twin troubled pools. 'If there is a local connection I don't know what it is. I should know the answer, it is somewhere in the depths of my mind.'

I asked if Helen was still commemorated in any way, and Arthur winced. 'She has been . . . slightly downgraded, I fear, but there is a feast day.'

He turned to his missal, its crisp leaves rustling as he ran his finger first through the list of daily offices and then the index.

'There's a thing. That's interesting. It's not there.'

As he searched, Arthur tried to explain the complicated hierarchy of Catholic celebrations, from solemnities every Sunday and Christian festival, to feast days for the apostles and memorials for the lesser saints. Each had a different colour, reflected in the choice of sash worn by the concelebrant, which also varied according to the season of the Christian year.

'There is a fourth category of feast, which is a founding memorial, when it would be obligatory for a parish named after someone to say mass for them. If it's in the missal it must be kept.'

But if not? Eventually, in a calendar produced by the Archdiocese of Liverpool, he found the reference he sought: 'August 18th, St Helen, Queen (3rd/4th century), Mass at choice'. Her festival was sandwiched between St Stephen of Hungary and St John Eudes, but unlike the feasts of these two luminaries the sacramentary prescribed no prayers for that day, nor did the lectionary advise any particular readings from scripture. Only a church named after her would be expected to observe any special rite, its priest wearing white for the occasion. I got the distinct impression that the church of St Helen in St Helens was not used to making much fuss about its patron saint on her special day.

Yet faith is a powerful phenomenon for those blessed with it. I supposed in my cynical way that once someone has made the spiritual leap required to believe that the leader of an obscure Jewish sect in the first century was the son of God, and rose from the dead to save the world from sin, it was a comparatively small step to accepting that several hundred years later a dowager empress could miraculously re-discover the very piece of timber on which the secular authorities had so horribly put to death a man they regarded as at best a political subversive, and at worst a common criminal.

'She had a lot of power. If she asked a question, she would get an answer. You would not argue with the mother of the Emperor of Rome,' said Arthur, sensing my hesitation.

'If you accept that the True Cross was found, she was the one that found it. There is no doubt in my mind.'

As far as the official status of Helen was concerned, Arthur said he had to be rather careful what he said about the church authorities in case it got back to the Bishop. Nevertheless, he went on to make some rather uncharitable remarks about modern theologians who undermined the simple belief of churchgoers with their nit-picking biblical scholarship. And then, as we moved on to the importance of physical relics in sustaining faith, he dropped his bombshell.

'We have one here. It's just a tiny thing, like a splinter. We believe it to be part of the True Cross.'

I was staggered. I had heard of such claims in Catholic countries but never in England. Mark Twain, in his classic account of a journey to the Holy Land, *The Innocents Abroad*, is forever joking about how readily his fellow pilgrims could identify some uniquely sacred object because they had already seen it countless times before in the cathedrals of France and Italy.

'Of course, if you put all of these relics together you would get a forest rather than a cross,' chuckled Arthur, his eyes twinkling. 'We almost certainly got ours when the church was founded, back in 1862. It is kept inside a little metal case with a glass front, in the shape of a cross. On Good Friday it is brought out and the people can venerate it. It is put on the altar during the particular service, and if people wish to they can come up and kiss the case.'

Could I see it? I blurted out the obvious question for a hack in a hurry, though a moment's thought on my part might have made me realise that an object so special it was only brought out once a year was not the sort of thing you readily showed to any curious passer-by.

'To be honest, I don't know where the Father keeps it,' said the diplomatic deacon. We talked instead of the healing powers attributed to some relics. Arthur described a miraculous tradition associated with a local priest, Edmund Arrowsmith, who was martyred in the 16th century. One of his hands, retrieved from the gallows after his body had been hung, drawn and quartered, was now preserved in a church at Ashton-in-Makerfield. Was the St Helens' fragment similarly revered in the region?

'No. Word would have got around, I think.'

St Helen and the Holy Cross is one of more than 20 Roman Catholic churches in the St Helens district, and by no means the most important, though it is the earliest remaining in its original form. Its foundation by the Jesuits reflected not just the belated flowering of authorised Catholic worship as a result of the emancipation Acts, but also the tremendous influx into the area of Irish migrants spurred by the potato famines in their homeland. On the way out, Arthur pointed proudly to the various devotional aids placed around the church: the plaster statues of the apostles ranged like wedding cake decorations above the nave; the relief sculptures marking the stations of the cross along the aisles; the shrine to Our Lady of Walsingham – the former parish of the priest-in-charge, Father John Pennington – bedecked with fresh flowers; the rose window overlooking the altar, unusually at the west end of the building rather than facing east but apparently a source of spiritual beauty when the setting sun streamed through. And, it seemed, almost wherever you turned, a lifelike bleeding Christ impaled on a ghastly crucifix.

✣

THE CROSS HAS become such a familiar object that it is easy to forget what it represents. To be honest, I had never really thought about this myself until embarking on my quest for St Helena, despite being brought up in an Anglican household, the hall of which was graced with a small family crucifix of wood and metal for as long as I could remember. I also spent my formative years singing in the choir of St Alban's parish church, Bristol – dedicated to the first British martyr – without taking in the grisly nature of the business, even though I recall with nostalgia that the highlight of our liturgical year was the annual passiontide performance of semi-operatic cantatas like *Olivet to Calvary* by J H Maunder and H Moore's *The Darkest Hour*. Yet the sheer horror of the Easter experience on which they drew for musical and dramatic inspiration never came home to me until I started looking into the subject.

I discovered that fixing criminals to a crude cross was the preferred Roman punishment for thieves, bandits, slaves and foreigners. It represented both a savage penalty for the individual and a collective signal of civic disgrace. Chiefly associated in Christian literature with the suffering of just one man, it was actually commonplace wherever and whenever the authorities sought to uphold the *pax Romana*. In 73 BC, for example, the victorious general Pompey thought nothing of crucifying 6,000 slaves after crushing the uprising of Spartacus, the bodies of whose followers lined the Appian Way outside Rome like a macabre human forest until the artificial trees along the road to Capua were picked clean by vultures and carrion crows.[5]

Although Roman citizens were automatically immune from such degradation, the practice spread as the armies of the empire conquered in their name. This painful, protracted and public process was taboo for Jews, who retained their own peculiar form of capital punishment for blasphemy and insisted on stoning religious malefactors to death instead, taking their cue from a verse in Deuteronomy which said that a hanged man was accursed in the sight of the Lord.[6] Yet in Palestine, during the lifetime of Jesus, several thousand Jewish rebels were put to death this way in order to suppress a revolt that broke out after the death of Herod the Great; while Gratus, Pontius Pilate's predecessor, crucified a couple of hundred Jews following an uprising in Judea. The Jewish historian Josephus later called it 'the most wretched way of dying' as he bewailed the fate of fugitives fleeing the siege of Jerusalem during the Jewish wars. 'The soldiers, out of the rage and hatred they bore the prisoners, nailed those they caught in different postures to the crosses, by way of jest.'[7]

The gruesome origin of the idea lay in the primitive pagan habit of putting the frighteners on one's enemies by impaling captives on the upright posts used for defensive fortifications. The Romans probably borrowed it from the Persians, or more particularly the Carthaginians, although the Etruscan tyrant Tarquin the Proud was a keen exponent. The Latin verb *crucio* initially meant simply 'to torment' and prolonging the agony seems to have been an essential part of the process. In early times, sticks were driven through the chest of the living from back to front, but some sadistic practitioners were not satisfied unless the pole passed right through the body from the fundament to the mouth, avoiding the vital organs so the poor wretch remained alive in agony if he had not first died of shock.

The Romans refined this to the practical form of punishment

with which we are familiar from the Bible. It became a judicial process in which a preliminary flogging while tied to a post, and the subsequent burden of carrying the crossbeam to the place of execution, were both as much a part of the penalty as being nailed up there exposed to the sun, insects and passing birds of prey under a placard proclaiming the name of the criminal and advertising the offence. Leaving the naked corpse on a cross, exposed to public humiliation on high ground or near the place of the crime, was intended to have a deterrent effect on the populace. The mad emperor Nero went one stage further during his persecution of early Christians in Rome: according to Tacitus, 'They were fastened on crosses and when daylight faded, were burned to serve as lamps by night.'[8]

The extent of the initial scourging was probably crucial to the subsequent suffering of the offender: with whips made of braided leather thongs, whose tails were embedded with pieces of metal or bone, the victim could have died of this alone. Josephus recorded luridly that some of his opponents were scourged until their entrails became visible. The gospels indicated that Pilate considered ordering a beating alone for Jesus, on the grounds that chastisement was a lesser penalty in a spectrum of possible uses, which also included inquisitional torture. In the case of Jesus, however, the mob wanted the death penalty.

As for how it was done, however, the Passion narratives are ironically the most detailed accounts we have, and all four evangelists record little beyond the stark statement that Jesus was taken out of Jerusalem to the place of execution and crucified, as if it was self-explanatory. Other Classical writers frequently referred to crucifixion but they too never actually described it, either because they were too fastidious or (more probably) because their readers were all too aware of the gory details, available for anyone to see on display outside the gates of any city. Seneca, a contemporary of the apostle Paul, gave a rare flavour in his *Dialogues* when he asked: 'Can anyone be found who would prefer wasting away in pain, dying limb by limb, or letting out his life drop by drop, rather than expiring once and for all?'[9]

For if they didn't collapse from massive heart failure, the poor victims died a slow, lingering death either by asphyxiation or dehydration, and that commonly took several days. As the muscles of the arms and legs tired of supporting the weight of the chest, the exhausted body would find it progressively difficult to raise the rib cage and draw in enough air to breathe. Each respiratory effort would increase the agonising pain of trying to lift the chest by either pushing down on the feet or pulling up from the elbows. Like drowning without the water, the unfortunate creature would gradually suffocate while suspended in mid-air. One does not have to be a Christian to acknowledge that such physical torture must rank as the most fiendish and barbaric method of judicial execution ever devised. Death by crucifixion was literally excruciating, an adjective we have since adopted from the Latin *excruciatus* meaning 'out of the cross.'

✠

JUST BEFORE LEAVING the Holy Cross church, another stained glass window in the south wall had caught my attention. The primary colours and simple outlines recalled a child's painting; though this stylised portrayal was no Bible scene. Instead a noble queen prayed humbly before a giant cross, watched by a plump mitred figure in green. Helena certainly, but with whom? Her son Constantine after his conversion, perhaps? Or maybe Macarius, the Bishop of Jerusalem, sanctifying her find? In the background a handful of legionnaires leant on a banner with the initials SPQR, *senatus populusque romanus,* the slogan of the senate and the people of Rome. Below the window, in the gloom of the chapel, knelt a solitary female penitent, clad in nondescript shades of grey and brown, her hands clasped before a face shaded by a fawn headscarf, the lips just visible but moving soundlessly.

Arthur the deacon, escorting me out, stayed me from drawing any closer, and dropped his voice to a whisper. 'We are one of the few churches that are open all day. It's a great act of faith these days.'

Indeed. Given the ignorance, or forgetfulness, the lack of any concern, or just absence of curiosity, that I had found during my own cursory expedition to uncover the heritage of St Helens, I had no desire to disturb a true believer seeking the intercession of her patron saint. I was touched by the simplicity of the sight; here in a relatively modern monument to a remarkable historical figure whose alleged accomplishments were something about which it was felt necessary to keep quiet in an increasingly sceptical age. I wondered if there was a parallel between Helena and Constantine, mother and son, and Mary and Jesus. Was Helena's reputation in mediaeval times an offshoot of the cult of the Virgin Mary, the woman chosen by God whose offspring brought Christianity to the world? Did Helena's role in giving birth to what became the Holy Roman Empire explain why in mediaeval times her name was attached to an ordinary wayside chapel in the Duchy of Lancaster? How and when was she supposed to have discovered the remains of the True Cross, a tale that was clearly once extremely popular but has gradually been lost from general view, preserved only in such physical reminders as the tiny relic in a provincial Catholic church now embarrassed about advertising its claim to one of the defining moments of history?

These questions crowded my mind as I took my leave of the kindly priest with profuse thanks. Returning to the burning summer streets of municipal St Helens I felt that the answers really lay elsewhere. The big event preoccupying the good burghers of the town that coming weekend was the annual St Helens Show. 'Fireworks, fairground, exhibitions . . . and lots,

lots more!' proclaimed the brochure. In other words, that other gift of the glory that was Rome, bread and circuses for the masses. I learned from a poster that the highlight of this three-day event, organised by the borough council, was a Mother and Baby competition. One of the largest in the country, apparently, then in its 21st year and no doubt the modern equivalent of the cult of the Madonna and Child. I did not wait around for the final, appropriately enough scheduled for the Sunday.

CHAPTER II

The Invention of the Cross

The very fact that a beam of wood should be found undecayed after so long a continuance in the earth would in most cases be a miracle.

Cardinal Newman[1]

EARLY IN THE 17th century a devout priest at the Jesuit College in Douai thought it would be a good idea to gather together everything that was known about the Catholic saints. Heribert Rosweyde's plan excited the church hierarchy, who gave the go-ahead to publish a chronological list of the lives of the saints according to the days of the year on which their feasts were celebrated, and he set about collecting relevant manuscripts and books. So enormous was the undertaking Rosweyde had unwittingly set himself, however, that by the time he died in 1629 not a single word had been sent to the printers.

The task was entrusted to another Jesuit, John van Bolland, who laboured for more than a decade over the mass of documents and with the help of an assistant finally managed to produce the first volume, covering the month of January, in 1643. The Pope was so impressed he invited the authors to Rome to study the Vatican's sources, and in the course of their subsequent pilgrimage through the libraries of Europe the pair accumulated even more material.

Bolland himself died in 1665, shortly after February had been completed, but posthumously gave his name to the mushrooming project which has continued sporadically from its base in Brussels ever since.[2] In the process, the founding principle adopted by the Bollandists, that every possible scrap of evidence should be collected and published, has given hagiography a bad name, turning the art of writing about the saints into a pejorative term for uncritical authorship. Their earnest intention was to bring some order and clarity to the study of lives and exploits which over the ages had been distorted by fantasy and popular imagination. So extensive is the *Acta Sanctorum*, and the learned commentaries it has spawned, that it has yet to reach a conclusion.

The chapter on Helena, widow and empress, which filled more than 100 pages of the folio edition published at Antwerp in 1738, is a case in point, rehearsing all that had been written before without coming to a verdict. Its tone was set at the outset by the combination of uncertainty about her date of birth, possibly in 248, and controversy over the place – 'some say Britain, some Drepanum in Bithynia, others Trevirorum . . .' Unfortunately it was also in Latin, which prevented me reading any further.

I found the August volume of the Acts of the Saints in the Jesuit library at Mount Street in London, whither I had gone in search of information about the St Helens relic. Father Tom McCoog, the librarian, issued a generous invitation on the phone.

'We should have something about relics in the records of our churches, though not all churches have relics. Relics are authenticated in Rome, but we have papers that go back to the 1700s. I'm not sure when the process began: the Carmelites? Relics are put in the altar – there's a way of going about it. We have dispersed some here, but usually you would have to contact Rome or someone who has a collection. What would have been done in the past I'm not sure. There may be something in our files about it.'

The headquarters of the Society of Jesus in the UK surrounds a quiet courtyard in the heart of Mayfair. I was escorted along a series of clinical corridors down to the basement where rows of leather-bound books on polished wood shelves testified to the accumulation of centuries of learning. A Barcelona football club scarf hung incongruously from a grille in the office where I found Fr McCoog. A white-haired, soft-spoken American from Philadelphia wearing a rugby shirt and cords, he gently corrected some of my preconceptions about the order's reputation as fanatical persecutors of heresy.

'We were nothing to do with the Spanish Inquisition. That was the bloody Dominicans,' he said. 'If you look at mediaeval paintings you see sheep surrounded by dogs. They're the *domini canes,* the dogs of God, the guardians and protectors of the flock. We got involved once or twice on the orders of the Pope, for example in the prosecution of Galileo, but our chief function was as educators, founding schools and colleges in the liberal arts tradition.'

'What do we do now?' He laughed. 'We die out. There are only 300 Jesuits in the British provincial, and for historical reasons that jurisdiction includes Guyana and South Africa. We have two dozen here in London and the average age of the house is 74. It's symptomatic of the decline of the Catholic Church. Those orders that survive are right wing, like Opus Dei and the Legionnaires of Christ. Their members thrive on nostalgia for a past they never experienced.'

Fr McCoog was rather vague about what might be in the records ranged around him. 'Relics of the holy cross are a dime a dozen,' he said cheerfully as he combed the files for me. 'You should go to Rome, they exhibit them there. I went hoping to see

Veronica's veil but all I found was a snotty handkerchief, so far away you could not see anything.'[3]

✝

THE JESUITS pulled out of St Helens back in 1932, but the musty boxes stored at Mount Street contained all sorts of scraps of paper, balance sheets, letters and notes about the order's efforts to proselytise in the district during the previous century and a half. After the Reformation, Catholicism in England went underground for three centuries, persecuted by penal legislation which made it treasonable to harbour a seminarian. Lancashire, identified as 'the very sink of popery' by the Privy Council in 1574, remained a hotbed of the Old Faith during this period. Many manorial families maintained their own chaplains, ordained abroad – particularly at Douai – and concealed at home in the 'priest holes' of the big houses.

One such was the Lowe family of Cowley Hill, whose pious daughter Winifrede became revered as the founder of the modern Catholic Church in the region. She married into the wealthy Eccleston clan, and, taking advantage of a recent relaxation in the laws that allowed Catholics to build their own churches once again, bequeathed the family home to the Jesuits on her death in 1793. Her will stipulated that the holy fathers should hold 14 masses a year for the repose of her soul, four more for various relatives, and two each for her late husband, her priest, and her best friend.

The succession of Catholic Relief Acts passed between 1778 and 1829, which gradually removed the threat of imprisonment, restored freedom of worship, and conferred the right to vote, set the stage for a public revival of Catholicism in the north-west in the Victorian era. In St Helens this peaked under Father Thomas Ullathorne, superior of the Jesuit mission for more than 20 years, who presided over a building spree which saw five more

Catholic churches spring up in the town, including Holy Cross. Its foundation stone was laid in 1860 on the feast of the finding of the True Cross, May 3rd, invoking the patronage of St Helen. At a celebratory dinner after the solemn opening two years later, Fr Ullathorne told a grateful audience including three bishops, four canons, six monks, 12 priests and 36 Jesuits: 'Now you have your church, take care to fill it.' Within months his clergy boasted of a potential congregation of 10,000, according to calculations based on the number of baptisms already taking place.

The surviving records suggested there existed an uneasy relationship between the original Jesuit mission base at Lowe House, also known as St Mary's, and the newly-founded focus of religious fervour at Holy Cross. At one point in the 1870s, Fr Ullathorne appeared to have borrowed several thousand pounds on the strength of the Holy Cross deeds to fund a presbytery at Lowe House, becoming 'pitiably weighed down with debt' in the process. The neo-Gothic building in Corporation Street itself cost £10,000 to construct, a sum largely raised through the munificence of Mary Stapleton, a local lady who married into the Bretherton family and acquired the grand title of Marchioness. Her name cropped up several times in the files as the donor of various expensive chalices and vestments, and her piety was displayed in an account of a pilgrimage she made to the Vatican in the early spring of 1862. Writing from Pisa, on her way home, she described an audience with Pope Pius IX, who had bestowed on her a selection of religious mementoes in response to a request to procure something appropriate in time for the opening of the church.

'I am very grateful to you for trusting me with this commission – not only have I a relic of the Holy Cross but also one of St Helena for you, which the Good Father procured for you,' she told Fr Ullathorne proudly.

'I am only too happy to have such holy things with me. At the same time I am afraid of losing them. If I do so, I cannot blame myself for I think I take very good care of them. I hope they will protect us during the journey home.'

✝

THE CUSTOM THAT every Catholic church should have a sacred relic of its own stems back to the earliest Christian times, when the first altars were raised to celebrate the Eucharist over the graves of the martyrs.[4] The remains that these first witnesses to the faith left behind on earth offered their successors a short cut to heaven. Their relics were never invested with magical properties, but simply provided a physical focus for worshippers invoking the intercession of God or seeking divine protection. They became much sought after, particularly following the example set by the death of Polycarp, the elderly bishop of Smyrna in Asia Minor – now Izmir in Turkey – who was burned at the stake in Rome around the year 155 for refusing to recant. Witnesses maintained that a wonderful fragrance 'like a breath of frankincense or some other costly spice' was given off by his charred remains, and resolved to commemorate his death annually. As Eusebius recorded their story in his *Church History*: 'We took up his bones, more precious than stones of great price, more splendid than gold, and laid them where it seemed right. When, if it proves possible, we assemble there, the Lord will allow us to celebrate with joy and gladness the birthday of his martyrdom – both to the memory of those who have contended in the past, and for the training and preparation of those whose time is yet to come.'[5]

However, there was a practical problem with such activities, particularly in Rome itself where the martyrs were mostly buried in the city's catacombs. Since permanent churches could not always be established as monuments over the actual graves of saints, the logical alternative was to move the dead bodies into new buildings. The shortage of suitable mortal remains for the purpose also became an issue as early as the fourth century, when substitutes became popular – such as handier shards of bone, pieces of cloth that had been in contact with a saint, or even particles of dust from a grave elsewhere. The discovery of the True Cross offered a less ghoulish and more convenient alternative. Such usage was first attested in an inscription found a century ago on a stone slab from north Africa, recording that 'the holy wood of the cross was brought and deposited here' in the year 359.[6]

A ruling by the second council of Nicea in 787, that no church should be consecrated without a suitable holy relic being sealed into the altar table, sparked a veritable gold rush. Possession of holy objects not only granted a church a special status among the faithful, but also conferred the power to attract pilgrims in large numbers, transforming the local economy. The usefulness of relics was broadened to include social as well as ecclesiastical functions, including oath-taking in courts, rallying troops in battle, and performing cures for medical ills. By mediaeval times the trade in relics was an international business, spurred on by waves of returning Crusaders armed with a wide and increasingly improbable range of souvenirs from the Holy Land. The sack of Constantinople by the Fourth Crusade in 1203 produced a rash of contributions plundered from the Pharos Chapel of the deposed Byzantine emperor Alexius III. One amazed knight, Robert de Clari, recorded a list of relics from the collection including two nails, the crown of thorns, the holy tunic, the tip of the lance that pierced Jesus' side, and 'two pieces of the True Cross as large as the leg of a man.'[7]

The attitude of the modern Catholic Church towards the veneration of relics is rather equivocal. Traditionally the position was laid down at length in canon law, which contained detailed provisions for the authentication of relics until the codex was revised in 1983. The updated regulations contain just one short section on the subject, whose formulation seems designed to distance the authorities from the practice while not actually condemning those who take comfort from it. 'It is absolutely wrong to sell sacred relics,' says Article 1190. 'Distinguished relics and others which are held in great veneration by the people may not validly be in any way alienated nor transferred on a permanent basis without the permission of the Apostolic See.'[8]

I sought guidance from the Vatican, and found the communications department still reeling from adverse publicity generated by a mischievous Channel 4 television documentary whose producers turned a serious proposal for an examination of the cult of relics into a populist hue and cry over the dubious claims of a church in Italy to possess the preserved foreskin taken from the infant Jesus at his circumcision ceremony. Nevertheless, officials did confirm that the recent reform of canon law meant that having a relic in an altar was no longer a mandatory requirement.

'Popular piety is no longer interested in relics, and in practice the church has followed that by reducing the amount of attention paid to them,' said Father Patrick Casserly. 'The old practice in Rome was that the contents of the tombs were given out to bishops visiting from around the world for use in setting up altars. That is still possible – bishops who come to Rome can still ask for relics, and are given a small amount from some of the many catacombs which are around the city.'[9]

Nowadays the business is handled by a special office at the Vicariate of Rome rather than in the Vatican itself. The pope used to have a small stock of relics 'for convenience' but some years ago this was handed over to the body at the Lateran Palace which is responsible for administering the diocese of the city and its network of necropoli. As for the relics of the True Cross, according to Fr Casserly that was a separate issue because the remains had been specially venerated for such a long time. 'The bit that was found was brought to Rome and over the years this was distributed,' he said. Fr Casserly seemed reluctant to be drawn further on the telephone. 'In the West we are very impious.'

✝

MARY STAPLETON SURVIVED to the age of 74, but I could find no corroboration of precisely what she had purchased on her trip to Rome in 1862. Father Pennington from Holy Cross told me in subsequent correspondence that the church possessed 'two tiny splinters' but no history of how they reached St Helens. Yet the Jesuit records in Mount Street did contain an official certificate attesting to the authenticity of a St Helens relic, signed by Cardinal Nicholas Wiseman, Archbishop of Westminster. In magisterial Latin script it stated that, having inspected the goods, he recognised them as 'sacred particles' from the wood of the holy cross of Jesus Christ 'which were extracted from authentic places' and were suitable for public veneration. Oddly, however, the certificate was dated December 1852 – ten years before Mary Stapleton's trip. Did this mean there was a rival relic in town?

Discussion of such a sensitive subject is avoided in modern histories of the St Helens churches.[10] A pamphlet published to mark the centenary of Holy Cross church in 1962 described in detail the stained glass windows, statuary and other items of church furniture donated by well-wishers yet made only an ambiguous reference to 'the Blessed Sacrament' hidden in a steel tabernacle inside the High Altar. Similarly, the most recent guide for visitors to Lowe House (1993) stated categorically that its only relic was the body of Winifred Eccleston herself, interred under the altar. Yet an earlier pamphlet on the history of the Jesuit mission, published in 1940 and lodged in the Mount Street archive, did acknowledge the existence of another fragment of the True Cross – not at Holy Cross, but at Lowe House.

The claim went back to a Father Thomas Eccleston SJ, who

testified before his death in 1743 that he had witnessed a section shaved off the 'Great Relic' which belonged to the Jesuits at Ghent, in Belgium. Another offcut from the same source is today preserved by Stonyhurst College, the Jesuit foundation in Lancashire, though it was never authenticated. The archivist, Father F J Turner, told me there was a close connection between Ghent and Stonyhurst but no proof that either had anything to do with St Helens.

'The evidence for the relics is based almost entirely on tradition. No written evidence goes back earlier than the time of James I, and any attempt to find further evidence has come to nothing,' he said.[11]

The provenance of the Ghent relic is based on an account by Father Edward Lusher, who studied there in the mid 17th century. He maintained that the wood had been 'cloven off a greater piece which was kept in the Tower of London, in an old bag of canvas, that had upon it this inscription: *A peece of the Stumpe of the Crosse of o'r Savio'r.* It was kept there among the King's jewels and was taken thence by a gentleman who was an officer of the Tower. His name was told me, but I have forgotten it.'[12]

Some time around 1620 the anonymous raider gave a piece of the wood to a mate from Yorkshire, Thomas Pudsey, whose wife passed it on to Fr Lusher, who bequeathed it to a colleague, Father Anthony Hunter, who took it to Ghent. At each stage of the chain the individuals concerned each kept a little bit back for themselves. One of these fragments ended up in a convent in Norwich, where it was further divided. Part was fashioned into a miniature cross and eventually passed into the hands of the Lovat family, together with a certificate from Cardinal Wiseman. The remainder went to Stonyhurst for safe keeping in 1824. Meanwhile the material dispatched to Ghent was itself spilt up, with at least three offcuts made, one of which ended up back in Britain with the Petre family accompanied by a certificate from the Bishop of Ghent which Cardinal Wiseman counter-signed

140 years later. On the suppression of the Society of Jesus in 1773, the surviving Ghent relic was given into the care of the city's cathedral.

All this carpentry took place at a time when Catholicism was proscribed in Britain, and amid all the secrecy which surrounded recusant activity no doubt the surreptitious passing-on of holy objects kept the flame of faith alight. In the early years of Elizabeth's reign even the presence of a crucifix on church altars was held to be illegal. Yet how did the original *peece of the stumpe* get to the Tower? According to the diligent investigations of Father John Morris, who researched the sources of English relics for a series of articles in the Jesuit periodical *The Month* in 1882, it must have come from Scotland when James I took the throne, since there was no earlier record of any religious relic among the post-Reformation inventory of Crown jewels. Fr Morris established that the King passed the remaining lump to John Tradescant as a reward, though on the adventurer's death it was restored to the Tower. Subsequently, on the outbreak of the English civil war, Queen Henrietta decided to send it to France for safe keeping but the ship foundered in the Channel and the cargo was lost. No doubt it was entirely coincidental that such a potentially valuable object should have made a brief appearance on the stage of British history just when the Stuart kings, James I and Charles I, were suspected of harbouring Catholic sympathies.

PROTESTANTS HAVE ALWAYS sneered at such idolatry and joked that if all the fragments revered by Papists around the world were brought together there would be enough timber to build a ship. Undeterred, a pious 19th-century French pastor once set about proving the doubters wrong. Charles Rohault de Fleury calculated that a crucifix made out of pine and strong enough to support the weight of a man, say four metres high with a two-metre cross-beam, would have a volume of about 178 million cubic millimetres. In the interests of verisimilitude he assumed that about one fifth of the upright would have been buried in order to provide stability, and that the victim's feet were at least 18 inches off the ground so that wild dogs could not tear out his entrails.

Monseigneur Rohault de Fleury then sought out all the surviving fragments – from two dozen separate pieces stored at the monastery of Mouth Athos in Greece to a huge chunk kept at St Gudule's Church in Brussels – measured them all minutely, and catalogued the results. On the publication of his *Memoir of the Instruments of the Passion* in 1870, the word whizzed round the Catholic world. Thanks be to God! The extant total accounted for less than four million cubic millimetres.[13]

'The marvel, then, is not that there should be so many relics existing, but that there should be so exceedingly few,' commented the Rev James Bellord in a penny pamphlet published by the Catholic Truth Society for an English audience in 1898. He reviewed Mgr Rohault de Fleury's work and concluded that his French counterpart actually left out quite a lot. He had ignored the relics of the Russian Orthodox Church completely, for example, and failed to take into account that much else had probably been lost over the centuries. The original relic preserved at Jerusalem was almost certainly subdivided after the Arab conquest in order to preserve it, he reckoned, with pieces distributed to various places including Constantinople, Cyprus, Alexandria and the Syrian cities of Antioch, Edessa and Damascus. 'It is probable that there is a relic of the True Cross in the royal sceptre of England,' added Mr Bellord, charting five other possessors of minor relics in the country to his certain knowledge – St Gregory's at Downside in Surrey, the Petre family, St Mary's Abbey at East Bergholt in Suffolk, St Mary's Convent at York, and Slindon in West Sussex. Even so, his revised calculations put the 'grand total of all known existing and lost relics' of the cross at just over ten million cubic millimetres, or still less than one tenth of Rohault de Fleury's calculation of its original size.[14]

CONSTANTINE THE GREAT formally abolished the practice of crucifixion in 337 in tribute to the suffering Jesus endured, replacing the cross he had himself frequently sanctioned for capital punishment earlier in his reign with the hangman's gibbet. Around the same time, representations of the cross first began to appear openly among Christian communities. Previously, during periods of persecution by the Roman authorities, the sacred mark was concealed in the form of an anchor, a trident, or even a swastika, the ancient symbol of the sun. A fish was also a popular substitute, fortified by the Biblical allusion to Jesus proclaiming the disciples 'fishers of men' and reinforced by the acronym formed by the Greek word for fish, *ichthys*, whose letters *ΙΧΘΥΣ* spelled out the initials of the phrase 'Jesus Christ, Son of God, the Saviour.'[15] Making the sign of the cross was often used as a coded greeting between the faithful: 'We Christians wear out our foreheads with the sign of the cross,' admitted Tertullian.[16]

However, in the wake of Constantine's edict of toleration, the development of Christianity as the state religion removed any stigma of subversion from the cross as a symbol of faith, and by the fifth century it was in universal use, not just on objects for liturgical purposes or on tombs but on household utensils too, like lamps, spoons, cups, plates, glassware, the seals of wine jars, and even water-pipes. The emperor Julian, known as the Apostate for his unsuccessful attempt to reverse the trend and revive paganism during a brief reign between 361–3, complained not only about the growing practice of signing the cross but also the popular veneration of pieces of wood from it.

The earliest reference to the existence of the remains of the actual cross on which Jesus died came in a series of lectures given by Cyril, the Bishop of Jerusalem in 348. 'The holy wood of the cross gives witness: it is here to be seen in this very day, and through those who take from it in faith, it has from here already filled almost the whole world,' he told his pupils.[17] Evidently the practice of displaying the relic in the holy city was already well established, though Cyril's words also hint at the idea of removing fragments and dispersing them among the faithful.

By the end of the century John Chrysostom, the bishop of Constantinople who was nick-named the 'gilded mouth' because of his eloquent preaching, said bits were frequently kept in golden reliquaries which people carried on a chain round their necks – the origin of the pectoral crosses still worn today. About 403 Paulinus of Nola received one from Jerusalem in a golden tube, so minute it was almost an atom. In a letter to a friend he started the rumour that the cross never got smaller no matter how many pieces were detached, and related the common belief that the miraculous wood had been discovered by Helena three-quarters of a century before. The friend had wanted a relic of the saints to consecrate a church but Paulinus passed on the fragment as better value than the current vogue for sacred ashes.

'In this almost indivisible particle of a small sliver, take up the protection of your immediate safety, and the guarantee of your eternal salvation,' he advised. 'Let not your faith shrink because the eyes of the body behold evidence so small: let it look with the inner eye on the power of the cross in this tiny segment.'[18]

Paulinus was a wealthy nobleman from Aquitaine who renounced his worldly goods and moved to Nola in Campania in order to join a monastic community near the shrine of a certain Felix. Each year this ascetic aristocrat renewed his vows by making a pilgrimage to Rome in order to take part in the annual procession round the tombs of Peter and Paul, guardians of the apostolic tradition. No doubt it was here in the holy city that he first heard the tale he later recounted to his friend Sulpicius Severus, of how Helena had asked her son the emperor to give her a free hand in clearing all the sites the Lord himself had visited. Using the resources of the imperial treasury, said Paulinus, she constructed a number of basilicas in Palestine, including one on the site of Jesus' ascension into heaven. There the ground was so hallowed that the imprint of the Saviour's last footsteps could still be seen, miraculously marked out in green turf from the surrounding sand.

✝

NOT LEAST OF the fascinating facts about Helena is that the mass of writings about her life and legacy over the ages has been based on the most slender of original evidence. Indeed, while she was alive, contemporaries appeared to have ignored her altogether. For example, Eusebius of Caesarea did not deign to mention her at all in his history of the early church up to 325, a work which celebrated the achievements of her son in unifying the Roman Empire and embracing Christianity as the state religion.

Helena did, however, receive an honourable mention in the same author's *Life of Constantine*, written 12 years later after the death of the emperor. Here Eusebius told in glowing terms of her pilgrimage to the 'venerable land' which the Saviour's feet had trodden, the dedication of the churches marking the birth, death and ascension of Jesus, and her death shortly afterwards 'having arrived at the eightieth year of her age.'[19] This belated recognition suggested that Helena undertook her journey after Eusebius had completed his church history.

The study of Roman coinage and inscriptions informs us that the honorary title of Augusta was bestowed upon Helena in 324, marking out for the first time a role for her akin to the Queen Mother of the day. However, since no new currency bearing her name was issued after 329 she must have died by then, basking in the unexpected fame which came to her in the last five years of her long life. Yet did her reputation amongst contemporaries have anything to do with the discovery of the remains of the cross? Probably not.

Eusebius did not have anything to say on the subject, though from the sanctimonious tone of his eulogy to Constantine in general and the piety of his portrayal of the Emperor's mother in particular we can assume Eusebius would have done had he been given half a chance. Cyril, the bishop of Jerusalem, said nothing at all about Helena in his later lectures, and neither did Chrysostom of Constantinople in sermons delivered just before the turn of the century. The first authority to link Helena with the discovery of the cross was almost 70 years after her death, when Ambrose, the bishop of Milan, related the story in his oration at the funeral of the emperor Theodosius in 395.

'Blessed was Constantine with such a mother!' declared the bishop with that sort of rhetorical flourish which makes the works of the early church fathers so difficult to read nowadays. 'Noble woman, who found much more to confer upon an emperor than she might receive from an emperor!' For Ambrose the discovery of the cross marked the beginning of a new age of Christian rule, in which Helena was accorded the status of a worthy successor to Mary, emulating the Virgin birth and thereby defeating Satan. 'She gave proof that he was born: I shall give proof that he rose from the dead,' the author made his heroine cry as he pictured her surveying the site of Golgotha, spade metaphorically in hand. 'And so she opened the ground and cleared away the dust. She found three fork-shaped gibbets thrown together, covered by debris and hidden by the Enemy.'[20]

Inspired by the Holy Spirit, but prudently checking the gospel records, this Helena had recognised one of the beams as the True Cross by the title plate conveniently affixed on it proclaiming 'Jesus of Nazareth, King of the Jews.' She also dug around for the nails, ordering a crown to be fashioned from one and a bridle from the other: both items were despatched as proof of the discovery to Constantine. The recovery of the nails became a crucial ingredient of the popular legend,[21] though I could not understand the significance of the emperor's headgear and the horse's harness until I went back to Ambrose's actual text. The point here was secular as much as religious, for Ambrose was speaking at a crucial time for the church. The Roman Empire had become a Christian state but the death of Theodosius left the western half in the hands of a boy of ten and the east ruled by a youth of 18. The bishop was anxious to remind the emperor's successors of their responsibility in maintaining the heritage of Constantine, in which the church both sanctified imperial rule and acted as a restraining force upon it. 'On the head, a crown: in the hands, reins. A crown made from the cross, that faith might shine forth; reins likewise from the cross, that authority might govern and that there might be just rule, not unjust legislation.'

Although Ambrose was the earliest author to make an explicit connection between Helena's pilgrimage in the early part of the fourth century and the veneration of the *lignum crucis,* the wood of the cross, towards the end, he does speak as if the association was common knowledge at the imperial court by then. His account of how the True Cross was recognised by the title plate echoed that given by John Chrysostom in his sermons on John's gospel around the same period: indeed it had been John the Evangelist who alone in his gospel offered the crucifixion detail that Pontius Pilate ordered a plaque be made identifying Jesus of Nazareth as King of the Jews.

However, Ambrose also had a thing about relics in general. More than any of the other church fathers he was responsible for developing the cult of relics as a powerful weapon for enforcing orthodoxy, playing on popular fears of demons and devils. The story of the recovery of the True Cross was just one element in a catalogue of recent finds that included the column used in the scourging of Jesus, the body of St Stephen, the head of John the Baptist, the chair of St James, and the chains of St Paul. Even at this early stage the trade in relics had become so intense that, shortly before his death, Theodosius stepped in amid reports that monks stole the remains of holy men and hawked portions for money. 'No person shall transfer a buried body to another place; no person shall sell the relics of a martyr; no person shall traffic in them,' the emperor decreed.[22]

Yet Ambrose was unabashed, providentially discovering the skeletons of two early martyrs, Gervasius and Protasius, in time for the opening of his new basilica at Milan, and followed up his success by unearthing the bodies of Agricola, Vitalis, Nazarius and Celsus as well. There is no reason to doubt that such a superstitious man was genuine in his convictions. He probably seized eagerly on the stories about Helena that pilgrims were already beginning to bring back from the Holy Land because they fitted into his grand scheme. For example, Rufinus of Aquileia returned to Italy in 397 after 20 years with the monastic community on the Mount of Olives. Later on he readily incorporated the story of Helena's involvement into the church history he started writing from the point where Eusebius had left off.

Rufinus also introduced a new ingredient to the tale in the person of Macarius, the bishop of Jerusalem, maintaining that he persuaded Helena to test the three beams at the bedside of a dying lady who was miraculously cured at the touch of the True Cross. A further refinement was the suggestion that the wood was sent to Constantinople along with those nails. Although Rufinus did not finish his history until well into the fifth century, his version has to be taken seriously because it appears to be closely based on an earlier source, now lost, compiled by Gelasius, bishop of Caesarea in the last third of the fourth century. Such a work would thus pre-date Ambrose, and directly reflect the beliefs of the Christian communities in the Holy Land. Nevertheless, there is no escaping the fact that the early Christian church left behind no contemporary evidence whatsoever for the cult status that Helena was so swiftly accorded.[23]

IN THE ROMAN CATHOLIC calendar the cross is everywhere venerated on Good Friday, the date of Jesus' crucifixion. Traditionally the missal also commemorated two other important moments in the history of the symbol: on May 3rd the church celebrated the original finding of the cross by Helena, and on September 14th it hailed the subsequent return of the relic to Jerusalem after it was stolen by the Persians several centuries later. The reasons for choosing these precise dates has become rather muddled over the centuries and harks back to a time when there were two separate liturgies in use among the Gallic churches of the western empire and the Roman churches of the east.[24]

The latter had since earliest times kept a special ceremony in September to mark the anniversary of the dedication in 335 of the Holy Sepulchre basilica by Constantine. As part of the festivities, the remains of the True Cross held in Jerusalem were exposed to the public for adoration. However, in 614, the invading Persian army of Chosroes II sacked the city (with the help of Jews within the walls) and massacred most of its Christian inhabitants. Priests vainly attempted to hide the sacred relics but they were unearthed and sent eastwards in the company of the Patriarch Zacharias as a gift to Queen Meryem, who was a Nestorian Christian. Eight years later the emperor Heraclius reasserted his control and set off to get them back, like a prototype Crusader fighting the powers of darkness. Eventually he defeated the Persians at Nineveh, Chosroes' successor sued for peace, and the conquered territories were returned in 629. The following spring Heraclius journeyed to Palestine to receive the True Cross back in person, and its restoration to the Holy City in triumph gave a double reason to celebrate the feast of the Exaltation of the Cross that autumn.

News of the recovery of the relic spread rapidly, and during the seventh century the Gallic churches too started to mark the restitution of the cross. However, they chose May because that was the actual date of Heraclius's return to Jerusalem. At some point the feast became associated with Helena's discovery instead. Since the 'exaltation' was also known as the 'elevation' of the cross, with the added meaning of bringing into the light, there may have been confusion with the popular account of how she found the remains buried in the ground. In Catholic jargon this feast soon became officially known as the Invention of the Cross. The derivation came from the Latin *inventio*, meaning to come upon, but remains resonant with irony because of the inadvertent implication that the whole story was made up.

In the modern liturgical year, September 14th retains its place as a day of devotion to what is now called 'the triumph of the cross.' However, the rest of the calendar has been rationalised, and the traditional commemoration of the finding of the cross on May 3rd was quietly dropped during the reforms heralded by the second Vatican Council in the 1960s.[25] Never again will the Roman church mark an anniversary in the manner last seen as recently as 1926, when good Catholics everywhere were encouraged to celebrate the 16th centenary of Helena's discovery. In a letter to his Prefect of Propaganda, William Van Rossum, the then Pope authorised a plenary indulgence to mark the occasion. The practice of granting remission of sins to those who repented harked back to mediaeval times, and was based on the notion that the church accumulated a treasury of merit through the good works of the saints, which could be expended on those who tried but failed to make the grade. In this particular case, any of the faithful who paid five visits to the basilica in Rome dedicated to the holy cross were entitled to receive forgiveness. Realising this was impractical for most of the faithful scattered around the world, however, Pius XI extended the concession to a number of other carefully selected locations. The Church of Helen and the Holy Cross in Corporation Street, St Helens, was the only eligible venue in the UK.

CHAPTER III

The English Connection

At this time Constantius, a man of exceptional kindness and courtesy, who had governed Gaul and Spain during the lifetime of Docletian, died in Britain. His son Constantine, the child of Helena his concubine, succeeded him as ruler of Gaul.

The Venerable Bede[1]

THE STORY OF Helena's miraculous discovery spread rapidly throughout Christendom, not only through the medium of Greek and Latin but also via Syriac, Coptic, and Georgian. So widely was it believed in an incredulous world that it soon cropped up in an early masterpiece of Old English literature. The Anglo-Saxon poem *Elene* described how the king of the Romans, rallying his troops to fight off the Huns and the Goths on the banks of the Danube, had a vision of the cross in the sky. Adopting the symbol as his standard, Constantine put his enemies to flight and in gratitude was baptised.

'Then the praise of Christ was in the emperor's heart, and henceforth he forgot not that famous tree; and then he bade his mother travel the road to the Jews with a troop of people, and

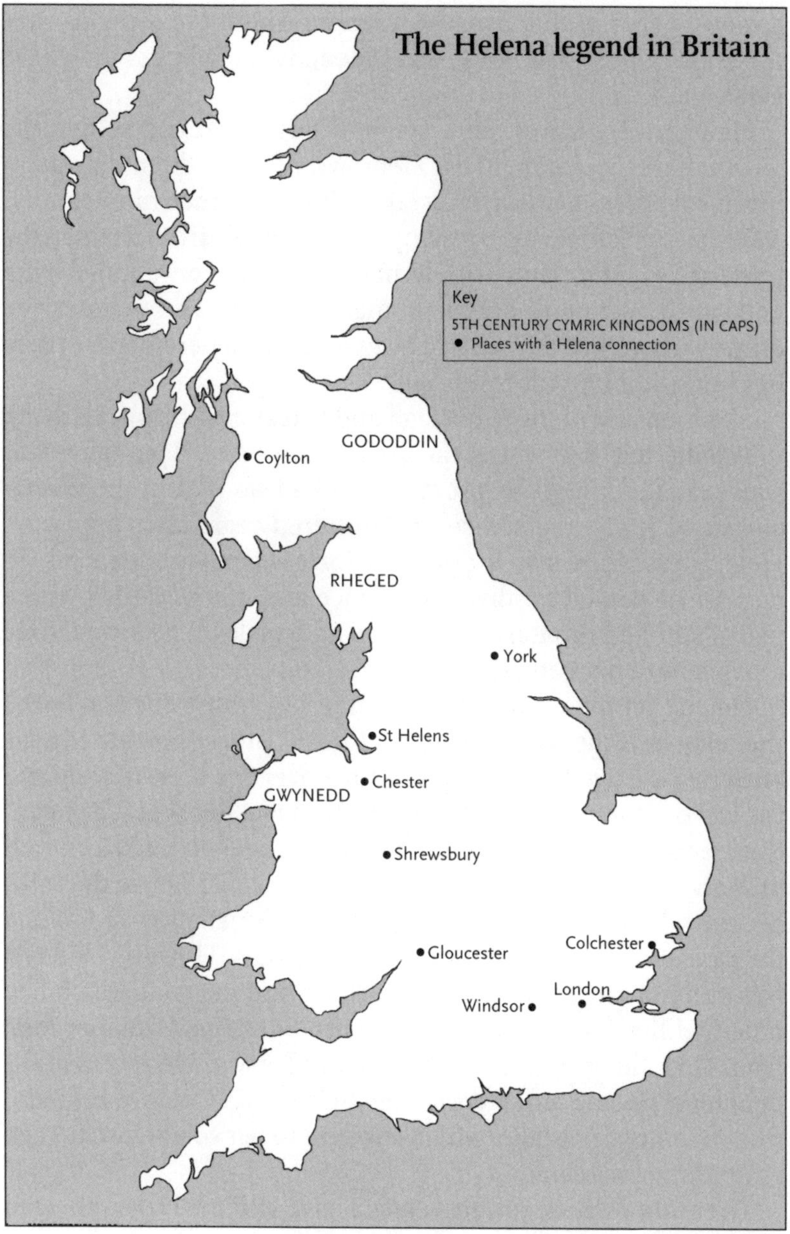
The Helena legend in Britain
Key
5TH CENTURY CYMRIC KINGDOMS (IN CAPS)
• Places with a Helena connection
GODODDIN
Coylton
RHEGED
York
St Helens
Chester
GWYNEDD
Shrewsbury
Gloucester
Colchester
London
Windsor

zealously seek with a band of warriors where the glorious tree, the cross of the noble King, was hidden in its holiness under the earth.'

Helena – for it was she – entered Jerusalem and sought the advice of the wise men of the Hebrews, offering them the opportunity to redress a historic mistake. 'Ye condemned him to death, who himself had raised up many of your people from death in the presence of men. Thus with blinded hearts ye confounded lying with truth, light with darkness, malice with mercy, ye contrived crime with wicked thoughts,' she told them. 'Wherefore the curse lies heavy upon you for your guilt.'

She took one of them hostage and threatened him with death unless he told her where the cross was buried. His name was Judas, and although he protested he had no idea of the whereabouts of Jesus' crucifix several hundred years after the event, Helena cast him into a dungeon for a week without food. In despair he prayed for divine guidance and was rewarded with a pall of smoke from the earth, where 20 feet down he found three crosses buried together.

Helena set them up and was pondering which one had borne the body of Jesus when a passing funeral procession gave Judas an idea: he waved the crosses in turn over the lifeless body and the last one caused the dead man to come to life. When he heard this news, Constantine commanded the queen to build a church on Calvary, not only to mark the site but also to house the relic. Meanwhile Judas promptly converted to Christianity and joined the priesthood, taking the surname Cyriacus. However, Helena was still not satisfied and demanded he find the nails which had crucified her Lord as well. After more prayer and another sign from God, this time a darting flame, Judas was successful and a delighted Helena ordered that the 'twisted wire' be wrought into a bit for a horse's bridle, which she sent to her son before herself embarking for home.

The author whose rolling verses I have so crudely paraphrased signed himself Cynewulf, but little else is known about him. He was thought to be a northerner writing towards the end of the eighth century, when the country was divided into three kingdoms: Northumbria above the Humber, Wessex below the Thames, and Mercia in between. Nevertheless, he remains the most celebrated exponent of the flowering of Anglo-Saxon poetry in the centuries before the Norman Conquest, combining echoes of an heroic age of battles and warriors with a strong moralising tone. Another poem attributed to him, partly on linguistic grounds but also because he was clearly interested in the Christian cross as a theme, is *The Dream of the Rood*, in which the teller recounts a vision of the cross, alternately bedecked with jewels or stained with blood. A voice coming out of the wood speaks of its brief part in the passion of 'the young hero' and how it was found years later by 'the followers of the Lord' – and the dreamer's faith is thereby reaffirmed. No clue is offered in the text, but it is at least plausible in the light of Cynewulf's other work that the dreamer was intended to be Helena.[2]

The Old English legend was in one literary respect quite different from the accounts of the early church fathers: the intervention of the character of Judas Cyriacus. While the heroine, Helena, experienced the vision, the newcomer actually found the wood and the nails. Cynewulf shared this extra ingredient in common with early Syrian versions of the legend which circulated among the eastern churches, and it was to become the most popular variant in the Middle Ages. Some of the sentiments strike modern sensibilities as uncomfortably anti-Semitic, holding the Jews responsible for hiding the cross because of their collective guilt in murdering the Messiah. This was probably deliberate in that, once Christianity had overcome the lingering threat from paganism by the beginning of the fifth century, propagandists in the east were increasingly anxious to distance the movement from its roots in Judaism. Thus, while Helena harangues the Hebrew elders in *Elene* for not believing their own scriptures, the Jews are offered a chance of redemption. One passage, between the discovery of the cross and the search for the nails, describes Judas wrestling with the Devil, who cries out: 'Erstwhile I was heartened by Judas and now once again by Judas I am humiliated.' In defying Satan – itself an echo of Jesus' temptation – Judas Cyriacus thus atones for the betrayal of Christ by Judas Iscariot. The theological rather than historical purpose is underlined by the character's name, for Judaeus Cyriacus is not a real person but a Latin translation of the phrase 'a Jew of the Lord.'[3]

Cynewulf probably got his raw material from a version of the Helena legend popularised in the West by Gregory of Tours after the sixth century. Quite possibly it was brought to Britain in the wake of St Augustine's mission to preach the gospel to the Angles, and the re-establishment of the Roman diocesan church in England over the native tradition of Celtic monasticism which held sway during the Dark Ages. During this period Northumbria was the literary centre of Western Europe, basking in the reputation of the Venerable Bede as a scholar and polymath. The stature of the monk from Jarrow is undimmed today, largely because of the reliability of the ecclesiastical history of the English nation he compiled in 731. Chronicling the fall of Roman Britain, he told his readers with admirable economy that Constantius, governor of Gaul in the time of Diocletian, had died in Britain and was succeeded by Constantine, 'the child of Helena his concubine.'[4] Bede's insistence on sticking to the bare facts cut no ice with his contemporaries, however. From the popularity of Helena in England, it was to be but a short step to the popular idea that Helena was English.

THE ENDURING AFFECTION for St Helena among the Anglican church-going classes in Victorian times was attested in 1863 by one Mrs Jameson, the devout author of a pious tome recalling the Legends of the Monastic Orders.[5] She enthusiastically branded Helena as a pioneering English saint in the mould of the martyr St Alban. 'From early antiquity the English have claimed her as their own and held her in especial honour: witness the number of our old churches dedicated to her and the popularity of her classical Greek name in all its various forms,' she trilled.[6]

Despite attracting the scorn of scholars, the notion was given a powerful boost as recently as half a century ago by Evelyn Waugh in an entertaining historical novel. The author made no claims to accuracy, admitting he picked out the picturesque in preference to the plausible when consulting the archives. 'The novelist deals with the experiences which excite his imagination,' he noted. 'The story is just something to be read: in fact, a legend.'[7]

Yet the flame of faith Waugh rekindled was still nurtured in Catholic circles, as I discovered when I consulted John Giblin. A retired engineer and resident of St Helens, he was chairman of the North-West Catholic History Society and occupied his spare time compiling records of the recusant families of Lancashire. One of his hobbies was disputing the birthplace of St Helena with the Anglican vicar of St Helens, the Rev Christopher Byworth.

'He has a degree in church history and reckons he is an expert, but I have studied the early sources. I went through them and nowhere could I find any reference to where she was born at all,' Mr Giblin told me over lunch at the Athenaeum, his Liverpool club. He waved his hand in the direction of the library across the hall, generously endowed by those 19th-century merchants who had founded this institution in the Athens of the North out of a firm conviction that its more famous namesake in London had no monopoly of wisdom.

'Evelyn Waugh regurgitated what was accepted for centuries. Of course you can never be certain but I am prepared to accept it is right. Helena was the daughter of Coilus, a Romano-British king who was ruler of a tribe at Colchester. This Celtic princess caught the imagination of the indigenous British, who had been pushed out to the remoter western fringes of the country by the Anglo-Saxon invasions. I would guess there was no leader of the Celts, but a memory persisted among the inter-married families. There are reasons to believe they were very proud of her.'[8]

Old King Cole was a merry old soul, they say, and a merry old soul was he, indulging his passions for smoking, drinking and dancing. 'He called for his pipe and he called for his bowl and he called for his fiddlers three.' The popular nursery rhyme was first recorded by William King in a 1709 collection entitled *Useful Transactions in Philosophy*.[9] It recalled a golden age in which a petty chieftain, also known as Coël or Caelius, presided benignly over a period of prosperity from his court at Colchester, administering the *pax Romana* on behalf of a grateful populace. The belief that he married off his daughter Helena to Constantius Chlorus, a Roman general serving in Britain, and bore a son who became Constantine the Great, was regarded by the antiquarian William Camden in the 17th century as 'the common and concurrent opinion of all writers . . . except one or two petty critics who differ among themselves.'[10]

The law on this matter was magisterially laid down by the Rev Alban Butler in the first edition of his comprehensive *Lives of the Saints*, published in 1842. 'We are assured by the unanimous tradition of our English historians, that this holy empress was a native of our island,' he wrote. Rattling off a list of learned antiquaries on the subject of Helena's roots, Butler accorded the honours to Colchester on the grounds that it was what most authorities agreed on. 'That town has for several ages boasted that it gave birth to this great empress, and the inhabitants, to testify their veneration for her memory, take for the arms of the town, in remembrance of the cross which she discovered, a knotty cross between four crowns,' he added.[11]

THE BOROUGH INSIGNIA is emblazoned all over 21st-century Colchester. It makes a fine tribute to the town's patron saint, though the chief function of this colourful coat of arms appears to be marking the iron posts which keep motor vehicles out of the historic centre, now pedestrianised for visitors and residents alike. Its ubiquitous presence at knee-height is an enduring symbol of a civic tradition that the town cannot shake off, even though officially the borough council's promotional literature readily admits the connection with Helena is a bit dubious. Nowadays Colchester is rather keener to promote its strictly historical charms as the oldest Roman settlement in Britain, with a wealth of excavated archaeological proof to back up the claims. Yet as I drove in for an exploratory weekend, the old links winked at unsuspecting motorists from roadside hoardings. From the sublime to the ridiculous, in the time it took to park a car I spotted advertisements for the St Helena Hospice, St Helena's grant-maintained comprehensive school, and the King Coel photographic studio.

Walking along the High Street, you can't miss the life-size bronze statue that dominates the town hall tower. Leaning on a tall thin cross on top of a classical folly, Helena watches over the borough, and virtually nowhere in the town centre can the local taxpayers escape her gaze. Neither can the councillors inside, for that matter, since she figures again in one of the stained glass windows illuminating the council chamber. It is visible from the street over the entrance to the Law Courts, as if she was Justice too. The magnificent town hall was one of the last great municipal monuments of the Victorian era, commissioned in 1897 but not completed until five years later, after the Queen's death. Drawings of John Belcher's winning design show that the architect envisaged a Baroque building adorned with sculptures of local notables and surmounted by a plain bell-tower. The style was retained but many changes made during construction, one of which involved adding the Helena statue to a modified clock tower. Alderman James Paxman, owner of an engineering firm and the town's largest employer at the time, was responsible for the adornment. Local lore suggested the figure originally depicted the Virgin Mary and was converted for the purpose, perhaps in Alderman Paxman's foundry.[12]

'Someone brought a Madonna back from Italy after their summer holidays,' confided the elderly Blue Badge guide who had just pointed out the landmark from the roof of the nearby castle, at the conclusion of her informative tour. She looked around to make sure the rest of the party had dispersed and lowered the piercingly cultured Edinburgh vowels that had carried through the Roman vaults so well during our 45-minute visit. 'We don't normally tell tourists this, but James Paxman had a bit of a reputation for the ladies. Some say they put Helena at the top of the tower because that was the only place he couldn't reach her.'

The castle is at the other end of the High Street, a curious structure which claims to be not only the oldest Norman keep in Britain but also the largest the Normans kept anywhere. Unfortunately it looks nothing like anything else the Normans built, chiefly because it was constructed from left-over Roman bricks, on the site of a pagan temple erected in honour of the emperor Claudius to commemorate his conquest of the Celtic tribes in AD 49. The Italianate outlook is further reinforced by the large windows inserted by a misguided 18th-century aristocrat, who thought the dilapidated structure he so carefully restored actually *was* a Roman fortress, and consequently re-roofed it with overlapping red tiles in the Mediterranean fashion familiar to those lucky few who had been on a Grand Tour of the Continent.

I asked the guide about King Cole, whom she had not mentioned at all, and she laughed as if recalling a memory of good times gone. 'According to the Red Book, which is now kept in the Record Office, Helena was here, but several hundred years out of date from the time she really existed,' she said. 'People believed it all for centuries. A circular earthwork outside the walls was called King Cole's Kitchen, there was a King Cole's Well in the High Street, and a bastion at the main Roman gate was called Colkyngs Castle.' So who exploded the myth, and when? She chuckled: 'It has not been disproved, but it has never been proved either.'

The Red Parchment, or Oath Book, bears the handwriting of the 1350s but its last entry was over a century beforehand, so the document itself is probably a copy of an earlier version. Folio 20, *Of Colchester and Coel*, set out the bare bones of the story with a precision that would be laudable if it were not completely erroneous. 'AD 219: Coel, Duke of the Britons, begins to build the city of Kaircoel. AD 238: Coel, Duke of Colchester, begins to reign over Essex and Hertford. AD 242: Helena, daughter of Coel, is born in Colchester.' And so on, through an alleged siege of Colchester by the Romans, which was only raised when Helena was betrothed to the general; and how she bore him a son while her father went on to rule over all Britain until his death in 297. 'In the second month,' added the author knowledgeably.

Sir W Gurney Benham, a civic worthy whose achievements are still recalled in the name of a small close in the modest suburb of Shrub End, offered a small commentary on the Helena connection in a monograph published in 1900, now in the public library. 'It was a matter almost of religion in the Middle Ages with the people of Colchester, and with the people of England generally, to believe that she was born in England and that she gave birth to Constantine at Colchester,' he wrote. Three times Mayor of Colchester, Alderman Benham also fancied himself as a bit of a historian. He investigated the archives of the College of Heralds and claimed to have found a precursor of the borough insignia in the coat of arms attributed to one King Coel Godebog. A genealogy from the same source drew a direct line of descent from Noah to James I, and put this intriguing character somewhere in-between the Ark and the end of the Elizabethan era. Any respect I might had had for his researches collapsed completely, however, when I also came across a song he composed for the 1909 Colchester pageant. The chorus made clear that by the Edwardian era, even in his adoptive hometown, the merry monarch was but a patriotic music hall symbol of the virtues of Merrie England.

> Old King Cole, rest his jolly soul,
> And may we all live like him in content and harmony;
> So keep the music going,
> And the bowl of friendship flowing,
> And the happy roses growing
> Over England fair and free.

✣

TRADITION HAS TO commence somewhere. Whenever historians hail longevity in order to value the contents of Britain's cultural treasury, it is time to start counting the spoons. Yet how on earth did Helena get linked to Old King Cole in the first place? I found one prime suspect in the work of a mediaeval ecclesiastic whose Chronicle first appeared around 1135. 'Tradition says,' wrote Henry of Huntingdon ominously. 'Tradition says that Helen, the illustrious daughter of Britain, surrounded London with the wall which is still standing, and fortified Colchester also with walls. But more especially, she built Jerusalem, adorning it with many basilicas purified from idols.' Henry, the canon of Lincoln cathedral, went on to record that Constantius, ruler of the Western provinces of Gaul, Spain and Britain, 'received in marriage the daughter of the British king of Colchester, whose name was Hoel or Helen, our St Helena, by whom he had Constantine the Great.'[13]

Pardon? I'm afraid that was a rather muddled passage, whose original Latin text is not clear. The translation deserves to be read again – this time as a question. *Whose* name was Hoel? Is this the daughter received in marriage, or the British king? Is this Hoel meant to be a spelling variation on Helen, leaving the king with no name? Or is there a missing comma which should separate Hoel from 'or Helen'? That would indicate he was a separate person, and allow the latter half of the sentence to stand as an explanation of who the daughter was. Nowhere does Henry of Huntingdon actually mention Helena's father being called Coel, but I wondered if a misreading of this misconstructed phrase had fuelled a misconception that the king's name sounded something like Hoel.

Remember, Henry maintained that Colchester derived its name from the king who first built walls around the city. This is a suspiciously circular argument of the kind that Rudyard Kipling immortalised in his *Just So* stories. How did Colchester get its name? Because it was the castle of King Cole, of course. Anyone with a smattering of Latin knows that *chester* is the Saxon form of the Latin *castra*, meaning an army camp. Therefore there must have been a commander called Cole whose base it was. Hence the mediaeval *Colecestria* – Cole's castle.

Yet the prefix *col* could equally well come from the River Colne on whose banks the settlement was built, a name which some believe may even have Celtic origins. Or more probably from the Latin *colonia*, since Colchester was in fact the site of one of the earliest Roman colonies in Britain, where veteran soldiers were settled in the first century.[14] Initially after the arrival of the Romans the town was called *Colonia Claudia* in honour of the invading emperor Claudius: later after the suppression of Boudicca's revolt it was changed to *Colonia Victrisensis*. With the departure of the Romans the Latin *castra* was initially dropped in favour of the Welsh *caer*, to give the old British usage of Caer Colun or Kaercolim – both meaning the castle of the colony – only for the Latin to be restored subsequently in the Anglo-Saxon *Colenceaster*.

There is a further remote philological possibility in the name originally used by the British for their initial settlement, which persisted after the Romans arrived and whose site is now being recovered at an archaeological park in a field on the outskirts of Colchester. This was Camulodunum, the fortress or *dun* of *Camulos*, the British god of war. The settlement was founded by Cunobelinus, the leader of the Catuvellani tribe of Hertfordshire and ruler of the Trinovantes from Essex, who was effectively king of south-east Britain during the interval between Julius Caesar's invasion in 55 BC and the Emperor Claudius's conquest in AD 44. It has even been suggested he might have been the historical personality behind a local folk memory which gave rise to the legend of King Cole, though such a possibility has to be set against the observation that even the slapdash mediaeval chroniclers recognised the two as separate characters from different periods.[15]

However, what if the name of Camulodunum was itself mistranslated by subsequent generations? Coel sounds suspiciously like *caelum* or *coelum*, the Latin word for heaven, or the haunt of a deity. Perhaps Colchester was not Cole's castle, therefore, so much as the Anglicised version of a Latin translation of a Romano-British name meaning the fortress named after a god. Whichever option you chose, it makes Old King Cole himself look like a literary error.

✣

ANYONE CONSULTING Edward Gibbon's monumental history of the *Decline and Fall* of the Roman Empire would have been under no illusion. The first best-selling volume in 1776 poured all the erudite scorn the father of modern history could muster on to the popular 'daughter of Coel' theory. 'This tradition, unknown to the contemporaries of Constantine, was invented in the darkness of the monasteries,' sneered Gibbon.[16] In other words, completely made up. Gibbon didn't waste his words on Henry of Huntingdon, but put all the blame for the misguided popularity of the falsehood firmly on the shoulders of a Welsh cleric called Geoffrey of Monmouth.

It was not the only charge Geoffrey has had to answer since offering to the world what purported to be a Latin translation of an ancient book written in the 'Brittanic tongue' whose original has never been found. He devised what amounted to a bible for the Britons, a patriotic romance about the leaders of a kingdom that no longer existed, ranging from a mythical Brutus who founded ancient Albion to the heroic Arthur who led the national resistance against the Anglo-Saxon invaders. His chronology mixed real names and places with characters from fiction in imaginary locations with such eloquent charm that generations of readers have been bewitched by his magic. The *History of the Kings of Britain* is riddled with fables, yet it has been called one of the most influential books ever written.[17]

This hymn to 'Britain, the best of islands' fired the imagination of Christendom. Almost 200 copies of the original Latin manuscript have survived, together with translations into Norman French, English and Welsh that make it easily one of the most popular mediaeval texts after the Bible. It inspired a stream of popular romances, provided the plots for several Shakespeare plays, including King Lear as well as Cymbeline (from the story of Cunobelinus), and continues to intrigue students of the Arthurian legend to this day. But the recipe did not go unchallenged by contemporaries, some of whom suspected an over-fertile imagination at work in the monk from Monmouth. A certain William of Newburgh commented acidly: 'It is quite clear that everything this man wrote about Arthur and his successors, or indeed about his predecessors from Vortigern onwards, was made up, partly by himself and partly by others, either from an inordinate love of lying, or for the sake of pleasing the Britons.'[18]

So we should keep a critical eye out for Geoffrey when he identified Coel as Duke of Kaelcolim, or Colchester, who became King of the Britons after putting down a revolt against Rome.

His story is that Constantius was sent to sort out the situation, but the wily Coel did a deal with the imperial envoy whereby he promised submission to Rome on condition that he could retain the title. 'After Coel's death Constantius himself seized the royal crown and married Coel's daughter. Her name was Helen and her beauty was greater than that of any other young woman in the kingdom. Her father had no other child to inherit the throne, and he had therefore done all in his power to give Helen the kind of training which would enable her to rule the country more efficiently after his death. After her marriage with Constantius she had by him a son called Constantine.'[19]

As far as I could ascertain, we only have Geoffrey's word for it that Cole's dukedom, Kaelcolim, was to be understood as meaning Colchester. Quite why the place should have this different name is not clear. Was it a misprint for Kaercolim? Perhaps because Kael sounded like Cole? Possibly *kael* was a variant of the Latin *caelum*, or heaven, thus harking back to the idea of the Roman colony named after a Celtic deity. Cross-checking my Latin dictionary, I even found the similar-sounding word *caelicolum* defined as an inhabitant of heaven. Perhaps, I surmised, the place-name Kaelcolim was no more than the latest version of attempts by successive Latin transcribers to make sense of a description they did not understand. In the guise of the Duke of Kaelcolim, Coel might be a tautology: the leading inhabitant of the place where Old King Cole lived.

GEOFFREY WAS a direct contemporary of Henry of Huntingdon, and the two men kept working and reworking each other's material in successive editions of their histories during the 1130s, which makes it difficult to work out who came first with what idea.[20] It remains possible that Geoffrey just copied a plausible story about the occupant of King Cole's castle which Henry had picked up through his East Anglian connections. Whichever of them was responsible for introducing and propagating the character of Coel to a wider audience, I had no doubt that both authors appeared on the mediaeval literary stage before any evidence from Colchester itself. Nevertheless, by the time their chronicles were circulating, the town was most definitely associating itself with Helena, and quite independently of any connection with Coel. The earliest surviving corporate seal of Colchester, from the 13th century, stamped on public documents an image of Helena in wax, identified not only by the cross and nails but also by a Latin inscription claiming her birthright.

When Henry V granted the borough a Royal Charter in 1413 the Helena legend was sufficiently entrenched for the opening letter of this particular parchment to be illustrated by an elegant figure in a blue robe, sitting under the arm of a wooden cross and wreathed with an inscription: 'Helena was born in Colchester. She was the mother of Constantine. Helena discovered the Holy Cross.' Underneath the illuminated capital – H for Henry – was the earliest known version of the borough arms, a red shield divided by a cross whose arms are of equal length but of unusual design.

The bits that the Rev Butler later called 'knotty' were supposed to represent the shoots of a living tree: indeed in early times the cross was green to signify the living truth of the cross, though this switched to white after the Reformation, ostensibly in deference to the Protestant hostility to religious relics. Today either colour is employed, but both versions show the cross pierced by three nails and adorned by three crowns. The nails I understood, of course, but the crowns left me baffled, especially as Butler had referred to four of them. Then I read the explanatory panel in the castle museum where the original charter is on display. The three crowns signified another twist to the Helena legend, in which among her miraculous discoveries in the Holy Land she also located the bodies of the three Magi and brought them back to Europe. Some feat, I thought, considering that the Three Wise Men were not identified by name until the sixth century, but apparently generations of pilgrims have proved the sceptics wrong by travelling to the shrine where something or other is stored in Cologne cathedral.[21]

Back in modern Colchester, literally as well as metaphorically, I went in search of other relics of the town's devotion to its patron saint. Somewhere a mediaeval aristocratic fraternity had met under the banner of the Guild of St Helen, but since the dissolution of the monasteries no site had been traced. Neither could I find any remains of the place of worship adjacent to the former Holy Cross Hospital for the Poor, run by the oddly-named Crouched Friars, an Augustinian order founded in 1240 by one William de Lanvalei, then constable of the castle. In a side street, however, I did chance upon the modern Church of St James the Less and St Helen, just as the priest was bidding farewell to his Sunday congregation. 'Why such an unusual joint dedication?' I inquired. 'It follows from the mediaeval monastery that used to be on this site. You will have to ask the abbot,' said Father James Hawes, a bustling man anxious to put the needs of his flock before the fancies of passing strangers. 'Helena obviously because of the mediaeval tradition that she was a British princess. Perhaps she was linked with James because he was the patron saint of pilgrims?'

Or wild geese, I muttered to myself, feeling chastened and resuming my circuit of religious sites within the old Roman walls like a penance. I found the centre of Colchester packed with mediaeval churches, many of them – just like the castle – imaginatively constructed using distinctive Roman building materials, but almost all of them either empty, ruined, or converted to more relevant uses. I passed a social history centre, a natural history museum, and an arts complex licensed to sell intoxicating liquor, before finally locating the oldest chapel in town on the corner of – surprise, surprise – St Helen's Lane. The building resembled a potting shed rather than a house of prayer, and was closed to the general public. Its most interesting feature was not the surviving 13th-century brickwork but the site on which much older foundations were laid. Not as old as the Roman theatre that archaeologists uncovered on the same spot, some remains of which are visible nearby, but certainly older than the Norman castle in whose shadow the abandoned St Helen's Chapel lay. Probably, therefore, Saxon.

The Blue Badge guide had put me on the trail of the Saxon kings during our brief conversation at the end of her tour of the keep. During the tenth century several held councils in Colchester, which had been re-fortified in 917 by Edward the Elder following the expulsion of the Danes from East Anglia. 'It would have been very unusual for the Normans to allow a building so close to the castle walls, which could have compromised its defence. We believe now that there may have been a Saxon court here, having found the remains of a great hall in the vicinity,' said the guide. 'The chapel may have been associated with the court, its east end abutting the Saxon stronghold like a private chapel to the royal demesne. So the Normans, as devout Christian knights, may simply have taken it over.'

The idea that the Normans continued an older religious tradition is supported by the foundation charter of St John's Abbey, a massive Benedictine foundation outside the Roman walls of which only the gatehouse survived the dissolution. Contemporaneous with the castle, the Abbey was part of the building programme undertaken by Eudo de Rie, steward to William I, to enforce his feudal will throughout the lands granted to him by the Conqueror. Dated 1096, just 30 years after the Norman invasion, the charter listed among the Abbey's estates 14 acres of land next to the Chapel of St Helen, which Eudo had recently restored. And I had now come full circle, tracing the veneration of Helena in Colchester back to the era of the

Saxons, among whom Cynewulf's epic poem *Elene* had been so popular.

✣

AS A POSTSCRIPT to this part of the story, some months afterwards I stumbled by accident across another element in the Old English connection, during a visit to the Cathedral of St Gudule in Brussels. Having some time to kill one weekend in the Belgian capital, I went to check out what remained of the relic that had been described there by Mgr Rohault de Fleury in his exhaustive treatise on the instruments of the passion. To my surprise, I found pride of place in the cathedral treasury taken up by a glass case containing a large wooden reliquary in the shape of a cross which hailed from England and was dated around the year 1000. Engraved along the edging of its beaten silver casing was a verse inscription in a late West Saxon dialect that echoed lines from *The Dream of the Rood*. Translated, this proclaimed: 'Cross is my name; of old I, trembling, drenched with blood, bore a mighty King.'

The reliquary apparently once contained what was thought to be the largest surviving fragment of the True Cross in the West, in a hollowed-out section of the transom. Whether the fragment is still hiding there or not is hard to tell, since what is on display to tourists and pilgrims is the silver covering on the reverse of the reliquary, prettily decorated in gold with the symbols of the Evangelists on the four arms and the Pascal Lamb in the centre. You can tell this is the back of the object because it also bears the manufacturer's mark carved across it in large letters, proclaiming 'DRAHMAL ME WORHTE' or 'Drahmal made me'. Who the artist was remains a mystery, although to experts the art and iconography suggest that he followed the tradition of the Northumbrian school. Another part of the inscription round the edge indicates he was commissioned by two brothers,

Aethelmaer and Athelwold, to commemorate the soul of their sibling Aelfric, but their identities are similarly unknown. Scholars believe from the distinctive prefixes to their names that the threesome may have been scions of the Royal House of Wessex, and that therefore the reliquary might have been constructed to take fragments of the True Cross that Pope Marinus sent to King Alfred in 883, according to an entry in the Anglo-Saxon Chronicle.[22] How and why it should end up in the Low Countries several hundred years later is another question which no one has yet fathomed, owing to the absence of any documentary record of this crucifix before the 14th century.

CHAPTER IV

The British Emperor

Nothing in the early existence of Britain indicated the greatness which she was destined to attain. . . . Of the western provinces which obeyed the Caesars, she was the last that was conquered and the first that was thrown away.

Thomas Babington Macaulay[1]

HELENA'S POPULARITY in England was not confined to Colchester or the Lancashire parish that was to become municipal St Helens. An official count at the turn of this century established there were 117 Anglican churches alone dedicated to her, all but four of which pre-dated the Reformation. They ranged from Helland in Cornwall, via Elstow in Bedfordshire (itself a corruption of Helen-stow), to the similarly misnamed Warrington parish of St Elphin.[2] However, the overwhelming majority of these dedications were found north of the River Trent, particularly in Yorkshire and Lincolnshire. Their geographical distribution indicated that even as the Colchester parchment extolled the false claims of the town in the time of Edward III, the balance of popular tradition was already weighted towards a more enduring link with the north.

This reflected the one fact of which we can be reasonably sure in this whole saga. Constantine, Helena's son, was proclaimed emperor at York in 306 on the death of his father, the general Constantius. Although Eusebius was silent on the subject, it was attested by Eutropius, who served as a later emperor's secretary: 'He died at York in Britain in the 13th year of his reign and is enrolled amongst the gods.'[3] The antiquarian Camden even told his 17th-century readers he was informed by 'credible persons' that Constantius was thought to have been buried in a vault beneath the site of the York church of St Helen-on-the-Walls.

Nicknamed Chlorus, the pale, on account of his pallid countenance, the general had restored order to the province of Britannia after a series of native uprisings and undertaken a massive building programme in the north symbolised by a new military fortress at York, the headquarters of the *dux britanniorum*. On his second and fatal visit Chlorus had been accompanied by his son, to whom the troops swiftly transferred their affections on his death, unilaterally proclaiming the young man *Augustus* and propelling him into the maelstrom of imperial politics in order to uphold that title against rival claimants.[4]

†

BEFORE I TRAVELLED north again, however, I had some loose ends to tie. One struck me forcibly quite by accident on the road out to Colchester. Trying to navigate my way through the City, just before the road still known as London Wall, I spotted a Corporation of London street-sign saying Great St Helen's. It reminded me of what Henry of Huntingdon wrote: 'Tradition says that Helen, the illustrious daughter of Britain, surrounded London with the wall that is still standing . . .' A few weeks later I went back on foot to explore the passageway and discover the church of St Helen Bishopsgate, a stone's throw within the circuit of the old city walls. A strange squat structure lacking either tower or spire, it was tucked away in a close occupied by the offices of investment fund managers and overshadowed by City skyscrapers.

'It's only hearsay but they say Constantine built a wooden church here in honour of his mother,' said Tony Thomas, the caretaker. 'Mind you, they probably say that about every church with the same name.'

Actually the first recorded reference to a church on the site was about 50 years before the Norman Conquest. The present building dated back to the 13th century, when a choir was built alongside the church to serve a newly founded priory of black nuns of the Benedictine order. After the dissolution of the nunnery by Henry VIII, the screen between the two was removed to create the unusual twin nave that charms the many office workers who attend prayers there on a weekday lunchtime. Visitors can still see the night staircase that led to the nunnery, and the stone grilles known as 'squints' through which nuns peered to get a glimpse of the altar. Yet the only reference to the woman who inspired them is Helena's name carved in a Latin inscription on the stone lintel of a restored Jacobean doorway.

'There has probably not been anything else since Catholic times,' grunted Mr Thomas. He proudly showed me the official annals, based on a scrapbook put together by a devoted churchwarden in the early 19th century. It relied heavily on the authority of a monkish chronicler called Richard of Cirencester for its account of the church's early history, and swallowed not only the London walls story but the daughter of Coel theory too as explanation for dedicating a church here to Helena.

I drew breath, without the heart to tell the helpful Mr Thomas that I already knew Richard of Cirencester was not guilty. A Benedictine monk studying at St Peter's in Westminster during the 14th century, he compiled an uninspiring history of the English kings from 447 to 1066 that cheerfully plagiarised both Henry of Huntingdon and Geoffrey of Monmouth. Unfortunately he almost became better known than either because his name was taken in vain by an ingenious 18th-century forger. Charles Bertram, an English teacher at the naval academy in Copenhagen, published in 1758 what he claimed was the translation of a long-lost text by Richard, a copy of which he had just happened to find in the Danish royal library. *On the Ancient State of Britain* played its own small part in the Helena legend by fuelling the London link. 'This city was surrounded with a wall by the Empress Helena, the discoverer of the Holy Cross, and if reliance may be placed upon tradition, which is not always erroneous, was called Augusta, as Britain is distinguished by the name of the Roman island,' it said.[5]

Bertram's audacity was exposed by an erudite article in the Gentleman's Magazine in 1867, but not before he had fooled the literary and historical establishment for more than a century. Among his most celebrated victims were Henry Bohn, publisher of the first popular library of classical texts, who unwittingly included the fabrication among his 1848 budget edition of *Six Old English Chronicles* (price 5 shillings), and even the pompous cleric-hater Edward Gibbon, who forced himself to praise Richard's unexpected grasp of detail in a footnote to the *Decline and Fall*. 'He shows a genuine knowledge of antiquity, very extraordinary for a monk,' he commented.[6]

Ruling out Richard's alleged new material as an alibi for Henry raises the question of where the story about Helena founding the walls of London came from. I can only assume that someone, somewhere, read too much into the existence of a church dedicated to Helena so close to the Roman walls. It is curious how these monkish chroniclers needed to credit Helena with some bogus British achievement when surely discovering the True Cross was quite enough to be going on with. After all it satisfied the nuns who built a priory in her honour. In the Bishopsgate annals I saw the common seal of the 'Nonnes Churche of Seynt Helyns' as affixed to a lease by Dame Mary

Rollesley, the last Prioress. This showed Helena clutching a fistful of nails and embracing the cross in the company of half a dozen adoring sisters of the cloth. There was also a drawing of an old stained glass window, but tragically its depiction of Helena finding the cross was savagely shot to smithereens by the blast of an IRA bomb which exploded 60 yards away outside the Baltic Exchange in April 1992.

The raw daylight that now floods into the church through the restored east windows illuminates a bright modern brand of Christianity. The evangelical tone is evident from the copies of the New International Version of the Bible which grace every pew, to the drum kit lurking at the back of the gallery alongside the organ. Even the tombs and tablets which dot the floor and line the walls in celebration of the lives of merchant venturers from Tudor and Stuart times looked out of place. Judging by the crowded autumn programme, the congregation would not lack for religious services, spiritual talks, prayer meetings or missionary work in the coming months. Nevertheless, I left feeling empty, disappointed that so little of substance could survive to link this living house of God to the person whose name it bore. Outside I passed by the entrance to St Helen's Place, a neoclassical arch framed by giant stone columns leading to the headquarters of the Leathersellers Company, which now occupies the site of the mediaeval nunnery. For a fleeting moment I thought I saw the ghosts of black nuns flitting through the courtyard – but they were only charcoal suits scurrying to worship at the temple of Mammon.

†

THE OTHER LOOSE END concerned Geoffrey of Monmouth. The Welshman's fabulous history made a much bigger impact on subsequent generations than his rival Henry from East Anglia. On the hunch that there could be no smoke without fire,

I was unwilling to let him be simply traduced as a teller of tall tales. For the science of critical history had yet to be forged in mediaeval times, and the chroniclers of the age were often guilty of no more than repeating what others had written, or writing down what had been passed by word of mouth through the generations. Take the well-loved Arthurian legend, for example, which Geoffrey both embellished and popularised but which has fascinated subsequent generations because sceptics have been unable to dispel the core of conviction that there was a heroic leader of the Britons who held out against the invading Saxons in the Dark Ages after the Roman withdrawal – even if Arthur's ardent supporters cannot agree among themselves on which particular historical figure he was based. I could not help wondering whether Old King Cole had a similar, if neglected, pedigree. Did he exist after all, a half-remembered figure in the background whose existence explained why Geoffrey could not let go of the name?

The idea came to me while perusing an alternative version of Geoffrey's text in a second-hand bookshop in Hay-on-Wye. For my initial researches I had naturally been referring to the easily available Penguin edition, which is based upon an 18th-century manuscript in the Cambridge University Library. Then I discovered that earlier generations would have relied upon the 1842 edition by one J A Giles. This was itself a revised reprint of a 17th-century translation, of an inaccurate 16th-century printed text, whose compiler collated and edited a number of French manuscripts with what subsequent scholars have pronounced a complete lack of judgement – but never mind.[7] Giles described our old friend Cole slightly differently, not as Duke of Kaelcolim but of Kaercolvin.

As we saw, *kaer* is the Welsh word for castle or camp, the ancient British equivalent of the Saxon *caestra*. As a prefix it is used by Geoffrey in the old British names of more than a dozen other towns in the Penguin version, including a number in

England. Later on in my inquiries, I came across a reference in Nennius, a ninth-century monk who wrote an earlier *History of the Britons,* to Caercollun as one of the 33 cities of the ancient island of Britain. J A Giles, who edited this work as well, thought the author meant Colchester here, presumably because it was not dissimilar to Kaercolvin. I wouldn't like to read much more into this mind-boggling word play, because we cannot rule out a copying error by the scribes who provided us with our versions of original texts long lost to posterity. Nevertheless, it seemed clear to me that, while Colchester may have strayed into the story by the accident of writing history, its persistence on the scene was not so much a scam by Geoffrey as an attempt to make retrospective sense of his sources. And this started me wondering whether Geoffrey's Welsh background might be an important clue to the origins of his myth making.

An answer of sorts emerged only after I had spent several days rooting around the dusty volumes of an obscure antiquarian library in Bloomsbury specialising in theology and the study of religion. Until the opening of the new British Library at St Pancras, the British Museum was home to the nation's storehouse of books, but discouraged casual callers to its famous Reading Room. It preferred to remain aloof as a last resort for those who could not find what they wanted at a wide variety of specialist libraries elsewhere in London – which was how I found myself entering an elegant building in Gordon Square housing a fascinating collection of miscellaneous oddments bequeathed to the nation in 1729 by a former Presbyterian minister from Wrexham called Dr Daniel Williams. It was there I came across a Welsh version of Geoffrey's history and groped towards a resolution of the confusion about Helena.

The authority on which Geoffrey of Monmouth rested his own claim to authenticity was his statement that he translated into Latin 'a certain very ancient book written in the British language' given to him by Walter, Archdeacon of Oxford, 'a man skilled in the art of public speaking and well-informed about the history of foreign countries.' Geoffrey mentions this 'ancient book' twice later on in his work but it has never come to light, though scholars accept that from internal evidence he probably had access to some written Old Welsh sources with which his account corresponds, including Nennius, an even earlier Welsh monk called Gildas who wrote the only surviving narrative history from the sixth century, and various Welsh genealogies and poems.[8]

What we do possess are several later Welsh versions of Geoffrey's history, dating from the 13th century.[9] These have always been presumed to be corrupt translations of the earlier Latin, and are traditionally referred to as the *Brut Gruffydd ap Arthur*, the latter being how Geoffrey of Monmouth was known in his native land. *Brut* is generally taken as meaning 'chronicle' although the derivation of the word is actually a tribute to Geoffrey's own popularisation of the idea that the first king of Britain was Brutus – another *Just So* story in which ancient Albion is said to have been conquered by a bizarre Trojan hero who called his companions Britons after his own name. This aside, I suspected that the significance of the various Bruts was not that the unknown Welsh scribes wrongly translated Geoffrey's Latin, but that they pointed us to the original source book which Geoffrey tells us Walter brought *ex Britannia*, that is, out of Wales. In other words, what if the extant Welsh manuscripts are more accurate versions of the missing Welsh original than the surviving Latin which predates them?[10]

I confess I cannot read mediaeval Welsh. Pouring over the various texts in Dr Williams' library, however, I compared rival references to Coel. The most obvious distinction I found is that the phrase which appears in the rival English translations as Duke of Kaelcolim or Kaercolvin is subtly different in the Welsh versions. One, which is generally accepted as a straight translation from the Latin, describes '*Koel jarll Kaer Coelin*' and thus appeared to repeat the canard about the eponymous steward of

King Cole's castle: *jarll* meaning earl. No progress there. However, another version, known as the *Brut Tysilio* – after a seventh-century Welsh saint who may have compiled an earlier manuscript on which it is said to have been based – identified '*Coel jarll Caerloyw*' and is properly translated as referring to Cole as Earl of Gloucester.

Curiously enough, the *History of the Kings of Britain* is dedicated to an Earl of Gloucester. Robert, the illegitimate son of Henry I, is hailed by Geoffrey 'with heartfelt affection' on behalf of the island of Britain as a worthy successor to his father. This reference has played a crucial role in the dating of Geoffrey's composition to before his patron's death in 1147, but raises the issue of whether Geoffrey had a political point to make on behalf of his 'most noble Duke' too. The death of Henry I in 1135 without heirs ushered in one of the most anarchic periods in British history, at a time when the Welsh laboured under the Norman occupation. The late king had appealed to the barons to acknowledge his daughter Matilda as his successor, but his nephew Stephen grabbed the throne instead. Robert mab Henri, as the Welsh knew the Earl of Gloucester, was the son of Nest, daughter of Rhys ap Tewdor of the royal line of Wales.[11] He was one of the chief supporters of Matilda and led an early rebellion against the kingship of Stephen. Although unsuccessful in ousting his rival, Robert nevertheless exercised undisputed sway over his feudal estates in Glamorgan and Normandy. As a patron of letters he took a great interest in the legendary tales of Wales and Brittany: he may even have commissioned Geoffrey and Walter to investigate them.[12]

Given the contemporary importance of the Earl of Gloucester to the author, it would be rather odd if the reference to '*Cole jarll Caerloyw*' had only been inserted by Welsh scribes writing several hundred years later, especially as by then the alleged link with Colchester had been taken up by English admirers as established fact. Of course we cannot be entirely accurate about what

Geoffrey wrote, since the oldest available Latin manuscript post-dates his death by several centuries. However, even this Latin version of the *History* contains a *Just So* story about the founding of Gloucester, the city of Claudius, to commemorate the marriage of the Caesar's daughter Genvissa to the British prince Arviragus. The passage is intended to symbolise the arrival of the *pax Romana*, but the town on the banks of the Severn is described first by its Welsh name, Kaerglou. Perhaps, therefore, Geoffrey was referring to Gloucester all along, and Colchester only came into the story at a later date, at the hands of English scribes who sought to make sense of a reference to Coel they did not understand?

†

CONSTANTINE'S HEAD, twice life-size, stared at me from a lofty pedestal in the Yorkshire Museum. Children busy drawing objects for a school project sprawled over the floor of the first room in the Roman exhibition area, oblivious of the significance of the ghostly white sculpture above them. It was probably the earliest portrait of the emperor, carved soon after his accession when the soldiers planted an imperial oak wreath on his head. It may also be more life-like than later versions fashioned when his power was absolute, and artists more careful to flatter their subject. Now weathered and pockmarked, the marble lump found during excavations of the city centre presented an ugly yet powerful image. The nose was eroded to an unappealing snub, the face fleshy with bulging chins and a fat neck. The full lips were pursed in a determined line, the heavy eyebrows furrowed with concentration. I stared back, thinking this was not a man to cross lightly.

The statue to which the bust belonged most likely stood in the legionary fortress, perhaps on a great stone pillar like the one recently erected outside York Minster. This massive column of limestone drums once stood in the great hall of the army headquarters, whose remains were buried beneath the graceful architecture of the Gothic cathedral. The site was excavated in the late 1960s, when engineers frantically burrowed beneath the largest mediaeval cathedral in northern Europe to secure its crumbling foundations lest the central tower collapsed. As a result of their efforts the bases of the other columns, together with the lower courses of the walls from the original Roman basilica, are today visible on an archaeological tour.

Wandering through a series of underground chambers, amid the huge concrete collars and giant steel pins that hold the cathedral in place just a few metres above, takes one through the foundations of the first Norman cathedral down to the ground level of Roman times. I trailed my fingers in the water running through a first-century culvert that drained the Roman camp into the River Ouse. I tried to trace the faded fragments of a rare military mural painted on the walls of the Roman barrack block. And finally, I stood on the dais of the great hall from which almost 1,700 years ago a Roman general called Constantine was hailed as the ruler of the known world.

York was as just important as Colchester in the story of the Roman occupation of Britain. Once the Emperor Claudius had arrived from Rome to take the surrender of the Celtic tribes in the southeast in AD 43, the rest of the country sued for peace. However, almost 30 years later a revolt among the Brigantes in the north forced the ninth legion into action, and it marked the subjugation of the rebels by establishing a permanent fortress at Eboracum. For hundreds of years before the Vikings arrived to give the city its present name, York thrived as the provincial capital of the north, the hub of a network of military roads and the base from which Roman troops were sent to guard Hadrian's wall against the barbarians after 122. The garrison, subsequently replaced by the sixth legion, encased their headquarters in a stone wall 6m high and 1.5m wide on large earth banks protected by a ditch. It provided the necessary security for a whole town to grow up on land south of the River Ouse in the third century; another *colonia* for army veterans modelled on Colchester.[13]

Today, however, York's Roman heritage has to fight for its share of proper recognition from the city's visitors. The magnificent minster church and the splendid city walls with their imposing gateways, watchtowers and posterns, all constructed in the 13th and 14th centuries, dominate the historic centre. A ruined abbey, a castle keep and more than a dozen churches all date from the same period, while the city's prosperity in the early modern era is marked by a plethora of fine guild halls and timbered houses. Even the local archaeologists, who have done such sterling work to conserve the remnants of the past in recent years, play down what they have discovered about the Romans. Instead they have won wide praise for marketing the city's unique selling point at the Jorvik Viking Centre, where tourists are invited to take a time-car journey back 1,000 years to a reconstruction of the Viking city that flourished here before the Norman conquest.

The Roman section in the museum, though excellent, competed not only with the Vikings, Anglo-Saxons and Normans to display some of the finest archaeological treasures in England, but with other quintessential aspects of national life at the turn of the century: such as exhibitions on Animal Magic (fun and fantasy for all ages), Claws (domestic and wild cats), and Homes of Football (for World Cup addicts). A casual weekend visitor spoiled for choice needed to be a mite obsessive to know that a pub called The Roman Bath in St Sampson's Square actually has the remains of one in its cellar, not to mention to appreciate that you get free entry if you purchase a bar meal. He or she may just be baffled by the modern bronze sculpture of an oddly dressed man reclining on a couch on the green by the Minster, as if he owned the place. Even the inscription sounds like a crossword clue: 'Constantine by this sign conquers: where Caesar is, there is Rome.'

†

LITTLE EVIDENCE EXISTS of early Christianity in York beyond a record that its bishop attended the synod convened by Constantine at Arles in 314, one of the emperor's earliest efforts to tackle the growing problem of heresy in the church. The present Minster is at least the fifth church on the site and its marvels of only passing relevance to my researches. Despite climbing the tower for a better view, I wished I had brought a telescope to focus on the two tiny stained glass images of Helena in the clerestory windows high above the chancel. Francis Drake, an 18th-century antiquarian, claimed there was an image of Constantine in the cathedral as well but I could not track it down.[14] Instead I went in search of the three churches he said had been dedicated to Helena in mediaeval times: on the Walls, out of Fishergate, and in Stonegate.

A stranger to York could be forgiven for being confused about the gateways to the city. Gate is in fact the Viking word for street, while the actual entrances through the walls are known as bars. (And every true Norseman knows that down south a bar is a posh word for a pub.) Fishergate, therefore, is the road south along the banks of the Ouse towards London, now the A19, and the vigorous pace of development over the years has left no trace of any church. Neither does St Helen-on-the-Walls exist any longer. It was demolished with several other city centre churches deemed surplus to requirements soon after the Reformation. The graveyard was uncovered in 1975 during the building of a residential complex sandwiched between a street called Aldwark, or 'old fortification', and the northern wall. Archaeologists found that over a thousand burials had taken place here but dated them all as post-Norman, on the grounds that the skulls were not as long and thin as those of Vikings found elsewhere in the city.

I climbed onto the city wall at the Monkbar and walked east along it, following the line of the original Roman fortress. After a couple of hundred yards, looking over the parapet I spotted the foundations of the corner tower where the Roman wall turned southwards.[15] The stones disappeared into the grass bank and I looked in vain for signs of any other ruins in the narrow strip between the wall and the back gardens of the modern housing estate. Continuing on, however, to the corner of the mediaeval wall, I came across a church dedicated to St Cuthbert, tucked away in a little-visited spot by Layerthorpe Bridge over the River Foss. This became the parish church after the 1547 amalgamation that spelled the death knell of St Helen-on-the-Walls, and has kept the legend alive with a notice in the porch informing visitors that the body of Chlorus was cremated only 250 yards away in a church built by Helena. I liked that touch: not only cremated, but the ashes sent to Rome. Like Jesus in the tomb, there was no body left as evidence. No wonder even Francis Drake was sceptical about the local lore which claimed for years afterwards that a lamp was kept burning in the imperial sepulchre there.

A tramp sleeping rough stirred himself from a pile of blankets when I suddenly yelped. Not at the sight of him, but a mouldy wooden cross planted in the shade of the churchyard. It was only a memorial to the Great War, yet carved on the tall upright was the *ChiRho* symbol adopted by Constantine after his conversion to Christianity – the first two letters of the Greek word for Christ, combined one upon the other. Underneath an inscription in Latin ran the length of the crossbeam, recalling Constantine's vision of the cross with the words *In hoc signo vinces* – 'by this sign, conquer.' Around the base a stonemason evidently bursting with local pride had carved: 'Constantine the Great proclaimed emperor in this parish AD 306.' I pondered what it was about the 1914–18 conflict that had prompted these parishioners to honour their dead by recalling an almost forgotten link with a Roman emperor. Relief at victory in the war to end all wars, despite the terrible cost in lives? That their faith in God had enabled them to vanquish evil and adversity? A flash of morning sunshine through the trees picked out the depth of the engraved letters through the accumulated green lichen that threatened to obscure its message. 'By this sign conquer.' The tramp settled down and went back to sleep.

The street that is Stonegate follows the north-south axis of the Roman fortress, and the civic church of St Helen-in-Stonegate roughly marks where the entrance used to be, just above the river. Like its namesakes the church came under threat of demolition after the break with Rome, but the thriving community of glass-painters who worked in Stonegate raised a petition and the building was reprieved by Act of Parliament in 1553. Two hundred years later the graveyard was paved over as part of the Georgian beautification of York, and the popularity of St Helen's Square today is chiefly derived from its proximity to that irresistible mixture of Continental chic and Yorkshire home-cooking known as Betty's Tea-rooms.

It is easy to pass by the scrubbed sandstone frontage that is characteristic of so many of York's municipal buildings without noticing anything special about St Helen's. Yet the view from the far end of the square cannot hide the unusual octagonal bell-tower, buttressed at the bottom where it emerges from the roof as if it were a rocket ready to be launched to heaven. Such a space capsule would send an uncompromising signal to the stars if the interior of the church was anything to go by. Stone gargoyles peered from the arches beneath a painted ceiling, from which hung a knotty crucifix bearing a writhing bloodied figure. Advertisements for a forthcoming pilgrimage to Walsingham and the availability of confession added to a distinctively Anglo-Catholic atmosphere. No one was about, but another notice told visitors not to pussyfoot around.

'Here the gospel of Jesus Christ is proclaimed and the sacraments of the one holy catholic and apostolic church are celebrated according to the custom of the Church of England,' I read out loud.

'The Church of England teaches and promotes the faith brought to this land in AD 597 by St Augustine and by his predecessors. At the Reformation the Church of England did not become protestant (a word nowhere found in the Book of Common Prayer or its alternatives) but retained the catholic credentials and ministry of the church.' Wow! I half expected a grateful Pope to pop in at any moment.

†

REVIEWING THE RESULTS of my investigation so far, I realised I had missed the point that perhaps the key to the British connection all along was not Helena but Constantine himself. While poking fun at Henry of Huntingdon, I had overlooked the fact that his glancing references to Helena were indeed overshadowed by a glowing tribute to her son, the supposed 'British' emperor, who himself had a vision of the cross and built churches in Rome to mark the deeds of the martyrs and house relics of the holy wood. Because I had been so keen to exonerate Geoffrey of Monmouth from the charge that he made up his history, I had forgotten that the use to which he sought to put history was more significant that what it actually said. For amid all the muddled Arthurian genealogy, Geoffrey also reminded his readers of the undisputed fact that the greatest emperor of the greatest empire that ever lived had arrived on the world stage in humble Britain. And by absorbing Constantine into the popular mainstream of British history, the Welsh cleric unwittingly offered the rulers of Britain a powerful propaganda tool.

I saw a glimpse of its potential in promoting the political ambitions of Geoffrey's patron, Robert of Gloucester. The emphasis the author put on Helena as a queen in her own right provided a glowing precedent for the embattled supporters of Matilda against the usurper Stephen, and the glorious dynastic lineage stretching back through Arthur and Constantine to Brutus may have been intended to heighten respect for the native British amongst their Norman conquerors. It certainly went down particularly well during the fierce outburst of patriotism that marked the Hundred Years War against France of the late 14th and early 15th centuries, around the time the original St Helens chapel was founded in Lancashire. It would even find diplomatic expression at the Council of Constance in 1414, when the English bishops invoked Constantine and Helena as scions of the royal house in order to establish separate national voting rights. A similar tactic was used 20 years later at the Council of Basle to establish English precedence over the Castilian delegation. And the process reached its apex when Henry VIII invoked Constantine's ancestry in his struggle against the papacy to obtain a divorce from Catherine of Aragon. For in 1533 the king insisted he had the power to appropriate papal authority and rule the church in his own lands just as the great emperor had done before.

Henry's claim was made explicit in the first humanist history of England the following year when Polydore Vergil referred to Constantine 'being begott of a British mother, born and made Emperour in Brittaine.' Subsequently this belief was reinforced by the recovery and publication in Italy of a number of Latin panegyrics dedicated to Constantine. 'O fortunate Britain, and now happier than all countries, which has first seen Constantine made Caesar,' declaimed Eumenius the Rhetorician on the occasion of Constantine's accession. Another anonymous Latin author paid tribute to the emperor's lineage through Constantius, telling his imperial patron: 'He delivered Britain from bondage, but thou by arising from thence hast made it illustrious.'[16]

In both cases it is obvious with hindsight how wishful thinking on the part of British propagandists could have read too much into these ambiguously worded passages. It was the close attention that Edward Gibbon paid to verifying the facts of Constantine's life that enabled him to explode the popular misconception. His famous explanation for the collapse of the empire hinged on the emperor who favoured Christianity over the pagan religion on which the Roman republic was founded. In any case, as an American analyst has pointed out, by the late 18th-century Britain was busy acquiring an overseas empire of its own. As the map of the world turned red through the force of arms and the power of commerce, the modern rulers of our island nation no longer needed to bask in the reflected glory of a bogus imperial ancestor.[17]

The repatriation of Constantine was a necessary historical corrective, but removing the emperor from the scene did not answer all the outstanding questions about the popularity of the Helena tradition in Britain. For a start I was still puzzled about the genesis of King Coel. For centuries after it was written, Geoffrey of Monmouth's history remained what amounted to an unofficial national doctrine. His bizarre stories contributed to the invention of the idea of Britain. The myth of an ancient and independent Albion helped reinforce a new Protestant identity for the country, confronting the Continental ideology of the Counter-Reformation with a home-grown notion of Christianity free from Roman hegemony. It received expression in the antiquarian researches recorded in Camden's *Brittannia* and in the literature of Spenser and Sydney. Given my suspicions that Geoffrey had unwittingly plundered a rich store of Welsh tradition, it seemed no accident that his vision should so happily underpin the age of the Tudors, on behalf of a royal family whose descendants had hailed from Anglesey, as seneschals to the kings of Gwynedd. I made tracks for the Celtic fringe.

CHAPTER V

The Welsh Princess

What of the Britons in the time of the Emperor Constantine, son of our own Helena? Were they not brave in the days of our own Arthur, call him fabulous if you will?

Giraldus Cambrensis[1]

EVEN IN SUMMER the thick sedge grasses were not quite green, as if the pale sun did not have the strength to bring out the correct colour almost a thousand feet above sea level. Instead, its thin rays were reflected off the yellow rain-sodden moorland, giving the bleak landscape a luminous quality that occasionally sparkled with an intensity that made you blink and narrow your eyes to see what was causing the blaze of light. Among a criss-cross of diverging mud tracks one in particular stood out like a beacon advertising civilisation, following the line of an artificial drainage channel covered in dressed stone slabs. After a few hundred paces the path led to a rough dam holding back a small pond, but it was not the sheen of the still black water that had caught the sun, for that was hidden from the track in a hollow of the hill. Instead, the light show lay straight ahead, on a narrow terrace up to six feet above the marshy ground, where a pavement of smooth grey slates had shattered into a myriad of sharp pieces that glinted in the sun as they marched off towards a quarry in the distance.

Forget the nuclear power station on the lake below. Blot out the crack of low-flying aircraft overhead and the grumble of a tractor on the nearby farm. Pretend there are no electricity pylons strung out across the pasture where those sheep are grazing. Ignore that ugly transmission aerial sticking up into the sky by the conifer plantation. Put the car park and the metalled path which brought you there off the A470 trunk road out of your mind. And never mind the weather, which would have been a degree or two warmer than the chill wind now swirling over the Vale of Trawsfynydd when the Romans arrived in north Wales almost 2,000 years ago.

Imagine instead the isolated fort at Tomen-y-mur, a lonely outpost of empire garrisoned by auxiliary troops recruited from friendly tribes to watch over a mountain junction on the most impressive road network the world has ever seen.[2] The outline of the camp is difficult to make out until you are virtually on top of the square earth bank which marks its walls, but the Normans built a crude castle upon it a thousand years later and their relatively modern mound acts as a convenient reference point for the comparatively ancient monument. It has the distinction of being the only auxiliary fort in Britain with its own amphitheatre, a place of entertainment usually reserved for full-blown legionaries, though the modest circle of turf that remains resembles a provincial boxing ring rather than the great imperial circuses where gladiators fought to the death and Christians were thrown to the lions.

Historians believe the Romans established their first roads in this wild land after Agricola subjugated the west Britons in AD 78.[3] The routes follow the commanding heights, striding along ridge-tops and engineered across steep hillsides. West across the

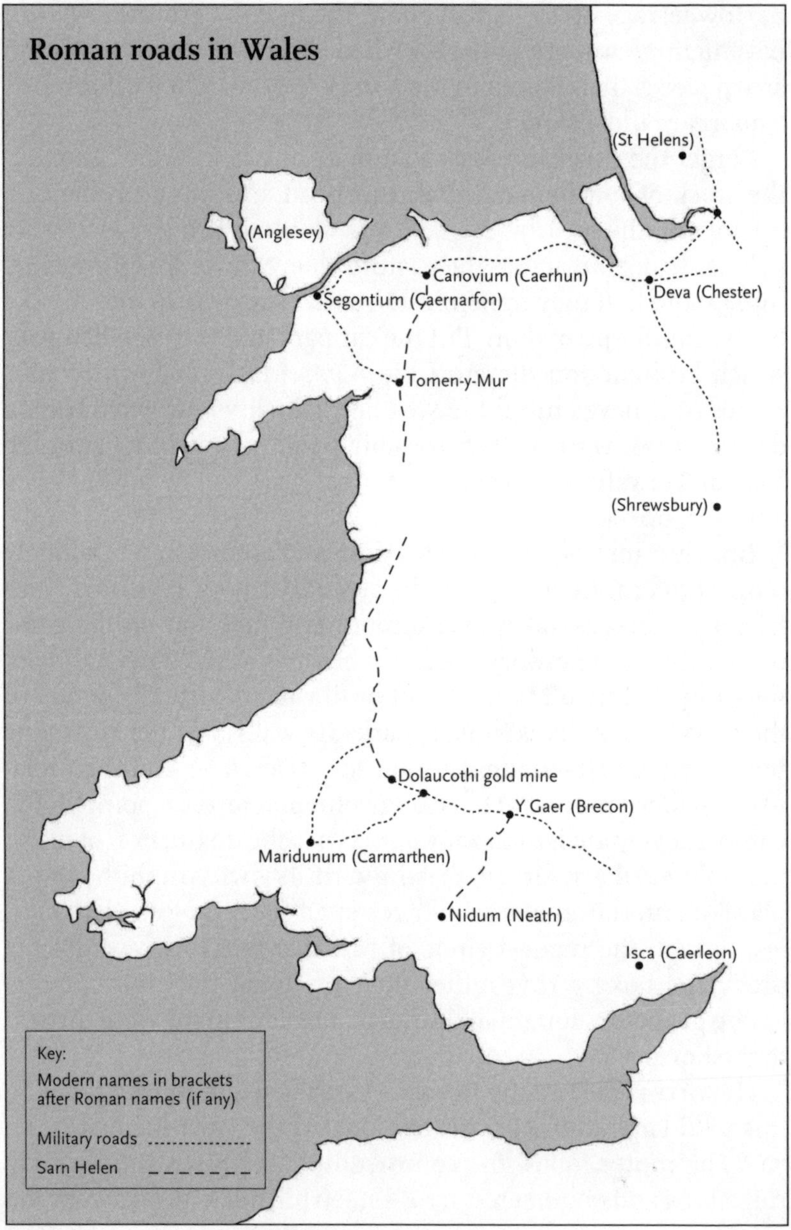
Roman roads in Wales
(St Helens)
(Anglesey)
Canovium (Caerhun)
Deva (Chester)
Segontium (Caernarfon)
Tomen-y-Mur
(Shrewsbury)
Dolaucothi gold mine
Y Gaer (Brecon)
Maridunum (Carmarthen)
Nidum (Neath)
Isca (Caerleon)
Key:
Modern names in brackets after Roman names (if any)
Military roads
Sarn Helen

mountain passes of Snowdonia they reached the sea at Caernarfon (Segontium). North led down the Conwy valley to a camp at Caerhun (Canovium). To the south along the coastal road, whose precise path is lost, was the stronghold of Carmarthen (Maridunum). And eastwards lay the stone fortress at Chester (Deva), home of the XX Legion, Valeria Victrix, and gateway to the great north road passing through the humble settlement of Newton-le-Willows, which so excited the imagination of the municipal archivist of St Helens.

For generations the Welsh have known these Roman roads by the name of Sarn Helen, which is roughly translated as Helen's Highway.[4] The Ordnance Survey marks two other tracks under this heading, one in West Wales leading towards Aberystwyth from Pumpsaint, near the old Roman gold mines of Dolaucothi, and another further east heading from Neath over the hills towards Brecon and the Roman fort of Y Gaer. Their romantic appellation may have a rather prosaic explanation, if, as some believe, it is simply a corruption of the Welsh phrase *sarn y lleng*, the paved way of the legions. Even more boringly, it might have been derived from *sarn heolen*, which simply means a paved lane.[5] But the bards of mediaeval Wales never let linguistic niceties get in the way of a good story. They sang that the roads were named after the wife of a Roman emperor, who had a son called Constantine, was accorded sainthood by the Catholic Church, and around whose exploits legends accumulated.

'Helen bethought her to make high roads from one castle to another across the Island of Britain. And the roads were made. And for that reason they call her Helen of the Hosts, because she was sprung from the Island of Britain, and the men of the Island of Britain would not have made those great hostings for any save for her.'

Thus recorded the *Mabinogion*, the acknowledged masterpiece of Celtic literature, handed down through the generations by word of mouth until preserved in a series of 14th-century manuscripts.[6] By the time Lady Charlotte Guest brought this collection of folk tales to a wider audience with her English translation 500 years later, Helen of the Hosts was firmly lodged in the mythological memory of the Welsh people as Helen Llwyddog. Though the story maintained that she received her epithet because she caused the roads to be built, the use of the archaic term 'hostings' was bursting with ambiguities for the future development of the legend. Were there a large number of roads, or were the roads constructed to carry large numbers of people? It was not long before Helen was to be credited with leading a military expedition from north Wales in person. There were Biblical allusions too that underpinned her eventual elevation to the sainthood: the parallel with the Lord of Hosts, commanding a heavenly army of angels, for example; not to mention the sacred host of the holy communion ceremony, the bread consecrated as the body of Christ. Inevitably, this holy Helen became muddled up with the mother of Constantine and the confusion not only fuelled the English belief that St Helena was born in Britain, but also the Welsh claim that it was Helen Llwyddog who discovered the True Cross.

✝

ELEN LLWYDDOG, as we should more properly call Helen of the Hosts in Welsh, was born about a hundred years later than her namesake yet the confusion between them lasted well into the 19th century. It was authoritatively cleared up by the Rev Sabine Baring-Gould, a prolific Victorian cleric who is best known as the author of the hymn *Onward Christian Soldiers*.[7] His inquiries into the Helena tradition in Britain followed the lead given by Edward Gibbon a century earlier, and blamed Geoffrey of Monmouth for muddling the two women up. Aiming to recover the actual acts of the martyrs from the accretion of fable and hagiography, the rector compiled a revision of Butler's *Lives* with particular emphasis on native British saints, based on his minute examination of early Breton texts. In that context Baring-Gould pointed out that the Welsh translation of Geoffrey's history, which we have already seen referred to Helena as daughter of *Koel jarll Kaer Loyw*, or Coel the earl of Gloucester, added as an afterthought *a honno Elen Luydawc*. Since there was no equivalent parenthesis in the Latin text, its appearance suggests an idle translator gratuitously added the 'also known as' to spice up the local interest for Welsh readers.

However, it was rather unfair of Baring-Gould to accuse Geoffrey of misleading the English on this basis. For in fact Geoffrey did go on to relate his own version of the separate legend of Elen a little later on in his *History*, though without mentioning her by name. This story starts while Constantine is still ruling in Rome with a revolt in Britain led by Octavius, Duke of the Gewissei, a tribe identified as the men of Gwent. After various setbacks Octavius became king and ruled to a grand old age, at which point he worried about the succession to the throne because he only had a daughter. One of his counsellors, Caradoc, duke of Cornwall, suggested marrying her off to a prominent Roman senator, Maximian, who had the added advantage of being a Briton descended from the House of Constantine. Caradoc's advice was contested by other claimants but eventually prevailed in a passage recalling Maximian's royal descent. 'For he is of the blood of Constantine. He is a nephew of our own King Coel, whose daughter Helena possessed this kingdom by hereditary right, as none can deny.' Geoffrey added: 'When Caradoc had made his points, Octavius agreed with him. With the consent of all, he gave the kingship of Britain to Maximianus, and his own daughter with it.'[8]

From these quotations it is clear that Geoffrey himself knew that Helena and the unnamed daughter of Octavius were two quite different women. Casual readers may not have been so careful in making the distinction, however, especially given the author's own carefree approach. For example, his chronology in this section of the *History* is all up the spout, compressing events encompassing several generations virtually into the lifetime of Constantine. The character of Maximian is also confusing: there was a Roman general of that name, who became ruler of the Western half of the empire, and who in 293 chose as his deputy Constantine's father Chlorus. Nevertheless, from the structure of the remainder of the story we can be sure that Geoffrey is actually talking about someone else with a similar name but rather different contribution to our national heritage. The problem is that Elen's husband was a Roman general who ran the Western provinces of the empire and fathered a son called Constantine. The parallels with Helena and Chlorus are uncanny.

✝

CLEMENS MAXIMUS was known in his lifetime as Magnus, making him literally 'the great.' A legionary officer who hailed from Galicia, the Celtic region of Spain, he made his reputation in Britain, driving the Picts away from Hadrian's wall, and was rewarded with the governorship of Valentia, the Roman province we now call Wales. Chafing at this effective exile in a remote corner of the empire, he was raised to the purple by his own troops in 383 and crossed the Channel in search of glory. So successful was he that the emperor Theodosius recognised Maximus as the de facto ruler of the Western Empire. Unfortunately, the extra power seems to have gone to the rebel's head. Summoning reinforcements from Britain, he crossed the Alps on a self-proclaimed mission to root out heresy in Rome. He entered the imperial capital in 388 but was vanquished in battle and executed at the Aquileia milestone.[9]

The sixth-century historian Gildas the Wise traced the end of Roman Britain and the arrival of the Dark Ages to the withdrawal of the legions in this period. 'Britain is left cruelly deprived of all her soldiery and armed bands, of her cruel governors and of the flower of her youth, who went with Maximus and never again returned; and utterly ignorant as she was of the arts of war, groaned in amazement for many years under the cruelty of two foreign nations – the Scots from the north-west and the Picts from the north,' he wrote.[10] His passionate appeal to native chieftains to rise up against the barbarian threat, soon compounded by the arrival of the 'fierce and impious' Saxons in the south, unwittingly set the scene for the myth of the 'matter of Britain' in which the Arthurian legend later took root.[11]

Magnus Maximus fatally weakened the British garrison and abandoned the last line of defence against the barbarians on Hadrian's Wall. Yet he became a hero to the Welsh. Within a few hundred years, genealogists were tracing the royal ancestry of the kings of Gwynedd back to him. He was renamed Macsen Wledig, taking the local military title of *guletic* or leader. Probably his posthumous reputation was aided by that glamorous link with Rome. Possibly he had concluded a series of deals with native chieftains in the west and north to defend Britain from the Picts in his absence. His own rehabilitation as a Welsh prince was helped by marrying a local heiress when he was strengthening the abandoned fortress of Segontium. Some said Elen of Caernarfon accompanied him on the crusade to Gaul, under his personal standard of a red dragon, later appropriated as the national flag of Wales.[12] According to the oral tradition recorded in verses known as the Welsh triads, it was by marching with the legionary hosts that she earned her own title of Llwyddog.

Bending history even further for the purposes of poetry, the bards of the Mabinogion told a more romantic version in *The Dream of Macsen Wledig*. This tale described how an emperor of Rome, 'the handsomest and wisest of men,' searched far and wide for the beautiful maiden whose vision had haunted his sleep. After crossing land and sea he found her in the far corner of an island (Britain), where there was a rugged land called Eryri

(Snowdonia), an isle off the coast (Anglesey) and a castle by a river (Caernarfon). Macsen fell in love with Elen, daughter of Eudaf, son of Caradawg, and made her his queen. But when his authority was challenged on the Continent, he left her behind, in charge of building on his behalf that eponymous network of roads across the country to link the three Welsh strongholds of Caernarfon, Caerleon and Carmarthen.

Nennius, the ninth-century historian who took over spinning the British myth where Gildas left off, maintained that the armies of Maximus never returned to Britain but were exiled to Armorica in Brittany.[13] (This observation was subsequently expanded by later writers as the explanation for the linguistic link between Breton and Welsh.) However, according to Welsh tradition his eldest son, another Constantine, did return from exile to north Wales, clearing the family lands of Irish settlers who had taken over in the meantime, and re-establishing the dynasty so that its seat at Caernarfon became known as Caer Gystennin, or Constantine's castle, for centuries thereafter. His reputation was to endure in Wales not so much as a warlord but as a soldier of the early British church, who founded a series of monasteries and become known as Custenin Fendigaid, or Constantine the Blessed.

The reality of his story carries echoes of what happened a generation earlier under his father, but coincided with an even more dangerous period for the British province perched precariously on the fringe of the Roman world. The empire in the West was now under the nominal rule of the boy Honorius. His military commander, the Vandal-born general Stilicho, had secured the northern boundaries in an early fifth-century campaign against the Picts, Scots and Saxons in Britain but was increasingly preoccupied by the broader threat from marauding barbarians on the Continent. When the Rhine frontier finally broke, Stilicho withdrew the XXth Legion from Chester to defend Italy. The Britons, peeved at being deserted and anxious for their own defence, responded by proclaiming their own Constantine as emperor.[14]

The Roman chroniclers dismissed this Constantine III as a jumped up private soldier elected from the ranks, but during his brief usurpation from 407–11 he led a native expeditionary force across the Channel in an apparent repetition of the failed ambition of Magnus Maximus. Ostensibly the enterprise was to repel the invaders from Gaul, but Constantine seems to have got as far as the River Po before being repulsed by loyalist forces, aided by a British general called Gerontius who switched sides. A magnificent confusion of rival imperial candidates all seeking to exploit the power vacuum caused by the barbarians was brought up short by the psychologically devastating sack of Rome itself by Alaric the Goth in 410. The British chieftains promptly abandoned Constantine and restored their recognition to the legitimate emperor, but it was too late. According to the contemporary chronicler Zosimus, the rulers of Rome, now exiled to Ravenna, had lost patience with the far-flung province. 'Honorius dealt with the states of Britain by letter,' he wrote, 'telling them to look to their own defence.'[15]

Constantine III retreated into the mythology of the Dark Ages that was to engulf Britain for almost 500 years. Nevertheless the very existence of a genuine Cymric ruler by that name, whose own son Constans maintained the local title of *imperator* after his death, created complications for the story-tellers of later generations. Nennius himself appears to have fallen foul of the confusion in noting in his *Historia Brittonum* that Constantius Chlorus had died in Wales. 'His sepulchre, as it appears by the inscription on his tomb, is still seen near the city named Caer Segont,' he wrote.[16] In fact the local tradition in Caernarfon is that it was Custenin Fendigaid who was buried at the former Roman settlement. The erroneous identification with the father of Constantine the Great came about through a misreading of an inscription on a stone tomb now in Llanbeblig church which referred to a 'son of the great, the very great.'[17] The Latin translation of that phrase should never have signified any more than that the dead man's father was called Magnus Maximus.

✝

NEITHER GILDAS NOR Nennius fell for the idea that Magnus Maximus was descended from Constantine. If it was not made up, why did Geoffrey of Monmouth assert it? Surely his claim must derive instead from contact with the lively Welsh tradition of fact, fiction and folktale handed down and elaborated through the generations. By Geoffrey's time the oral tradition was being written, not only in the emerging literature of the *Mabinogion* but also in the first recognisable historical documents in the Welsh language.

Take the *Bonedd y Sant*, or *Lives of the Saints*, for example, an early attempt to record the genealogies of those Celtic saints excluded from the official Roman martyrologies. Though there is no reason to doubt the authenticity of the individuals mentioned, many were given bogus links to local dynasties in an attempt to boost their status. One was *Elen 'ch Goel godeboc* or Helen daughter of Coel the Splendid, that strange character who featured in the heraldic archives consulted by the amateur historians of Colchester. 'Elen found the blessed cross after it had been concealed in the earth by the Jews,' reported the genealogy, and thereafter the bards sang:

> Without difficulty, Elen Godebog
> Found the cross for Christendom.[19]

There was also the *Annales Cambriae*, compiled by the monks of St David's, which traced the pedigree of the tenth-century kings of Dyfed back to the ancient times in order to legitimise their dynastic claims. They sought to show that the ancestry of the pioneering law-maker Hywel Dda, or Howell the Good, went right back to Constantine the Great. Interestingly, however, they made the connection through the maternal line of Hywel's wife Elen in order that she could be a descendant of Elen Llwyddog.

'*Constantii magni map Constantii et Helen Luitdawc que de Brittannia exivit ad crucem Christi querendam usque ad Ierusalem,*' ran the relevant entry.[20] Loosely translated, this made Constantine the Great the offspring of Constantius and Helen Llwyddog 'who left Britain to find the cross of Christ in Jerusalem.'

Aside from this pedigree, the *Annales* primarily consists of a list of dates recording key events from the fifth century to mediaeval times. It records that Hywel Dda's queen – given the Latinised form of her name, Helena – died in 928, the same year the great Welsh king made a pilgrimage to Rome. And it contains one of the few 'facts' that have fuelled the legend of King Arthur by noting that in 516 the Battle of Badon took place, 'in which Arthur carried the cross of our Lord Jesus Christ on his shoulder for three days and nights and the Britons were victorious.'[21] Although this is generally assumed to refer to the symbol of the cross emblazoned on the shields of the warriors rather than an actual relic carried into battle, it reinforces the close contemporaneous association that was made between the story of the British resistance and the Christian faith.

Hywel Dda was ruling most of Wales at the same time the Saxon kings were venerating Helena in Colchester. Modern scholars suggest his celebrated codification of the Welsh laws was not so much a declaration of independence as part of a process which acknowledged the over-lordship of London.[22] Nevertheless, until the Norman Conquest was extended to Wales in the 13th century, the two traditions were effectively kept well apart by the artificial land barrier that had been erected by Offa, King of Mercia, in the eighth century. The dyke that ran from north to south, utilising natural features as well as extra-ordinary earthworks that can still be seen in places today, represented more than a border: it was the boundary between two cultures.

The dyke was intended to shut out the strange-speaking West Britons, thereafter permanently designated *wealhas* or 'foreigners', from the land of the Angles. This etymology of the word 'Welsh' has its origins in the Teutonic term *Walsche,* which denotes any group of bordering tribes, and is reflected across Europe from the Walloons of Flanders to the district of Wallachia in Bulgaria.[23] The Welsh themselves branded the hostile people who barricaded them into their own homeland as *Sais,* or Saxons, from the *seax* or sword that was the most distinguishing feature of the English enemy.

✝

THE SARN HELEN survives in stretches of Roman causeway that are too far off the beaten track to be useful highways any longer.[24] Like the quarry road I saw exposed near Tomen-y-Mur, they are often associated on maps of present-day Wales with related Roman remains, such as kilns which used to produce pottery and tiles, or earthworks which marked where the troops practised constructing their camps. A group of 19th-century antiquarians who founded the Cambrian Archaeological Association specialised in tracing remains of these roads.[25] A report in 1846 described visiting one section at a place called Ffynnon Helen, or Helen's fountain, somewhere on the mountain pass through Snowdonia on the way to the city of Segontium. The authors said Helen was resting here with the van of the Welsh army when she heard of Constantine's death. The king was further north, at Castell Cidum in the shadow of Mynydd Mawr, when he was killed by an enemy arrow. I found the Great Mountain on my map, just south of Caernarfon, but the other places, like the rest of the story, could not be verified.

Instead, I tried to retrace another branch of Helen's Highway north from the isolated amphitheatre above Trawsfynydd Lake. It traversed Forestry Commission land, necessitating an early detour, before spanning the sparkling waters of the Arfon Cynfal at a crossing whose Roman origins are now obscured by the modern tarmac of Bont Newydd, or Newbridge. From there the Roman road which marched boldly across the map, east of the slate-mining village of Festiniog, was but a grassy ridge on a hill-side pasture, intersected by wire fences where impatient farmers had interrupted the walkers' right of way in order to restrain the wandering of their livestock. The footpath continued uphill past the unobtrusive Iron Age hill fort of Bryn-y-Castell and disappeared into naked moorland where all traces of the Roman road had been destroyed by quarrying. But it could be picked up again on the far side of the mountain, descending the steep wooded slopes of Cwm Penamnen via a way-marked terrace down to the auspiciously named settlement of Dolwyddelan.

Despite the pronunciation ('doll-with-elen') I was disappointed to find no direct link with the legend that had brought me to Wales, although how the village got its name is reassuringly confused. Local lore insisted *dol* meant 'meadow' and Gwyddelan was a sixth-century saint commemorated at the quaint 16th-century church by the river. There was an Elen's Well in the grounds of the hotel, a natural spring in the long grass, but the proprietor of Elen's Castle, Frank Ratcliffe, only laughed at my tentative queries over the bar of his hostelry. After all, Elen was the name of a Celtic fairy, guaranteed to bewitch the unsuspecting.[26] Frank directed me further down the Lledr Valley to the magnificent Dolwyddelan Castle, suggesting this distinctive Welsh fortification was named after a native princess called Elen. There the representative of Cadw, official curators of Wales' built heritage, politely disagreed, insisting that Dolgwyddelan came from *dol gwyddelig*, meaning Irishman's meadow.

I feared I had reached a dead end. Yet as I turned my attention from following half-forgotten Roman roads to exploring a restored 13th-century castle, a new line of inquiry opened up. For I learned that the fortress might once have sheltered a Helen, the daughter of Llewellyn ab Iorwerth.[27] From his itinerant court, Llewellyn the Great sought to consolidate his rule by establishing dynastic alliances with the English, and married off his Helen to John the Scot, the Marcher lord of Chester. Dolwyddelan was traditionally the birthplace of Llewelyn, and he refortified the castle at the height of his powers between 1210 and 1240. I couldn't help wondering if it was more than coincidence that the last great Welsh king should name his daughter after a Christian saint.

THE FLOWERING OF Welsh literature in the mediaeval period coincided with a national uprising against the Normans, just as the leading families among the invaders were themselves struggling to assert a single hegemony in England. As a rebellion it was an on-off affair, in which the Welsh most successfully raised the standard of revolt when the English were busy fighting amongst themselves. While Geoffrey of Monmouth was taking sides in the English civil war of the early 12th century, for example, there had been a flurry of flag flying in Wales under Owain Gwynedd, prince of Aberfraw on the island of Anglesey. In the early years of the next century, the rise of Llewelyn ab Iorwerth was facilitated by the civil war raging between Richard the Lionheart and King John.[28]

Later Llewelyn's grandson, Llewelyn ap Gruffyd, benefitted from another bout of infighting with the barons back in England which forced Henry II to recognise him as Prince of Wales in the 1267 Treaty of Montgomery. There matters might have remained in uneasy equilibrium if the younger Llewelyn's younger brother Dafydd had not been addicted to fomenting revolts of his own. Perhaps he had fallen for all the literary propaganda produced on behalf of the House of Gwynedd?

The upshot was Edward I's punitive expedition of 1282, which did not rest even when Llewelyn had been defeated in battle at Builth Wells and his head posted on the Tower of London. The ruthless King ordered the fugitive Dafydd to be hunted down so that he could be hung, drawn and quartered in the streets of Shrewsbury as a warning to other would-be traitors. The English victory was enshrined in the Statute of Rhuddlan, described by nationalist-minded historians as the first colonial constitution, and sealed by the series of great stone castles stamped across the map of north Wales. In addition to Caernarfon, whose walls were said to have been modelled on the city defences of Constantinople, these solid English fortifications included a new square tower at Dolwyddelan. Edward also inaugurated the tradition that the eldest son of the king should be proclaimed Prince of Wales, since his heir was born at Caernarfon in 1284. For my purposes, however, the interesting discovery was the steps Edward took to wipe out any traces of an embryonic Welsh state by securing all the insignia of an independent Gwynedd. Among the symbols it was feared might service a revival was a relic of the True Cross found on Llewellyn's dead body.

Edward's capture of the Welsh Regalia is less well-known than his seizure of the Scottish Regalia, since the results of his campaigning against chieftains north of the border included possession of the famous Stone of Scone and its attendant throne, on which English monarchs have been crowned at Westminster Abbey ever since. The Welsh equivalent was attested by several contemporary chroniclers, and said to include the crown of Arthur and the ancient British kings, together with a relic called the *croes naid* contained in a gilded and bejewelled reliquary which was carried on important occasions before the Prince of Wales. Matthew of Westminster described that when Edward took Caernarfon the Welsh surrendered 'a large portion of the cross of our Lord, which in the language of the Welsh is called *Croizneth*.'[29] Six hundred years later a nostalgic Catholic pamphleteer of the 19th-century Roman revival described it fondly as 'the greatest treasure of the British people in the old days.'[30]

According to an entry in the Welsh Rolls of Edward's reign,[31] one Einion ap Ivor and a group of compatriots delivered to the king while he was at Aberconwy a portion of the cross which had belonged to Llewelyn and his ancestors. In return, they were excused military service for themselves and their heirs in perpetuity. There is confusion about the origin of the relic, with some monkish writers assuming it must have been brought back by Helena from the Holy Land, and a strong Welsh tradition claiming it was supplied to the local princes by a certain St Neot. However, the real sixth-century saint of this name hailed from Cornwall, gave his name to a village in Cambridgeshire, and seems to have had nothing to do with Wales: he may have entered the story inadvertently through a corruption of the archaic Welsh word *naid*, which means refuge, or fate.

Edward was a pious king, whose own coronation had been delayed because he was off crusading in the Holy Land under the banner of the cross when his father died. He ordered the visible signs of his Welsh triumph to be conveyed to Westminster Abbey and placed on the high altar as an offering to God. Later they were transferred to the shrine of Edward the Confessor, where they joined the crown and sceptre of the Scottish regalia and other spoils of the Welsh campaign, including the golden coronet and jewels of Llewelyn which had been salvaged by Alphonso, the king's younger brother. 'And so the glory of the Welsh, though against their will, was transferred to the English,' wrote Matthew of Westminster.

✝

THE TOMB OF Edward the Confessor had become a repository for sacred relics ever since the saintly king died in 1065, shortly after completing his abbey church at Westminster. Tradition held that he endowed it with an improbable variety of Biblical bits and pieces, ranging from the frankincense offered by the three *magi* to the bread which Jesus blessed during his mission in Galilee, and not forgetting the vestments of the Virgin Mary. The confessor's bones were removed from the high altar to a special tomb on his canonisation in 1163 with no further mention of any extraneous objects, but the veneration of relics really took off with the arrival of a fresh collection of holy wonders during the course of the 13th century.

The most spectacular was the portion of the blood of Christ encased in a crystal vase that Henry II received from the patriarch of Jerusalem in 1247. The king was so pleased that he personally paraded the vessel through the streets of London with solemn ceremony before depositing it at the Abbey. Twenty-two years later Henry III inaugurated a cult of devotion to the Confessor after constructing a brand new shrine to house the saint's remains. The chapel of St Edward the Confessor subsequently became the resting-place of the English kings until Henry VII built the Royal Chapel. One wonders how sacred the site actually was, since its inaugurator earned a reputation for borrowing the jewels he kept there when he was short of funds. Nevertheless, the official history of the Abbey recorded an impressive haul of relics at this period, which also include a stone marked with the imprint of the Saviour's foot at his ascension and a thorn from the mock crown which adorned his head at the crucifixion.[32] The large piece of the cross brought from Wales became the *pièce de resistance* of the display.

And where is it now? Some say Edward I carried it with him on his campaigns to subdue the Scots in 1300 and 1307, after which the relic was stored in the Tower of London for safe keeping during the reign of his less spirited son. Others argue that Edward II's hated favourite, Piers Gaveston, was forced to swear on it that he would never again set foot in England after his relationship with the king precipitated civil war. Yet the most persuasive tradition asserted that the relic of the cross was transferred to the royal chapel at Windsor Castle shortly after Edward III founded the Order of the Garter there in 1348.

Although the original records of the order have been lost, it is believed the king was inspired to recreate his own version of the Arthurian round table, consisting in this instance of himself, the Prince of Wales, and 12 knightly companions, as part of a plan to exalt the prestige of the monarchy. One document that survives, however is an inventory from 1384 compiled by the Dean of Windsor, Sir Walter Almaly, who gives pride of place among the ornaments on the High Altar of the royal chapel to 'one noble cross called Gneth.' Seven years after the king died, however, the symbol of his chivalrous vision of chivalry was looking rather tarnished, for Sir Walter went on to give a fuller description of what had been the national palladium of Wales in terms of what it lacked – 'in which there are seven various stones missing of the same type as those set in the same cross. And in the foot of the same cross there are eleven pearls lacking and three small emeralds on the edges. Three tops of pinnacles are wanting.'[33]

The story of the Cross Gneth is commemorated to this day in two carved and painted wooden bosses on the underside of the roof of St George's Chapel in Windsor. Both depict a golden Celtic cross with a distinctive circular ring linking the four arms, which is believed to represent the reliquary in which the treasured remains of the True Cross was stored. Although the cross-shaped container became known locally as the Cross Gneth, the name would appear to derive from the contemporary belief that it contained the *croes naid* rather than the alternative suggestion, fuelled by an ambiguous phrase in another inventory 150 years later, which implied it had hailed from the Cistercian abbey in Neath.

The relic itself was presented in 1352 to the College of St

George's, the monastic community whose role was to act as the spiritual home of the Garter Knights, and the priests spent more than £315 – a small fortune in those days – encasing it in gold and silver and adorning the whole with pearls, rubies and emeralds. Twice repaired by goldsmiths within the next half-century, it became a focus for pilgrimage, and the sick and crippled came from all over England to be healed at a shrine which also boasted three other smaller remnants of the True Cross, a couple of thorns from the mock crown worn by Jesus at his scourging, a part of the table used at the last supper, the veil of the Blessed Virgin Mary, the cloth with which Veronica wiped the face of Jesus on the road to Calvary, and (naturally enough) some bones belonging to St George.

The precise location of this shrine is now unknown, for the royal chapel fell into disrepair and more than a century later Edward IV commissioned a new one at Windsor which took the west wall of the original as the starting point for the east wall of its successor. This took 35 years to build and remains to this day one of the finest examples of Gothic Perpendicular architecture in the country. Here is where one can see the Cross Gneth roof bosses today, concealing two of the joints where the rib arches meet in the magnificent vaulting completed in the early years of the 16th century.

One of the pair, high above the south aisle of the nave, at its easternmost end, shows Edward kneeling before the reliquary in the company of Richard Beauchamp, the Bishop of Salisbury, who was appointed the first Dean of the new chapel.[34] It is thought the Cross Gneth itself was exhibited somewhere in the immediate vicinity, a practice attested by a couple of contemporary Papal bulls which granted indulgences to any penitent who visited St George's Chapel to venerate 'a cross of great length of the wood of the cross brought by St Helena.' An inventory taken in 1501 to mark the hand-over of liturgical goods for use in the new chapel gave pride of place to 'a golden cross, containing within it part of the precious wood, ornamented with many precious stones, without the foot' but gave the reliquary no name. Although no one can be sure where it stood any longer, a plaque marks a likely spot by a niche near the south-east corner where modern pilgrims are invited to light a candle and say a prayer in remembrance of the generations who came there in times past.

Most of the religious treasures and sacred relics accumulated in England during the mediaeval period disappeared from history altogether with the dissolution of the monasteries under Henry VIII. The 1534 Act of Supremacy unilaterally declared him to be head of the new Church of England and the loyal priests of St George's promptly conducted another stock-taking of what were now royal treasures. Amongst them was a detailed description of 'the holy cross, closed in gold, garnished with rubies, saffires, hemerods, lacking of the same stones in number 15 as it appeared in the place where they were set.' This is recognisably the same Cross Gneth referred to in the earlier inventories, and indeed the entry specifically mentions it being donated to St George's by Edward III. This object appears to have regained the foot that was missing at the beginning of the century, a splendid base covered in gold, garnished with pearl and precious stones, and mounted upon a pride of golden lions.

Four years later Thomas Cromwell banned the veneration of relics altogether, but the reference to the lions enables us to keep track of the relic in a later inventory conducted in 1548, soon after the accession of Edward VI, when the Protestant reformation was in full flood and all churches in the country were ordered to adopt the Book of Common Prayer and hold services in English. However, this inventory recorded only 'the foot of the holy cross' with no mention of the wooden relic or its casing. Indeed according to an affidavit given to the King's Commissioners in 1552 by John Robins, a canon of Windsor, the gold from the back of the reliquary had been disposed of by his colleagues three years earlier. 'To whom they sold it I cannot tell but I think surely that Wygg the Goldsmith had a great portion of it,' he wrote. The Commissioners had been despatched to check that all church plate had been delivered to the Crown and no embezzlement was taking place: but their interest was financial rather than spiritual, and so the list of valuables which they carted off to the Jewell House in the Tower of London included that ostentatious pearl-encrusted base mounted on golden lions-feet – yet gave no inkling of what it had been created to carry.

Meanwhile, the fate of the abbey church of St Peter's in Westminster was no exception to the rule of the reformers, despite the exalted status of the building today as the national parish church. The monks here had last compiled an inventory of their most precious possessions in 1520, 15 years before Cromwell ordered them to be seized, and were still claiming to possess their own piece of the True Cross and other relics of the passion. 'As to the Relyks, first a cup of gold with stones with the blood of our Lord. Item a white marble stone with the print of our Lord's foot. Item a great part of the holy cross. Item a long coffer of crystal with our lady's girdle with cases belonging to the same girdle. Item a point of the nail and three thorns closed in gold . . .'[35]

The document rattled on in like manner, offering once again a tantalising glimpse of what was important to earlier generations in a past we so easily forget from behind the curtain drawn by the Protestant settlement. No doubt the gold, silver and jewels were subsequently all recycled for the royal Treasury. William Benson, the Abbott at the time of dissolution, probably found delivering up the abbey treasures to the king rather easier on his conscience than resistance, for he was subsequently appointed the first Dean of the new administration. Yet the fate of the English relics followed that of the Welsh regalia into obscurity. They became just bits of wood and stone, blood and iron, glass and glitter, of no relevance to the newly forged Anglican Church which had just freed itself from all taint of popery and superstition. Only the folk memory remained, fuelled by the literary fancies of popular history.

CURIOUSLY, GEOFFREY of Monmouth ignored Helena's sainthood. Neither did he claim for her the discovery of the cross.[36] These are notable omissions, considering either the extent to which both were regarded as self-evident in his time, or the weight of ordure heaped upon him as a fantasist by subsequent generations. Indeed, for a cleric Geoffrey appeared remarkably uninterested in sacred history at all, making no attempt to link the Celtic world of myth and magic he explored with the Christian orthodoxy of his day. One could add that for a Welshman he was also curiously lacking in national consciousness. For example, he apparently did not know the name of Maximus' bride. And although his edited version of *The Dream of Macsen Wledig* suggested he had access to some repository of Welsh lore, it was probably not the Welsh triads themselves, or he might have made more specific use of them.

I was also troubled by another curiosity. In the same way we saw that the Welsh text of Geoffrey's *History* referred to the Earl of Gloucester in place of the Duke of Colchester, there is an intriguing variation in the ancestry of the unnamed Elen Lwyddog too. The daughter of Octavius, duke of the Gewissei, in the Latin version mysteriously becomes in the *Brut* the daughter of *Eudaf jarll Ergig ac Euas*. In fact Octavius the Old was indeed the Latin name of Eudaf Hen, prince of Arfon in north Wales and ruler of substantial estates in the south through marriage.[37] The Welsh form of Gewissei, Iwys, is still preserved today in the Herefordshire village of Ewyas Harold, which like the ancient kingdom of Erging lay between the rivers Wye and Monnow. But why describe Elen with reference to her father's acquisitions in the Marches rather than the family seat in Snowdonia? It may be coincidence, but I couldn't help feeling that the fact the border area was Geoffrey's birthplace had something to do with it.

An analysis of geographical references in the *History* shows that he is familiar with south-east Wales although does not have much of an opinion of it. Such residual local loyalty no doubt accounted for his siting Arthur's capital at Caerleon, the ruins of whose Roman fortress was well-known in Geoffrey's day. Yet to make his career, the monk from Monmouth took the high road to Oxford rather than gravitate towards the nearest Welsh centre of learning, at Llandaff Cathedral in Cardiff. His signature appears in the charters of several 12th-century religious foundations in Oxford, then not yet a university, and towards the end of his life he went to London to be consecrated bishop of St Asaph in north Wales, though it is unlikely he ever visited his see before his death.

While clearly aware of the Welsh legends, his writings are surprisingly free of either Welsh words or any other sense of interest in the traditions of the country, leading one analyst, J S P Tatlock, to conclude he might actually have been a Breton whose ancestors came over to Britain with the Norman conquest. More likely he was simply a product of that borders mentality which is still displayed today by Welsh television viewers who turn their aerials towards England rather than tune in to S4C broadcasts in the language whose roots are evident even in the names of the places where they live. Geoffrey was exposed to Welsh influences yet did not have much empathy with the culture in which he grew up, and on which he turned his back in favour of the bright lights of Oxford. There he expounded a wider sense of Britishness than merely a folk memory of a greater Wales, but by drawing on a Welsh tradition he did not really understand, he sowed the seeds of magnificent confusion in the minds of subsequent generations.

IN A POSTSCRIPT Geoffrey left the later history of the Saxon kings of England to others, like Henry of Huntingdon, but advised them to steer clear of British affairs because 'they do not have in their possession the book in the British language which Walter, Archdeacon of Oxford, brought from Wales.' He added: 'It is this book which I have been at such pains to translate into Latin in this way, for it was composed with great accuracy about the doings of these princes and in their honour.' A *pps* in the *Brut Tysilio* went even further, purporting to be a note from Walter, Archdeacon of Oxford, explicitly admitting responsibility for turning a Welsh original into Latin and then back into Welsh again. More than 800 years later it is difficult to know where the truth lies, but I am convinced that the key to a proper understanding of Geoffrey lay in the Welsh dimension to his work. This appears to have been largely ignored by mainstream English scholars out of an understandable anxiety to avoid being sucked into the quicksand of myth and legend which have been such a pitfall for Arthurian studies.

Imagine my astonishment, therefore, to discover quite unexpectedly that there was an historical figure called Coel after all – and he was Welsh. Coel Hen, or Coel the Aged, cropped up as the shadowy ancestor of the *Gwyr y Gogledd*, or Men of the North, whose heroic exploits are related by the Welsh bards in the poems of Aneurin, Taliesin and Llywarch Hen. I said Coel was Welsh, but he never lived in the Wales we know. Our best modern guess[38] makes Coel an early fifth-century commander, possibly the last *dux britanniorum* appointed by the Romans to defend the northern half of the province when they pulled their own armies out to deal with the growing continental threat that was eventually to engulf the imperial capital itself. This general, whose Latin name could have been either Coelius or Coelestius – there was a contemporary Irish monk of that name in Rome who won notoriety as a follower of the heretic Pelagius – was probably based at York, and possibly responsible for garrisoning Hadrian's Wall.

Following the Roman withdrawal, the kingdom of Coel's successors stretched from the River Dee and River Humber to the Firth of Forth and the Firth of Clyde. Two of the 'sons of Coel' specifically mentioned in the verses of the *Gododdin*[39] were Urien and his offspring Owain, the last rulers of a realm called Rheged (in the area we now know as Cumbria) and leaders of the local resistance against invading Angles who had already overrun Northumbria. The Welsh bards sang the praises of 'the three hundred spears of the tribe of Coel' and attributed to them the mythic qualities of a golden age, for 'on whatever expedition they might go together, they would never fail.'

Echoes of these exploits reappeared in Scotland in the late 18th century with some of the earliest recorded versions of 'Auld King Coul' being collected by Robert Burns.[40] They linked up with a local tradition that commemorated Coel in the Ayrshire district of Kyle, and asserted that the merry monarch was buried in a tomb in the grounds of Coilsfield House.[41] However, this burial mound was excavated in 1837 and found to date from the Bronze Age, while modern linguists suggest the derivation of Kyle is more probably the Gaelic word *caol*, meaning thin or strait, and thus signifying a narrow arm of the sea dividing two pieces of land – as in the kyles with which the coastline of western Scotland is riven. Nevertheless, the tradition persisted because this part of the country was also one of the last to remain in the hands of the north Britons, and their descendants preserved a folk memory of native resistance to the barbarians, in which the civil society formerly enjoyed under the Roman protectorate lived on in the Kingdom of Strathclyde and eventually became a key ingredient in the forging of the Scottish national identity.

Just as it was the Picts who poured across Hadrian's Wall from Scotland, and the Scots who actually invaded from Ireland, so west Wales during the Dark Ages was in fact populated by Celtic people of Irish extraction, while the Welsh who populated the eastern borders had more in common with the inhabitants of the north of England. They called themselves *cambroges*, fellow-countrymen, to set themselves apart from the invaders from overseas, both the barbarian tribesmen further north and the heathen Saxons in the south. Their strong sense of identity as the last upholders of the Roman civic tradition survives in the English word for their geographical stronghold, Cumbria, and the Welsh word for the new homeland, Cymru, to which they retreated after the military failures of the sixth century.[42]

Resettled in Wales, the bards preserved in popular poetry a record of the Cymric resistance under a series of native leaders in an area which had once been the most sensitive outpost of the empire. Gradually the story of the *Gwyr y Gogledd*, the men of the north, became conflated with the origin legends of Gwynedd in the north of Wales. In an attempt to relate the old battle songs to new locations the Welsh past took on increasingly mythical characteristics, a process further fuelled by the introduction of the Arthurian legend from Brittany. Yet while Arthur went on to inspire a national fantasy, poor Coel became a figure of fun. His name survived in an ordinary Welsh word, initially meaning omen or portent, then in mediaeval times belief or faith. Although the noun *Coeling* can still be used in Welsh to describe a descendant of Coel, it is rather ironic that the verb *coelio* now means ' to believe or trust', and *coelus* one who is credulous or foolish. Although serious Celtic scholars started to unravel the history from the Welsh literature during the 19th century, the real king Coel Hen has yet to emerge from the shadow cast over the popular imagination by the mythical Old King Cole.

CHAPTER VI

Trier

The veneration of relics, in fact, is to some extent a primitive instinct, and it is associated with many other religious systems besides that of Christianity.

The Catholic Encyclopaedia[1]

THE WELSH TRADITION was never coherent, but fluid enough to accept both the assertion in *The Dream of Macsen Wledig* that Maximus left his bride at home and the popular belief that she marched with his armies to the Continent. In fact, we do have independent evidence that Elen visited the regional imperial capital of Augusta Trevirorum (present-day Trier), where for three years Maximus presided over a glittering cultural circle that included the poet Ausonius and the ascetic Martin of Tours, the founder of Western monasticism.[2] A contemporary description of the court portrayed Maximus' wife as a particularly devout Christian. Sulpicius Severus, a scholar who attached himself to St Martin, does not actually mention her name, and indeed is clearly well aware that St Helena's discovery of the cross is a quite separate story since he relates it independently in his own 'sacred history' from the origin of the world to AD 400. Nevertheless, he provided a touching tribute to Elen's piety in his biography of Martin, as she waited on the saint at a banquet. 'In the meantime the queen hung upon the lips of Martin and not inferior to her mentioned in the Gospel, washed the feet of the holy man with tears and wiped them with the hairs of her head.'[3]

While at Augusta Trevirorum, Maximus corresponded with the pope, and was twice visited by Ambrose, the influential bishop of Milan who played a major part earlier in this inquiry as the originator of the legend that Helena discovered the True Cross. Ambrose was actually born in Augusta Trevirorum, his father having been the Praetorian prefect of Gaul. However, by the time he returned as imperial ambassador, more than 40 years later, he had no truck with provincial politics. Maximus was offering peace on condition the legitimate emperor, Valentinian, paid homage at his court. The latter wanted to recover the body of his brother Gratian, slain by the usurper, for burial at Rome. The first embassy resulted in an agreement to respect the territorial status quo. Two years later Ambrose had barely submitted his credentials than he was summarily dismissed.

In a letter to his patron, Ambrose described a prickly interview with 'a man who is cloaking war under the mask of peace' but had nothing whatsoever to say about his wife.[4] A shame really: is it too fanciful to think that the cleric who was shortly to credit Helena with finding the True Cross could himself have prevented the Welsh from coming to believe their Elen was responsible for the discovery? Or is that an unhistorical anticipation of what was to be, on behalf of both sides? As in so much of this story, would later generations have simply seized on yet another coincidental connection as false proof for what they wanted to believe anyway? As, indeed, they did with the account of Elen's piety towards St Martin. For, just a minute. Did we not encounter this author, Sulpicius Severus, earlier in the story? As the recipient of a small piece of the True Cross from his friend Paulinus of

Nola, recording for the first time the belief that the original would never get smaller? So maybe . . .? Unpicking a legend is a bit like unravelling a conspiracy theory.[5]

To return to reality in Trier: neither bishop nor emperor was surprised when Maximus crossed the Alps on his fateful final campaign. The invasion forced the youthful Valentinian to flee Milan, and he recovered his throne through the armed intervention of Theodosius, the emperor in the east. Ambrose was already responsible for entrenching Catholicism among the aristocracy of the west; his subsequent relationship with Theodosius laid the groundwork for the mediaeval notion of the Holy Roman Emperor as son of the church. The brief reign of Magnus Clemens Maximus became a mere footnote in the grand sweep of European ecclesiastical history, his vaulting ambition remembered only in the fertile imagination of the *cyfarwyddion*, the patriotic band of poets, bards and myth-makers in the faraway Celtic land from where he launched his ill-fated adventure.[6]

†

I MAKE NO apologies for having dwelt so much on the twin conceits of Constantine as an English emperor and Helena as a Welsh princess only to conclude that both were bogus. Nobody nowadays seriously advances either thesis. To modern sceptical minds they are self-evidently wrong, and not particularly relevant to the world at the start of a new millennium. Yet for generations, centuries even, ordinary people in Britain believed otherwise – and didn't give the matter a second thought.[7] Paradoxically, the reign of Helena and Constantine in the British national consciousness became a fact of history even though it was untrue. In retrospect it may seem extraordinary how such easy convictions held sway for so long, rooted in religion and reinforced in literature, undisturbed by the critical scrutiny we take for granted. But their persistence as beliefs which affected the conduct of clerics and churchgoers alike is intrinsically no odder than anything else people believed about Helena over an even longer time-scale. They collapsed under the rational gaze of an Enlightenment which gradually put paid to the remainder of the Helena legend too, though since that had the full might of the Roman Catholic church on its side it took some while to give way.

With all the advantages of historical method, we can say with absolute confidence that Constantine was not British, though as it happens the circumstances of his birth are disputed.[8] This is partly because in their retrospective search for auspicious signs the imperial panegyrists sought to stress the emperor's youthfulness at the time of his accession, and link his place of birth to the site of an ancestor's famous victory. It was probably somewhere in the Balkan provinces, whence his father Constantius Chlorus hailed, sometime between 272 and 282.[9] Whether he was in his mid-twenties or early thirties at the time of his father's death, however, Constantine could not have been born in Britain because Chlorus did not first visit the island until 296, when he landed with his army to put down the rebellion of the usurper Allectus.

By then all the evidence suggests Helena had been divorced by her husband. Indeed, until rehabilitated at the imperial court by her son after 306, Helena barely figured in the official records at all. For Chlorus was a soldier of humble birth who had earned himself the status of honorary Roman through his military service. Where or when he had met Helena in the course of his campaigns has been a matter of spirited speculation ever since Eutropius, secretary to a later fourth-century emperor, noted that Constantine was born *ex obscuriore matrimonio*. Even the loyal St Ambrose acknowledged the suggestion she had been a lowly *stabularia*, although whether this meant the landlady of an inn or a simple barmaid has also been the subject of much debate. Later pagan historians claimed she was a prostitute, but that may be a harsh interpretation of the Roman custom of concubinage. As a Roman officer Chlorus would have found it difficult to marry a woman from a lower social class, though living together was quite acceptable.

What is not in dispute is that almost immediately after his promotion to Caesar in 293, Chlorus dumped Helena unceremoniously in favour of a more upmarket match. This was a common practice – Constantine himself was to follow the example in similar circumstances not long afterwards – and politically astute in uncertain times when power could be underpinned by dynastic alliances. Chlorus hitched himself to Theodora, stepdaughter of his boss Maximian. She bore him six other children in the 13 years he policed his quarter of the empire. His base was none other than the regional imperial headquarters at Augusta Trevirorum in Gaul. Extensive remains of this administrative complex are still standing in the provincial German town of Trier, and I hoped that among those ruins on the banks of the Mosel river I might find some clue about what had happened to the real Helena.

THE SOLEMN CEREMONY started like a scene out of a comic opera. A plump burgomeister in a long red coat and a tea-cosy hat led the procession out of the cathedral. An escort of sheepish young soldiers in red, white and blue uniforms followed, their pillbox caps perched rakishly at an angle to the sun. Bearing the banners of three traditional religious orders, they waded across the plaza in thigh-high black boots, clanking heavy broadswords on the cobbles. Behind them fluttered a huge flock of nuns in grey and black, hands clasped over their prayer books as they softly chanted *kyrie eleison*, Lord have mercy, over their charges – a clutch of young blonde girls in virginal white frocks.

Then came the priests in full regalia amid clouds of incense, leading the singing to the accompaniment of the beat of a thousand feet and the rhythmic tinkle of bells. The bishop himself walked slowly in the shadow of a magnificent embroidered palanquin, held over his head by four attendants. Yet the bright summer sunshine still sparkled off his golden robes and episcopal mitre, and caught the edge of the gilded sacrament-holder he bore aloft just a few inches in front of his face. Dazzled into a respectful silence, the congregation which had poured out of the cathedral to watch the proceedings themselves fell in behind the parade as it wound round the town. Well before the bishop reached a makeshift altar under the mediaeval cross in the Market Square, the Hauptmarkt, it was clear this was no costume drama being put on for visitors.

In fact the tourist office in Trier was rather hazy about the annual festival of *Fronleichnam*. 'It's a Catholic thing,' said one harassed counter assistant brusquely when I enquired later. 'I think it was the day Jesus died and his body disappeared – or something like that,' volunteered a colleague, who admitted she had been brought up in the faith.[10] Their uncertainty was a shame considering the Catholic Church has played such an enormous part in preserving the history of this settlement on the Mosel River in Germany.

Two thousand years ago it was one of the most important cities of the civilised world, the administrative nerve-centre from which the Romans ran the northwest corner of the empire, including Britannia. Julius Caesar first introduced the Celtic tribe of the Treveri in the commentary on the Gallic wars he wrote after his invasion of Britain in 44 BC. Settlement was rapid and the stone bridge over the Mosel, the town walls and monumental gates, the forum and amphitheatre, and the Barbarathermen public baths – the largest outside Rome – were already in situ by the second century. Even the ravaging of the city by barbarian Franks and Alemanns around 276 was turned into an opportunity when Constantius Chlorus took charge and restored civic order on an even greater scale than before. Today it houses the most impressive collection of Roman ruins north of the Alps. Yet without the intervention of the churches over the years, none of this heritage would have survived.

The sandstone entrance the Romans built to their regional capital of Augusta Trevirorum, nicknamed the Porta Nigra because the encrusted soot of centuries had blackened the gate, endured because it was converted into a church by Archbishop Poppo in the 11th century. The imperial palace constructed for Constantine the Great in the early fourth century was adapted into a basilica when the emperor adopted Christianity, and in turn provided the walls and pillars for the nave of the Romanesque cathedral of St Peter built 800 years later. Constantine's magnificent throne hall, the Aula Palatina, became the seat of the mediaeval Archbishops until replaced by a purpose-built Renaissance palace and falling into disuse. Appropriately, however, the massive brick structure was rescued from being a stables and is now itself a church, albeit a Protestant one, restored to its imperial size and shape if not its former marble-clad finery. Some of the buildings of the huge public bathhouse whose remains loom over the town's park today were also transformed into churches, though these have long since disappeared. The remainder, in common with the Roman amphitheatre dug into the slopes of the nearby hill, was incorporated into the defences erected by the Archbishop-Princes who ruled their own state under the patronage of the Holy Roman Emperor.[11]

But even outside these great monuments, just wandering the streets of Trier provided constant reminders of the city's religious past. It still has more than 30 Catholic churches. 'When it is not raining the bells are ringing,' is a local saying, and many houses carry chalk marks over the doorway recording their owners' annual contribution to a religious charity. Architectural oddities feature on every corner: here a Madonna and child carved into a wall, there a decorated stone lintel from an older structure preserved above a modern window. One day on the way back to my hotel, on a hillside overlooking the town centre, I stumbled across a series of red sandstone pillars on which Biblical scenes had been carved. Some were free-standing next to the pavement, others mounted in walls. It was only after following them up the path that I realised they represented the Stations of the Cross, the representation of Jesus' path to his crucifixion that adorns the walls of every Catholic church. At the summit of Holy Cross Hill was a restored chapel whose sacristan said Christians had worshipped there since Roman times. Apparently early believers regarded the location as sacred because they thought its distance from the centre of Trier echoed the geographical relationship between the Mount of Olives and Jerusalem.

†

HELENA PROVIDED the link between the two cities. Her husband, Chlorus, was elected emperor in Trier, and made it his capital in 293 when he became ruler of the Western Empire. A gold medal struck in the city portrays a swarthy man, with creased forehead and baggy eyes, a hook-nose, and a thick but close-trimmed beard. The reverse shows Chlorus on horseback, having crossed the Channel, receiving homage from the defeated rebel Allectus at the gates of London under an inscription hailing the 'restorer of eternal light.'[12] On his death in 306, Constantine was declared Augustus and used Trier as a base to launch his own bid for control of the empire. It seems reasonable to suppose that Helena lived in the imperial palace here, even though she had been put aside by the ambitious Chlorus in favour of a more politically correct marriage to Theodora. Local tradition preserved her memory in the belief that Helena was responsible for transforming the palace into a basilica under the guidance of Bishop Agritius.

Certainly the early history of the cathedral is contemporaneous with Constantine's foundations in the Holy Land, and some authorities believe Trier may even have been an architectural model for the work carried out in Palestine.[13] Archaeological investigations suggest the original basilica was twice the size of the present building: its west door extending all the way across the plaza outside to the edge of the Hauptmarkt, and its southern walls enclosing all the space now taken over by the adjacent church of Our Lady. The roof was supported by massive granite columns, one of which lies outside the main door today, broken after bursting in the heat of a fire which engulfed the basilica in the sixth century. Another is planted like a tree in the cloister linking St Peter's with Our Lady, while others still form the core of four huge pillars in the centre of the nave. If you look carefully you can see where the brick has been cut away in one place to reveal a head of the god Jupiter peering out from the original imperial column.

Inevitably destruction through war and fire entailed rebuilding over the years, but the history of the basilica through the generations is graphically illustrated by the external view of the north wall. Here the core of the original building is marked out in distinctive Roman red brick, with later Romanesque additions at either end. The outline of the original arched windows is clearly visible, a fan of thin red bricks picked out in white mortar, but the openings were long ago walled up and narrow Norman-style slits subsequently cut into them to provide what little natural light now illuminates the interior. The two Italianate towers at the west end overlooking the plaza are what strike visitors today but my interest was in the apse in the east where a precious relic was walled into the high altar when the mediaeval church was consecrated in 1196.

Whether Helena came back to Trier after her pilgrimage to the Holy Land at such an advanced age must be debatable. Yet for centuries, Trier has thrived on the idea that she not only returned to donate her palace to be converted into a church, but also installed in it a souvenir of the journey, the tunic worn by Jesus before his death. Housed today in a special reliquary, it is officially described as a symbol of Christian unity and put on display to be venerated every 30 years or so. Unfortunately I had just missed the last pilgrimage, in 1996. 'People were queuing on their knees all the way from the Porta Nigra to the door of the Dom,' recalled Heidi, the vivacious tourist guide who showed me round town. 'I saw wizened peasants wearing the suits they got married in, which now barely fitted them, and elderly women from the villages with the sort of braided hair you see in old pictures. I didn't know there were so many pious people nowadays.'

Even during my visit there was a steady stream of visitors, no doubt drawn by curiosity as much as faith. The Baroque shrine in which the Holy Robe is now kept dominates the interior of the cathedral. The eyes of the congregation are naturally swept up towards two small openings in the rococo facade which give a tantalising glimpse into the relic chamber. In the upper window a cross hangs in a starry sky – an effect achieved by studding the backdrop with rock crystals – while below a glass case houses the tunic. Spread out inside a gold crucifix that is itself hidden in a box inside the glass case, it's a bit of a disappointment for those who climb the stairs behind the altar in the hope of a closer look.

Given the scepticism that surrounds the much more famous Turin Shroud, almost certainly a clever mediaeval forgery, Trier would be wise to avoid testing the authenticity of the Seamless Robe of Christ by subjecting it to scientific analysis. Like the shroud in which Jesus was buried, however, it owed its existence to the Bible story. The four Gospel accounts of how Jesus was tormented by the Roman guards after his arrest, being forced to wear a purple robe and a crown of thorns, agree that afterwards the soldiers divided up his ordinary clothes and drew lots for them.

John offered the most detail of the scourging, noting that Jesus was arraigned before Pilate wearing 'the crown of thorns and the purple garment' and implying he was still in this garb when presented to the crowd. The mob rejected the mocked-up 'King of the Jews' for fear of offending the civil power of the Romans, and demanded his death as an impostor under their own religious laws for pretending to be the son of God.

'The soldiers therefore, when they had crucified Jesus, took his garments and made four parts, to every soldier a part; and also the coat: now the coat was without seam, woven from the top throughout. They said therefore one to another: Let us not rend it, but cast lots for it, whose it shall be, that the scripture should be fulfilled.'[14]

Although the cross was an early Christian symbol, artists were slow to depict the crucifixion. Perhaps they feared any representation of such cruelty would be repugnant to believers, or smacked of pagan idolatry in the face of the second commandment, 'thou shalt not make unto thee a graven image.'[15] Instead they preferred to portray the good shepherd, which had the added advantage of being a pagan symbol of humanitarian concern, or the equally ambiguous figure with its hands uplifted in prayer. In Helena's day, Eusebius curtly dismissed a request from Constantia, the emperor's sister, for a picture of Jesus. Just because they were on sale to souvenir-hunters in the bazaars of Palestine did not mean they were Christian, thundered the bishop.[16]

The first drawings of Jesus actually on the cross appeared in the late sixth century.[17] Though pinned to the wood by four nails he was shown alive, showing no signs of suffering, clad in a long, flowing, and sleeveless tunic called a *colobium* which reached the knees. The head was erect, framed in gold, and bearing a crown: the image of Christ triumphant. The tunic remained a key feature of the scene until at least the ninth century, early Christians being rather prudish, though he stayed fully robed in the east until much later. The Eastern Church always preferred to stress divinity rather than humanity, and even when it did accept nakedness, eschewed realism. However, in the west the *colobium* had by the tenth century become a shorter garment, reaching from the waist to the knees, the familiar loincloth of conventional Biblical illustrations. At the same time artists began to depict the agony of such a death, with bent arms, a twisted body, a tormented face, flowing blood and a crown of thorns: the humiliation of the Passion.

It struck me as intriguing, in passing, that the earliest historical references to the existence of a venerated tunic in Trier should correspond with the general disappearance of such a fashion accessory from western religious art. But the church authorities had anticipated such doubts. The official guide to the cathedral highlighted the original design of the podium which acts as the focal point of the modern structure, and which contains the remains of a 12-cornered memorial in the middle dating from Roman times. 'This unusual arrangement can best be explained – even though watertight evidence can no longer be produced – by the ancient Trier tradition according to which the Cathedral's most precious relic, Christ's tunic, the Holy Robe, was kept and venerated in this place,' said the pamphlet welcoming visitors to Germany's oldest diocesan church. Unfortunately the location is now obscured by the new altar platform constructed during restoration works 30 years ago, and buried beneath pseudo-ecumenical engravings of scenes from the Greek epics and the Hebrew scriptures intended to symbolise the roots of Christianity.

Although the famous tunic remained hidden to me, there was plenty of literature available containing photographs taken at its last public display. Funnily enough, it looked remarkably similar to the pair of 1,500-year-old Coptic garments on show with a lot less fuss in the textile section of the town museum. Worse, a shop in the Simeonstrasse had a job lot of pottery brooches in the shape of a miniature tunic for sale at five marks, with matching items to wear round the neck. Apart from the size and the colour, a muddy brown, the style was indistinguishable from the gaudy garments hanging on racks in the clothes shops of the pedestrian precinct. I tried to imagine Constantine's disappointment when Helena arrived home bearing souvenirs. 'My mother went to the Holy Land and all I got was this lousy T-shirt.'

†

BACK AT THE Hauptmarkt, the Fronleichnam procession had dispersed. The altar was taken down, the local bums regained their usual perches under the market cross, and the flower sellers set up their stalls again. The bells from St Peter's stopped competing with the chimes of St Gangolph's and gave way to chatter from pavement cafes as Trier assumed a secular air. Cyclists in Lycra gear and hikers in leather shorts fought to make their way through parties of schoolchildren clutching questionnaires. I found a table at a cafe in front of Zur Steipe, the mediaeval town hall. Its brightly-painted facade featured a gallery of life-size sculptures on the first floor, four saints flanked by a pair of soldiers. One statue in particular caught my eye, clad in a purple robe with a golden crown above a white wimple, the tell-tale cross and bunch of nails in either hand giving her identity away.

It was only a modern plaster model, however: I discovered later that the stone carvings carried out in 1483 by one Meister Steffan are now hidden away in the Stadtmuseum, as for that matter is the original market cross as well. I felt cheated that some of the town's distinctive public ornaments were contemporary copies. They mocked the excitement I had felt trying to bring history to life, as if I had strayed into a theme park. No doubt such compromises are inevitable in order to preserve the artefacts of the past from pollution and decay while retaining the illusion of how they might have looked in situ. In Trier, the pressure works both ways. I was reassured to learn that even the all-powerful Macdonald's chain was forced to convert its crude yellow 'big M' logo into an inconspicuous gilded Gothic-style motif before the municipal burghers would allow it to open a franchise a few doors down the historic Hauptmarkt.

A couple of days later, I unexpectedly encountered another religious ceremony, this time a group of nuns taking their vows at the Gothic church of Our Lady which adjoins the cathedral. I accosted an elderly priest wearing a purple skullcap and matching sash round his cassock to inquire what the earlier festival had been all about, not realising until half-way through our conversation that this was actually the bishop himself. Dr Hermann Josef Spital did his best to explain the theological significance of the feast of Corpus Christi as officials looked on askance at my impertinence. Yet when I seized the opportunity to ask about the tradition of Helena, the old bishop's eyes lit up.

'She is not so popular in the West now, but many people from the East come here. She is still venerated in the Orthodox Church.' He smiled. 'We have her head here in the crypt, you know. There are holy masses said there regularly in her honour.'

Intrigued, I popped back into the cathedral. In a gloomy chapel under the altar I found a brass casket, surmounted by the bust of a woman shouldering the cross, and holding three nails in her spare hand. An inscription in Latin proclaimed: *Ave caput ecce sanctae helenae fundatricis verae ecclesisae cathedralis vetuestae treverensis*. I guessed at a rough translation: 'Hail, here lies the head of the holy Helena, founder of the true church and ancient cathedral of the Treveri.'

The box had miniature arched windows but I couldn't see through, and in any case it was clearly sealed. Here was one relic that would not be brought out. As I examined it in the fading light, a bad-tempered sacristan wearing a grey apron started collecting up the offertory candles and shooed me out. 'Schliessen' he hissed. 'Closed.'

✝

THE HELENA TRADITION in Trier received a major boost immediately after the Second World War as a result of excavations in the bomb-damaged cathedral. Archaeologists exploring the remains of a room from the ancient imperial palace found thousands of fragments of a plaster ceiling which had dropped on to the ground and shattered. Piece by piece, the fragments were recovered and laboriously put together like a giant jigsaw puzzle. Where their place in the overall design was not clear, scientists studied the imprint of wooden lathing on the reverse of the fragments. The grain of the wood and the woven pattern of the lathing acted like fingerprints in identifying how and in which order they had been attached to the ceiling.

In 1983 the reconstructed results were put on show in the Episcopal Museum as a display of 15 panels featuring a mixture of dancing cupids and life-sized human heads. The brightly-painted scenes appeared to epitomise wealth and wisdom, with a smattering of rich purple robes, horns of plenty, sacrificial bowls, a globe, and a learned philosopher with a scroll. By far the most interesting panels, however, presented four women, not only each decked with abundant jewels and wearing golden diadems but also with their faces dramatically framed by a spotlight against a deep blue backdrop. In the fashion of Roman art this device, known as a nimbus and the origin of the halo in Christian iconography, denoted persons of special status. Were these pictures in fact portraits of members of the imperial family?

The archaeologist Theodore Kempf thought so, and was so excited by his find that he boldly identified the women.[18] The one bang in the middle, her face partially obscured by a veil, was Helena, he insisted. Below her and to one side was a plump, vain woman drawing her veil aside with a fat, fleshy arm to look in a mirror: this, he decided, was Fausta, Constantine's wife. Along the far edge of the ceiling, their faces turned towards the nearest wall, was a girl with tousled hair plucking at a lyre whom Dr

Kempf named as a younger woman also called Helena, who was the wife of Constantine's son Crispus; while an unkempt woman with a mean look in her staring eyes, taking a string of pearls out of a jewellery box, he decided was Constantia, the emperor's stepsister, married to Licinius.

Dr Kempf's convictions were not shared by the curators who put the restored ceiling frescos on display without daring to attribute a name to any of the panels which now grace the walls of the exhibition. Nevertheless, they are a startling sight. Pride of place goes to the panel from the centre of the ceiling, number eight in the sequence. Her dark eyes stand out across the room, flashing beneath a tightly curled fringe of auburn hair, as the veil is drawn back with one hand and the other proffers a golden bowl. 'Who are you? What do you want?' she seems to say, as if slightly taken aback by the visitor's presumption in questioning her identity, while simultaneously suggesting, 'Go on, take a closer look.' The invitation drew me hypnotically, to the point where I suddenly realised that the nose and mouth were missing, and the clever colouring of the reconstruction had conned me into thinking I had just seen the face of Helena.

'The question is not so sure,' said Marcus Gross-Morgen, a young art historian working for the museum. 'The bishops, they still believe, and everybody comes here to see Helena, but they do not admit this is all a legend from Dr Kempf, that there is no document.'

Marcus explained that the tradition claiming the cathedral was the house of Helena could not be traced back before the ninth century, and appeared to have originated from a rival cathedral at Rheims, which claimed to be the guardian of Helena's body. Inspired by the belief that her remains had been moved from Rome to the premier cathedral of France in the fifth century, an eager scribe called Altman of Hautvillers wrote a life of the saint to buttress the dubious authenticity of the relics. In the process he spun the tale that she hailed from the local aristocracy and had donated her family home to the bishop of Trier. This was subsequently seized on by the town to demonstrate its primacy over the rest of Gaul, a claim which was underscored in tradition if not in fact by the symbolic detachment of what purported to be Helena's head from the rest of her body and its preservation in the see. Marcus shrugged the whole story aside as a mediaeval fantasy which had retrospectively muddled the popular perception of a fourth-century imperial court about which we knew very little for certain. He implied that Dr Kempf had assumed Helena must be in the centre of the ceiling because he presumed he was excavating her palace.

'We have no proof about the paintings except they must be very rich Romans. Perhaps the one in the centre is Fausta. It seems to me impossible it is Helena because she was 70 years old, yet next to the picture is a panel representing Eros, and the god of love does not go with an elderly woman. The wife of the emperor would be more important than his mother, so I think she is positioned in the middle. She also has a hairstyle from the time and is the only person who matches contemporary descriptions.'

A gold coin was found at Trier showing Fausta, who was – like Helena – proclaimed Augusta in 324.[19] It portrays her in frumpish fashion, with a thin mouth under a severe frown, wearing her hair scraped back in a bun so big it looks more like a Pharoah's head-dress. To my inexpert eye it was impossible to tell whether this sideways view represented the same woman in the middle of the ceiling fresco, missing so much of her face. Nevertheless such coins represented the only contemporary descriptions we have, in which a likeness is linked to a name, and luckily Trier possesses a fine collection of gold, silver and bronze currency in the Landesmuseum. The city had a prolific mint, whose output offered a tantalising glimpse of all the characters in the dynastic drama that was to unfold.

So what about Helena? Of the remaining women in the ceiling

fresco, we can rule out the self-absorbed young girl with the lyre on the grounds of age. But was the empress-mother the carefully coiffeured matron adjusting her perm and inspecting her fading beauty in the mirror? Or the dishevelled dame surprised sneaking a string of pearls from the jewellery box? For the latter portrait does indeed have a superficial resemblance with another coin found at Trier, this time a bronze. There are the same bug eyes, the long straight nose and pinched mouth with the faintest hint of a moue. On the coin she wears a necklace and a diadem holding her hair in a neat bob, though by the look of the profile this could equally be an elaborately coiffeured wig. It resembles a coalscuttle helmet rather than the natural curls, barely restrained by a wreath, which spilled into the nimbus of the painting. Nevertheless, the connection put a face to the name for the first time, and I didn't like what I saw. That sly look in the eyes, added to the primness of the lips, suggested butter wouldn't melt in *her* mouth. The hand prising the pearls out of the casket had its little finger daintily up-raised, but the thumb and forefinger were rubbing the string between them as if assessing the quality. 'A covetous look, furtive, casting her eyes around to see who else is in the room,' I had written in my notebook at the time. 'Yet she already has a massive weight of gems around her neck!' This unflattering portrait suggested deviousness at odds with the pious image of the holy Helena handed down through later generations.

†

AMONGST THE COINS now displayed at the Rheinisches Landesmuseum is another member of the imperial family who resided at Trier, Crispus. Constantine's eldest son appears as a cross between a muscular sportsman and a bull-necked thug; a smirk on his face framed between a thickset jaw and cropped hair. He was the product of the emperor's liaison with Minervina, a relationship that echoed that between Constantine's father and Helena. In this case, not only is it disputed whether Minervina was a wife or concubine, there is also some doubt whether she died or was put aside when Constantine married Fausta in 307. A year after his accession to the purple, this was a diplomatic alliance with the daughter of Maximian, whom Constantine had succeeded as emperor in the west. She bore him three more sons who were later to rule in succession in their own right, but Constantine's enemies were quick to put the stigma of illegitimacy on Crispus.

Nevertheless, he was named Caesar in 317, alongside Fausta's eldest son, also called Constantine, and despite his youth ran his quarter of the empire from Trier. He was tutored by Lanctantius, the historian, and was said to have fought with distinction against the Alamanni and Franks. Still in his teens he was promoted to the rank of consul in 321, married another Helena, and played a key role in the campaign which established Constantine as sole claimant to the imperial throne. His efforts were rewarded with promotion to Caesar in 323. Three years later Flavius Julius Crispus disappeared from the coinage altogether, without explanation.

It was said later that he was put on trial and found guilty. The chroniclers were embarrassed. 'Being forced to it by necessity, he executed that exceptional man,' said Eutropius about Constantine.[20] The Christian writers avoided mentioning the subject altogether. Its omission from Eusebius's history is one of the key factors that enable us to date the work to 325, yet this prolific author never referred back to the episode in the later panegyrics either. In the absence of fact, salacious gossip proliferated. One story claimed Fausta had fallen for her stepson, but her advances were repulsed so she accused him of rape. Constantine was sensitive to sexual irregularities, and around that time he passed laws against abduction and concubinage. Another version maintained that Fausta complained to Constantine that Crispus was plotting against him. Maybe she was jealous and wanted to promote the interests of her own sons. Perhaps she insinuated that his illegitimacy would provoke an excuse for civil war over the succession. Either way, Constantine's reaction was pretty extreme. He put her to death as well – in the steam baths at Trier.

Walking round the site in spring sunshine it is difficult to imagine the horror of such a tragedy. The remains of the baths are to be found on a terrace at the foot of the Petrisberg, the hill marking the east end of the *decumanus maximus*, the main road that bisected the town from the river. Supplied by a well, a small brook, and two aqueducts from a reservoir in the hills fed by the Ruwer, the giant structure originally planned was never actually finished. The whole complex was redesigned on a smaller scale later in the fourth century but no longer used for public bathing, probably because Christians did not approve of the practice. Yet the walls of the caldarium are still intact, layers of limestone ashlar interspersed with horizontal strips of red brick to a height of 19 metres.

Bathers would have left their clothing in a cloakroom, and visited the sweat room for scraping and cleansing before entering the caldarium – a vaulted triple-conch building with hot baths in the apses. Its double windows give an indication of the scale but we have to imagine the roof soaring even higher, the fine marble claddings on the walls, and a colourful mosaic floor leading to the warm air room, the cold plunge bath, and an exercise area. Nevertheless, traces remain of the furnaces which fed the underfloor and cavity wall heating, the chimneys for exhaust gases, and the network of subterranean service corridors and drains three metres below the bathing halls. The baths would also have been the social centre of the town, with a library among the host of snack vendors, shops and even restaurants. That makes it a rather public place for an execution.

Such considerations did not affect the verdict of Zosimus, the sixth-century historian. The pagan counterpoint to Eusebius, he based his hostile account of Constantine's reign on the lost works of Eunapius, a Greek sophist who anticipated Gibbon's anti-clerical theme that the Roman empire collapsed because of the decline of the old religion. Of the emperor, Zosimus said: 'Without any consideration for natural law he killed his son Crispus on a suspicion of having had intercourse with his stepmother Fausta. And when Constantine's mother Helena was saddened by this atrocity and was inconsolable at the young man's death, Constantine, as if to comfort her, applied a remedy worse than the disease: he ordered the bath to be over-heated and shut Fausta up in it until she was dead.'[21]

Zosimus had an axe to grind against Helena. Elsewhere in his work he gratuitously branded Constantine the 'son of a harlot' and the product of 'the illegal intercourse of a low woman.' Writing at a time when the story of Helena and the discovery of the cross was in full swing, he would have taken any opportunity to discredit her. Ironically, he only fuelled the legend by portraying her son as a tyrant, whose remorse at his crimes propelled him towards a full and final acceptance of Christianity after dithering for a decade. The idea was seized on by later generations as a convenient explanation for Helena's mission to the Holy Land. She must have been sent as a personal emissary by the emperor to expiate his sins. Once this idea caught hold, it was then applied in reverse, to suggest that Helena was herself suffering guilt for persuading Constantine he had made a dreadful mistake over Crispus and encouraging him to punish Fausta. The empress-mother and the imperial wife were no doubt rivals at court and quick to do each other down. It is equally plausible, however, that St Helena once again became the victim of a confusion of names, and it was Helena the young widow of Crispus who sought revenge for her husband's untimely death.[22]

CHAPTER VII

Rome

And in this altar are two phials of the blood and water from Christ's side, moreover there is part of Christ's cradle, the coat without seam, and his purple robe. Moreover there is the napkin that was about his head, and the towel that he washed his disciples feet withal.

Mirabilia – the Marvels of Rome[1]

PONTE MILVIO IS a modest piece of architecture, inconspicuous amid the glorified museum that has become Rome. Once the principal crossing of the Tiber, the Milvian Bridge now carries little traffic except for scooters taking short cuts. A ubiquitous Vespa buzzed past as I watched a man fishing in the sluggish green river, another walking his dog, and a third jogging in the cool of an early spring evening. Litter was strewn over the cobbles, the iron lampposts were rusted, and graffiti scarred the low walls: *Claudio ti amo! Danilo.* The brickwork beneath the scrawl was distinctively Roman, those long thin tiles barely thicker than the mortar between them which are seen all over the Italian capital and in countless pizza houses everywhere else. Any antique charm the crossing now possessed was ruined by the massive fortified gateway at the northern end built by Pope Pius VII in the first years of the 19th century. Yet such a crass structure would have been entirely in keeping with the character of the man who, 1,500 years previously, here led his armies into the city after a fateful encounter which changed the world.

Constantine the Great subsequently ascribed his military victory on the north bank of the river to divine intervention, in the form of a blazing cross which appeared to him in the sky on the eve of battle. Or rather, Eusebius did, recording the vision after the emperor's death as a sign from God which marked his patron's conversion to Christianity.[2] The emperor told his confidant, a long time after the event, how he saw a cross of light above the sun bearing the inscription 'conquer with this.' As Constantine struggled to interpret the phenomenon, Jesus appeared to him in a dream and instructed him to make earthly replicas of the sign which would protect him thenceforth. The emperor promptly ordered it to be inscribed on the shields of his soldiers, and thereafter revered the God who had granted him the prize on 28th October 312. Shortly afterwards he issued an Edict of Toleration which officially proscribed the persecution of 'the cult of the Christians' and allowed them to worship freely throughout the empire.

The fight was the climax of almost unrelieved civil war in which the general proclaimed emperor of the west at York back in 306 had to deal with a series of rivals in order to take up his seat at Rome. The last of them, Maxentius, was so confident of success that he took his troops out of the capital to confront Constantine's invasion force, destroyed the 200-year-old stone crossing behind him, and constructed a temporary bridge of boats which could be unfastened if the enemy tried to enter the city. Unfortunately for Maxentius, the bridge collapsed beneath the weight of his own retreating soldiers, many of whom followed their leader and fell into the river to drown. The liberation of Rome was later declared a miracle: Eusebius drew a parallel with

Pharaoh perishing in the Red Sea after Moses had parted the waters. At the time the senate stuck with pagan custom, and voted to build a gigantic arch on the road which Constantine followed on his triumphal procession to give thanks to Jupiter on top of the Capitoline Hill.

Completed in a hurry, this monument at the base of the Palatine hill, in the shadow of the Colosseum, was a composite structure re-working white marble panels from Asia Minor that were originally commissioned for earlier emperors. There were battlescapes taken from the time of Trajan, scenes of hunting and sacrifice culled from the era of Hadrian, and material designed for Marcus Aurelius thrown in for good measure. The only carvings contributed by Constantine's own workshops were friezes depicting the vanquishing of Maxentius and some decoration on the plinths of columns. They can still be seen today, but only if you have binoculars for, despite being one of Rome's most popular tourist attractions, the Arch of Constantine is now fenced off to visitors. As an official war memorial its theme was the continuity between the present and the past, represented by those passé second-century emperors whose features were replaced by those of the latest conqueror. The inscription ran: 'To the emperor Flavius Constantinus, greatest Augustus, pious and favoured by fortune, the Senate and the People of Rome dedicated this arch to mark his triumphs, because at the instigation of the divinity, in his greatness of heart, he came with his army and exacted instant vengeance on behalf of the commonwealth from the tyrant and all his minions in righteous warfare.'[3] Unveiled three years after the vision of the cross granted to the first Christian emperor, it hardly read as a ringing endorsement of his faith.

☧

WHILE THERE IS no doubt that Constantine's reign was a defining moment in history of Christianity, when precisely in it that change came about is still disputed. Clearly he had a firm conviction by the time he despatched his mother to the Holy Land and authorised an extensive church building programme there. Indeed, one of the engaging beliefs that stuck to Helena through the ages was that she always was a Christian and used her influence at court to convert her son.[4] In his church history Eusebius noted that her husband Chlorus was favourably disposed towards the Divine Word when he ran Britain during the Diocletian persecutions. 'He took not the smallest part in the war against us but preserved the pious that were under him unharmed and unabused. He never threw down church buildings nor did he devise anything else against us,' said the bishop.[5] Another Christian scholar of the time, Lactantius, disagreed with that judgement about Chlorus' attitude to religious property, yet added: 'but the temple of God which is in men's hearts he left untouched.'[6] However, Eusebius later scotched the rumours he himself had started, recalling in his biography of the emperor Helena's last days in the presence of her son. 'He rendered her through his influence so devout a worshipper of God (though she had not previously been such) that she seemed to have been instructed from the first by the Saviour of mankind.'[7]

The trouble with Eusebius is that he was always operating to an agenda, one that was hinted at in the conclusion of his history in 324, when the empire is united and all is well with the world, and made explicit in his unctuous biography of the first Christian king 15 years later. Discounting the bishop's enthusiasm to rewrite the past in the light of Constantine's undoubted conversion leaves us with indications that the emperor kept his personal options open. After all, he put off baptism until he was on his deathbed. Ever since, cynics have claimed that Constantine simply saw in Christianity a useful propaganda mechanism which could be harnessed to the purposes of the state, via an imperial cult, in order to achieve his overriding secular end of unifying the fissiparous empire. In the process, this theory goes, he so transformed early Christianity that thereafter the new religion became synonymous with what the emperor himself believed.[8]

One of the oddities about the incident on the bank of the Tiber is that if the whole army witnessed the vision, as Eusebius maintained, why has so little independent corroboration been found? There is also an ambiguity about the actual sign that appeared in the sky, for Constantine did not adopt the cross as we know it as his symbol, but instead adapted the old Roman imperial standard into a new form, the *labarum*. Eusebius described it as a spear with a transverse bar, giving the shape of a cross, surmounted by a wreath in which was set the mark known as the *ChiRho*, from the first two letters of the Greek word for Christ, *XP*. 'The emperor constantly made use of this sign of salvation as a safeguard against every adverse and hostile power, and commanded that others similar to it should be carried at the head of all his armies.'[9]

Lantanctius confirmed the story, and the *ChiRho* indeed appeared on imperial coins struck from 315 onwards. However, it was not a particularly Christian symbol, since it also stood for the Greek word *chreston* and was already used as a literary marker by readers of pagan papyri. It also looks remarkably like the Egyptian *ankh*, the hieroglyphic symbol of life, and thus carried a mystic pagan significance in addition to the new one imposed by Constantine. This would not have posed a problem for the emperor; since a majority of the population were unbelievers, it would suit him to proceed cautiously with his enthusiasm for Christianity. A pagan orator some years earlier claimed Constantine had witnessed a vision of Apollo during a campaign against the Franks in Gaul, and instructed his troops then to put the 'celestial sign' on their shields.[10]

Sun worship and the cult of Apollo was popular throughout the empire, and Constantine may have deliberately blurred the boundaries between the old solar religion and the creed of Christ. He continued to issue coins with the symbol of the unconquered sun, *sol invictus*, until about 320, around which time he also endorsed the Christian custom of resting on the weekly anniversary of the resurrection by forbidding legal business to be undertaken on 'the venerable day of the sun.' Tertullian had long before observed that many pagans believed the Christians worshipped the sun not only because they met on Sundays but also because they prayed to the east, and Clement of Alexandria once described 'Christ driving his chariot across the sky like the Sun-God.' No one knows who started the trend, or precisely when it began, but it was also during Constantine's time that Christian feasts took over pagan festivals, like marking the nativity of Christ at the winter solstice. Up until this point Jesus' birthday was marked on January 6th, if at all. The annual re-birth of the sun on December 25th, the feast of *natalis invictus*, fitted conveniently with the new doctrine hailing the arrival of 'the light of the world' who had been heralded in the Old Testament as 'the sun of righteousness.'[11]

☧

CONSTANTINE SPENT JUST four years in Rome before launching a campaign to win over the Eastern Empire as well. Although he subsequently transferred the imperial capital to Constantinople, he embarked on a building spree during that short period which was to fix Rome thereafter as the headquarters of the Catholic Church. He erected a basilica on the site of the barracks used by the army of Maxentius, for example, and in 314 Pope Sylvester took up residence in the Lateran palace next door. The property may have been the residence of Fausta, Constantine's wife, who was actually Maxentius' sister. She had already lent her house to Pope Melchiades in 313 for the first council of bishops. The church was dedicated to the Holy Redeemer and intended to signify the triumph of Christianity over paganism. Now called St John's, San Giovanni in Laterano remains the Cathedral of Rome, the most senior of all the city's churches.

The new emperor also put another one over Maxentius by completing a basilica his predecessor had started in the Forum. It was the last secular one of its kind; a huge covered hall used for business transactions, providing shelter from the heat or cold, where judges and litigants retreated to hold hearings away from hubbub. Before the edict of toleration, Christians had tended to gather in private houses to celebrate their faith rather than public buildings where they could be the focus of hostility. With Constantine's intervention, the characteristic architecture of the basilica became indissolubly linked to the construction of churches rather than law courts.[12] A key feature of the design was the raised end opposite the entrance, the apse, in which the judges and assessors sat. Before them was an altar on which sacrifice was usually offered before beginning any important public business. This arrangement was taken up by the early church virtually unchanged, though by the Middle Ages the layout had been revised so that the altar itself was in the apse and the priest stood before it with his back turned on the congregation, so that all faced in the same direction.

The custom of praying towards the rising sun was probably older than Christianity itself, but by the third century one of the earliest liturgical works, the Apostolic Constitutions, was recommending that any church should be oblong 'with its head to the east.'[13] However, Constantine's model basilica in the Forum already faced towards the west. All the ancient great basilicas of Rome followed the same orientation, as did both the major churches soon established under Constantine's patronage at Antioch and Tyre, and indeed the Holy Sepulchre at Jerusalem itself. Apologists justified the variation by pointing out that at least the bishop, seated *ex cathedra* on his throne in the apse, was facing east.

Is this the face of Helena? The centre panel of the ceiling of the palace of the Empress, reconstructed in the Episcopal Museum at Trier.

Life-size bronze coin showing the head of Helena Augusta, in the Rheinisches Landesmuseum Trier.

Gold coin struck in Trier in AD 297, showing bust of Helena's husband, Constantius Chlorus, on his triumphal entry into London: from the Rheinisches Landesmuseum Trier.

Sancta Helena Augusta – the official papal memorial at the base of one of the four great pillars of St Peter's Basilica in Rome.

The porphyry sarcophagus in the Vatican Museum that was constructed for Constantine – but temporarily housed the remains of his mother instead.

The Relics of the Passion: three pieces of the True Cross in a 19th Century reliquary in the chapel of Santa Croce in Gerusalemme, Rome.

Agrippina or Helena? The mysterious marble bust in the Capitoline Museum, Rome.

Larger than life – the carved stone head that once surmounted a colossal statue of Constantine, now in the coutyard of the Conservators' Palace, Rome.

A mosque on a mound at the modern Turkish village of Hersek: all that remains of Drepanum, Helena's birthplace in ancient Bithynia?

The rocky face which General Gordon saw on Skull Hill in 1883, now badly eroded, looks out over the Arab bus station in East Jerusalem.

Enthusiastic American pilgrims re-enact the tormenting of Jesus by Roman soldiers along the *Via Dolorosa* in the streets of Old Jerusalem.

Scenes from the Holy Sepulchre (I): Abed Joudah, Custodian of the Key, unlocking the Church on Good Friday morning, to release the Franciscan monks from their overnight vigil.

Scenes from the Holy Sepulchre (2): Greek Orthodox pilgrims create their own holy water by swabbing the unction stone, on which they believe Jesus was laid after being taken down from the cross.

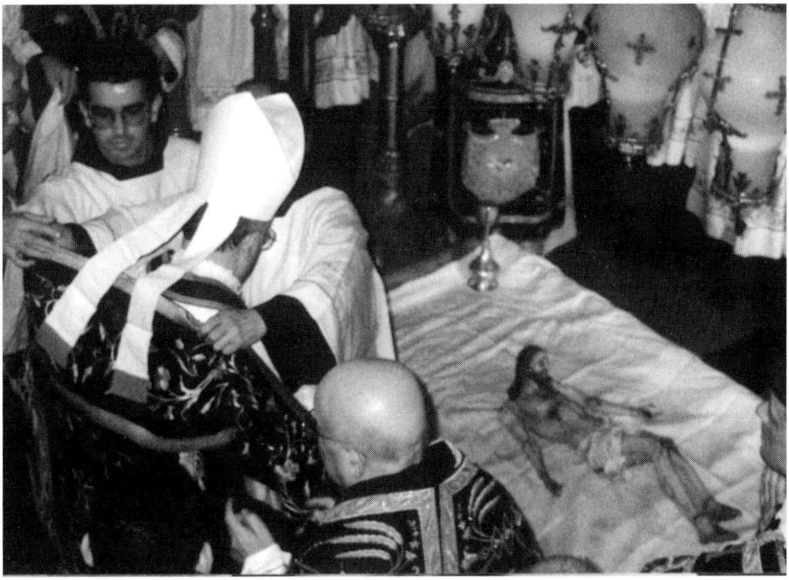

Scenes from the Holy Sepulchre (3): On Good Friday evening, the 'body' of Jesues is symbolically taken down from the cross on the altar of the Franciscan chapel of Calvary and placed in the Tomb of Christ.

Scenes from the Holy Sepulchre (4): The Archbishop of the Ethiopian Orthodox Patriachate, His Grace Abuna Matheus, leads the traditional Palm Sunday rooftop procession round the dome over St Helena's chapel.

Scenes from the Holy Sepulchre (5): The Latin Patriarch, His Beatitude Monseigneur Michel Sabbah, pauses to pray at the unction stone during his ceremonial entrance before High Mass on Easter Sunday.

In the case of the Forum the first priests seem to have been competing for space with a giant statue of Constantine. The ruins of the transitional basilica are still impressive today, with their portico of four porphyry columns, though the bronze tiles on the roof were stolen by St Peter's and the figure of the emperor now lies in fragments in the courtyard of the nearby Conservators Palace museum. This is worth a look, too, if only to appreciate the sheer scale on which the Romans operated. At ten metres high – and that seated – the statue was a colossal representation of the subject's stature. Perhaps only half was made of stone, while the clothed parts of the huge body (which no longer survive) probably disguised a wood and bronze frame. Nevertheless the bust alone, now resting on a makeshift platform alongside a plinth carrying the remains of a giant foot, dwarfs all onlookers, its angular chiselled features still fastened on some distant ambition far above the heads of mere mortals.

Constantine was also responsible for commissioning a sanctuary over the tomb of St Peter some years later. The chief apostle had been crucified in the circus at the foot of the Vatican hill during the persecutions of Nero – he who fiddled while Rome burned, blaming Christians for the fire. The former fisherman from Galilee requested his execution be carried out upside down in order to be distinguished from Jesus. His bones were so sacred to early followers that they were probably moved from place to place to avoid desecration, but a tomb was discovered in 324 that fitted the bill and was promptly encased in red marble.[14] I strolled through the underground crypt below the present floor, retracing the outline of Constantine's church, to get a flavour of the period. Beneath my feet modern excavations had discovered a necropolis containing the oldest known Christian mosaic. Interestingly, it portrayed Christ as the Sun on a horse-drawn chariot.

As for the Renaissance pile on top, mostly Michaelangelo modified by Bernini in the 17th century, I could take it or leave it.

The only aspect which captured my attention was the statuary overlooking the main altar from the four central pillars. Helena graced one, below a high balcony framed by two twisted pillars rescued from the remains of the original Constantinian church after Rome was sacked by the barbarians. A small chapel invisible from the ground stored the Vatican's own fragment of the True Cross, displayed only on Good Friday. 'They hold it up high, it's tiny, you can really see nothing,' said an official in the Ufficio Technico. Apparently I had just missed a showing of Veronica's veil, kept behind another pillar. If I stayed long enough I might see the spear which pierced Jesus' side, kept on number three, or even the head of St Andrew. Only members of the Vatican chapter are allowed inside the four relic chapels, accessed not through staircases hidden in the piers themselves, as some believe, but from a network of secret passages in the hollow walls and vaulting of the basilica itself. Officially this is to maintain the holy relics safe from robbers, though such arrangements also have the advantage of keeping sceptics at bay.[15]

Visiting the Vatican without being remotely interested in its Renaissance treasures of either art or architecture was a strange experience. Like everyone else I queued outside the walls for hours to get into the palace museum, yet instead of following the crowd for the Borgia Apartments and the Sistine Chapel I whizzed upstairs to the Greek Cross room. This displayed neither Greeks nor crosses but a pair of sarcophagi, twin blocks of porphyry perhaps two metres wide, one-and-a-half high, and another deep. The one decorated with wreaths, angels and cherubs was intended for Constantia, the daughter of Constantine. The other was not identified, and from the graphic figures on the front showing spirited Roman cavalry trampling barbarian prisoners you might think it was designed for an emperor. It was – but became redundant once Constantine moved his court to Constantinople, and was reputedly used to house the mortal remains of his mother instead. The sight of a solitary spectator mesmerised by an unmarked block of polished purple stone must have looked odd to the masses still winding their way through the one-way system to the Sistine. I wanted to tell them: this was the closest I had got to Helena so far.

☧

HER HOME IN ROME was the Sessorian palace, just inside the Aurelian walls at the eastern-most corner of the city. The other boundary of the palace is still marked by the impressive remains of a Claudian aqueduct, but nothing remains of the nearby baths of Helena except their reputation as another monumental piece of architecture. In memory of his mother Constantine converted the palace itself into a church in order to house the cross she brought back from Jerusalem. Or so they say now at Santa Croce in Gerusalemme, where the largest extant fragments are still kept. I arrived on a Saturday morning to find queues at the confessional and a priest telling the story of the finding of the cross to a congregation of mostly women and children. He illustrated the tale by pointing to the frescoes in the apse, behind an altar where a statue that once represented the pagan goddess Juno had for centuries done service as Helena.

A flurry of nuns disappeared through a side door in white dresses, black coats, and white shawls, gesticulating eagerly. I followed them into a bare antechamber whose only striking feature was a length of weathered timber, more than a metre of mottled and pockmarked wood with a large hole in the centre. An iron grille set into the wall kept visitors at a distance from the exhibit labelled *pars crucis boni latronis* – part of the cross of the good thief. The Gospel writers all concur that Jesus was crucified along with two robbers, one on either side of him. The idea that one was good and the other bad, and the former was called Dismas and the latter Gestas, came much later.[16] Even though Helena was supposed to have found all three crosses, it surely strained the credulity of even the most devout pilgrim to suggest that one of the two unholy versions should have been preserved, let alone identified . . .

The nuns had not tarried here, so I passed into an antechapel with a small organ in the corner. The far doorway led into a small, dark box whose oppressive grey and white marble walls owed more to Mussolini's fascist style of the 1930s than Christian architectural tradition. Four black pillars supported a canopy over an altar in the middle but the centre of attention was a glass case recessed into the far wall. The contents were not easy to see in the light, refracted by the glass security screen and reflected by the gold casing of the cross-shaped reliquary inside. I peered to make out three fingers of wood, several inches long. The two suspended in either arm of the reliquary were pale, as if dried out, while the vertical one was a dark, rich brown. These purported to be all that remained of the True Cross after that multitude of bits and pieces had been broken off and distributed elsewhere.

Still sceptical? How about the rusted nail displayed nearby? Or the two thorns miraculously saved from the crown the soldiers put on Jesus' head? Bone from the index finger of Doubting Thomas, with which the apostle touched the wounds of Jesus to prove he had come back to life? Or the cluster of small stones purporting to come respectively from the tomb where Jesus was buried, the pillar where he was scourged, and the stable where he was born? They are all here, if you want them to be. Even part of the actual placard Pilate put on the cross mocking Jesus of Nazareth as King of the Jews! Just a small part of the inscription is etched on the wooden fragment but in three languages, Hebrew, Greek and Latin, one on top of the other. Here apparently is the vital accessory described by Ambrose, with which he claimed Helena identified the True Cross among the three 'fork-shaped gibbets' she found discarded among debris. According to the Bishop of Milan: 'She adored the King – not the wood indeed, because this is an error of the gentiles and a vanity of the wicked

– but she adored him who hung on the tree whose name was inscribed in the title.'[17]

☧

THE ABBREVIATION INRI, from the Latin title popularised by Ambrose, *Iesus Nazarenus Rex Iudaeorum,* became a banner for generations of Christians, affixed above the cross in countless artistic representations of the crucifixion scene down the centuries. Yet historically it is highly unlikely the *titulus* or charge-sheet would have been shortened in this way, since the whole point of public display was that the message should be understood by the masses. Carved, written or painted on a wooden board, it would only need to have lasted a couple of days while life ebbed out of the subject whose crimes were listed on it. It is also inherently unlikely that an artefact of such transitory purpose was capable of preservation, although there have been dogged efforts to claim that the Santa Croce relic is made from the sort of walnut-wood prevalent in Palestine at the time, and that it bears traces of having originally been painted white with the letters picked out in red or black, conforming to contemporary Roman style. There are also complicated arguments over the type of writing itself, though after the embarrassment of the Turin Shroud the authorities appear reluctant to seal this controversy by subjecting the material to carbon dating.

The inscription on the cross is mentioned in all the gospels, but the only phrase common to each account is 'The King of the Jews.' That is all Mark said was on the superscription. Matthew added the preface: 'This is Jesus . . .' Luke dropped the name, reverting to, 'This is the King of the Jews.' John was the only evangelist to report that Pilate personally wrote out the charge, and identified Jesus the Nazorean – in the original Greek, *Iesous ho Nazoraios* – as King of the Jews. 'This title therefore read many of the Jews, for the place where Jesus was crucified was nigh to the city, and it was written in Hebrew, and in Latin and in Greek,' said John. In one of those many details that convince many that the evangelist was an eyewitness, he went on to describe how the chief priests disputed the charge of kingship, and told Pilate he should have made clear this was a claim being made by Jesus rather than by the Jews. The procurator replied, famously: 'What I have written, I have written.'[18]

The first point to note about the Santa Croce *titulus* is that the order of languages on the relic is different from that given by John, with the Greek coming before the Latin after a top line of half-a-dozen squiggles that could be the remnants of Hebrew. Through the protective glass case I was unable to make out the upper two lines, even with the aid of a reconstruction helpfully carved into the wall nearby, yet it was clear from the Latin line at the bottom that what survived was the reference to 'the Nazorean' found solely in John, the distinctive part of what was potentially the longest inscription. Yet as I carefully copied down the letters in my notebook I realised two odd things: not only was the phrase

NAZARINVS R

actually spelled backwards, from right to left, but also each letter was reversed, as if reflected in a mirror.

Я ƧVИIЯAZAИ

My first thought was that some poor mediaeval tradesman, commissioned to construct a fraud, had been told that Hebrew was written backwards and took his instructions rather too literally. Subsequently I found that my suspicions had already been anticipated by the Catholic apologists. In 1870 a certain Monseigneur John Virtue, chaplain to the forces at Colchester and later Bishop of Portsmouth, inspected the relics and pronounced them quite plausibly the work of a simple Jewish craftsman who, knowing neither Latin nor Greek, did not realise those alphabets were written left-to-right but followed Pilate's orders to the letter.[19]

This argument against forgery was recently revisited by the German scholar Carsten Peter Thiede and the British journalist Matthew D'Ancona after the pair were granted a rare up-front examination of the relic by its Cistercian guardians. In *The Quest for the True Cross* these two collaborators argued that a forger would have attempted to make his work correspond as closely as possible to the conventional wisdom, thus following John by engraving in the order Hebrew, Latin and Greek. The fact the relic was in the order Hebrew, Greek, and Latin fuelled their belief that this was actually the original *titulus*, rediscovered at the time Helena found the True Cross. The reversal of the writing, from right to left, only confirmed their view that the artefact was the genuine product of a contemporary Hebrew scribe unfamiliar with Greek or Latin, and working in haste, rather than a fake. 'A falsifier working, say, on behalf of Helena or Macarius, or for a mediaeval cardinal, would simply not have risked something so abnormal if his purpose was to establish the supposed authenticity of his work,' they argued.[20]

In support of their thesis, Thiede and D'Ancona re-examined the early Biblical texts. In particular they pointed to the existence of an alternative language order offered in some versions of Luke, traditionally regarded by scholars as a later interpolation, which said the superscription was written in Greek, Latin and Hebrew. This longer reading of the relevant verse in both the Codex Sinaiticus, written during the second quarter of the fourth century, and the Codex Alexandrinus of the fifth century, was clearly not simply copied from pre-existing versions of St John's gospel, but must have had an independent source. At the same time the authors observed that the traditional authority of St John's eyewitness account was also undermined by later, and influential, versions of his manuscript, including the Codex Alexandrinus, where the order of languages was given as

Hebrew, Greek, and Latin. Together these observations raised the intriguing possibility that many later Biblical manuscripts were amended or corrected to accord more closely with what Helena's archaeologists had found on the *titulus*.

The argument in *The Quest for the Cross* prompted me to take a closer look at what was actually carved into the Santa Croce fragment. As Thiede and D'Ancona pointed out, the traditional reconstruction etched on to a brass plaque above the reliquary, and displayed on a wall nearby, is misleading, adding extra letters that cannot be seen by the naked eye. For example, the reconstructed Latin line puts an 'E' instead of an 'I' in NAZARINVS, thus conforming to the Vulgate spelling of the familiar phrase as used by Ambrose (writing in Latin) at the end of the fourth century – precisely what a mediaeval forger would have done in following conventional wisdom. The use of the 'I' by the original carver is technically correct in the suffix for a classical Roman place-name, which in this case would be pronounced 'Nazar*ee*nus.' However, as the authors acknowledged, the accurate Latin should have its counterpart with the double-e sound of the Greek *eta* (H) in the line above. The fact that the Santa Croce fragment does not have the letter H as would be expected, but the short Є of *epsilon* instead, is only one of a number of oddities in the way the Greek line has been carved.

According to Thiede and D'Ancona, the Greek line reads:

NAΣAPЄNȢC B

We have to take the 'B' for granted since it is not on the photographs they publish, nor was it visible to me during my visit to the sanctuary in Rome. However, this would be the first letter of *basileus,* or king, as in King of the Jews, corresponding to the 'R' for *rex* in the Latin line above. The letter Ȣ is the Greek *upsilon,* a distinctive form of Y, which the authors point out was commonly used in the first century to represent the dipthong *ou*. (It was also, incidentally, the ancient Hebrew symbol for *shekel*.) Yet no gospel papyrus uses the symbol, further evidence for these authors that no forger could have copied it from a Biblical manuscript.

Clearly the actual Greek word used in John's gospel, transliterated as *Nazôraios*, would be properly spelled ΝΑΖΩΡΑΙΟΣ rather than ΝΑΣΑΡϵΝꙊC. But there are other discrepancies that Thiede and D'Ancona either do not investigate or cannot explain. The Santa Croce relic is unusual in having an 'A' for the second syllable instead of an *omega* (Ω), for example. This echoes the Latin, NAZARINVS, in the same way we saw the Greek version preferred the long ϵ of *epsilon* to the short H of *eta*. Also the *-os* ending in classical Greek should be properly written 'ΟΣ' rather than 'ꙊC'. Despite the artistic flourish of the Ꙋ symbol, the use of 'Ꙋ' for the last syllable would provide the u-sound of *upsilon* and thus more closely correspond to the Latin ending of NAZARINVS. Meanwhile the strange concluding 'C' does not exist in the classical Greek alphabet at all. Here it may be a bastardised form of *sigma*, which traditionally appears as ς in lower case when used at the end of a word. It seemed to me that all these philological oddities suggested that the engraver was more familiar with Latin than Greek.

Thiede and D'Ancona admitted they could not prove that the wooden fragment in Santa Croce was the headboard of Christ, but claimed to have restored the artefact to its rightful place in the spectrum of historical probability. To my mind their arguments worked both ways. For, if textual variations about the order of languages on the placard existed in the immediate post-Constantinian period, surely that represented an acknowledgement that at this time there was no conventional wisdom for a faker to follow?

I was also much troubled by the reversed writing on the Santa Croce fragment. In their account of why the Greek and Latin lines were written right-to-left, Thiede and D'Ancona glossed over the more fundamental point that almost every letter was also reversed in a mirror image of what it should be – except, that is, for the Σ in the Greek line, which was already reversed so actually appears normally. What you see in Greek is:

ꓭ ƆƔИƎꟼAZAИ

To me this remains the greatest puzzle of the Santa Croce fragment. While it does not prove the relic to be a forgery, a careless attempt at copying by a semi-literate craftsman seems to me the only credible explanation for such sustained error.

Certainly it beggars belief that a first-century Jewish scribe, commissioned by Pilate to draw up the charge-sheet for a condemned criminal, would so lack a grasp of Greek or Latin as to carve the individual letters backwards, even if he was in such a hurry he thought the characters should be written right-to-left like his native tongue. After all, Greek was the *lingua franca* of the eastern world in which he lived, while Latin was the language of the imperial power that employed him. Even a Hebrew-speaker taking down dictation from a Roman official must have been able to recognise the sounds and shapes of Latin and Greek letters to be competent for the task at hand. And if anything, such an engraver would have been more at ease with Greek than Latin, in contrast to the impression given by the fragment.

Even if fraudulent, there is no reason to suppose the Santa Croce relic was connected to Helena. Evidence of the existence of the *titulus* goes back almost as far as references to the True Cross itself, but there is a significant gap. Egeria, the Spanish noblewoman who visited Jerusalem in 384, mentions both items in the same breath, being kept in a small gold-plated silver box and displayed for veneration on Good Friday. Unfortunately, she assumed her readers knew what was written on the inscription, and gave no further details.[21] There is no reason to doubt Egeria's testimony, but what she witnessed at Jerusalem happened more than 35 years after Bishop Cyril first disclosed that the holy wood itself was being venerated in the city. Yet only ten years after Egeria's return from the Holy Land, the story that Helena discovered both the cross and the *titulus* had reached Ambrose in Milan, and was preached as fact. Such a quickening of the pace of the legend suggests that the latter half of the fourth century might have been the time in which some constructive carpentry would have had most impact on the credulous. Two centuries later an Italian pilgrim to the holy city, Antoninus of Piacenza, appeared to describe the whole thing. 'I also saw and held in my hand and kissed the title which was placed over the head of Jesus upon which is written Jesus of Nazareth, King of the Jews,' he said.[22]

How or whether a fragment came to Rome remains a mystery, however, since the fragile remnant kept at Santa Croce was only discovered by accident in 1492. Workmen repairing the church mosaics under the direction of Cardinal Peter Gonzales de Mendoza found a cavity closed by a brick with an inscription on the inner face, *titulus crucis*. Behind the brick was a small leaden casket, inscribed *Ecce Lignum Crucis* and tied with a cord bearing the wax seals of Cardinal Caccianemici, later Pope Lucius III, who had earlier restored the basilica in 1143.

'He must have found the inscription during restoration work

The puzzle of the Santa Croce fragment: is this the original placard identifying Jesus *the Nazorean,* King of the Jews – or a later forgery?

	The reversed mirror-image writing you see	What it would look like if written normally and L–R	Approximate transliteration and pronunciation
The text of St John's Gospel		ΝΑΖΩΡΑΙΟΣ Β	Na-zôr-ai-os
The Greek line on the original relic	ᗺ ƆȣNЭꟼAƩAИ	NAΣAPЄNȣC B	Na-sa-ray-nus
The Latin line on the original relic	Я ƧVNIЯAƩAИ	NAZARINUS R	Na-za-ree-nus
The Latin line in the mediaeval reconstruction	Я ƧVNƎЯAƩAИ	NAZARENUS R	Na-za-ray-nus

he initiated and placed it in the roof,' wrote Heinrich Drenkelfort, author of the official Santa Croce guidebook. Significantly, he made no grandiose claims for the items in the church's collection, approaching the issue of their significance with circumspection. 'Modern scientific criticism of the intrinsic worth of these relics will interest the believer in Christ less than their value as signs of the Passion,' he said. 'One must distinguish clearly between what they are and what they represent – the reality that Jesus of Nazareth was crucified in Jerusalem under Pontius Pilate.'[23]

☧

I RETRACED MY steps into the main church and wandered underneath the apse into the crypt. The flagstones and low barrel ceiling here marked the remains of Helena's palace. After the chapel was consecrated by Silvester I in the fourth century, the relics of the cross were traditionally stored here and successive popes made the short journey from the Lateran to venerate them each Good Friday: the altar in the church above was reserved for the bones of two martyrs, Caesarius and Anastasius. A cleaner in a lumberjack shirt and jeans pulled off his rubber gloves and took a break from his chores to explain that the relics of the cross were removed to a balcony above the choir in the 16th century because the subterranean chapel was so damp. Although this protected the collection, it also made it less accessible. Until the modern shrine was built almost 70 years ago the relics were only displayed once a year on September 14th, the feast of the exaltation.

Rolando Almoneda learned his English when working in the Saudi oil fields and was a mine of information. He explained that the church got its unusual name, 'The Holy Cross in Jerusalem,' because Helena had the ground covered with earth she collected from the Holy Land on her pilgrimage. 'The soil was brought here from Calvary too. The floor was sealed because people kept on digging for it to take pieces away, destroying the pavement. Before you go you should see it,' he advised.

The sacristan disclosed there had been such a surge of visitors during Lent that the church had instituted an appointments system, so few priests were available to meet the demand. The lot upstairs were pilgrims from the provinces. I asked him about Helena and he launched into a faultless recitation of the Golden Legend, the version of her pilgrimage and discovery popularised by Jacobus de Voraigne, Archbishop of Genoa in the 13th century. More than a thousand manuscripts of his *Legenda Sanctorum* have survived, in every European language, making it the most widely read mediaeval book after the Bible. William Caxton printed the oldest remaining English translation in 1483.

Voraigne cheerfully admitted that some of the stories he compiled were probably apocryphal but insisted that accuracy about dates and places took second place to the moral significance of history as revealed by God's chosen agents. In any case the Legend of his title did not then carry its modern connotation of a myth: the ecclesiastical Latin word *legenda* simply meant matter to be read aloud in church at the divine office. Among his list of Helena's achievements was the recovery of the hay on which Jesus was laid in the manger: being thereby sanctified, the ox and ass had refused to eat it, preserving what Helena was able to bring back to Rome. As far as I was aware no one claims this relic today, but patrons of the other great early Christian basilica in town, the church of St Maria Maggiore, do still venerate a silver casket under the altar said to contain several pieces of wood from the crib at Bethlehem. Fortunately for my sanity, Rolando stuck to an edited version of how Helena identified the True Cross by laying a dead man on it, so he came back to life.[24]

'Archaeologists in Jerusalem have been trying to find any trace of the cross but they are unable to do so even now. That proves the real cross was first brought here,' he concluded triumphantly.

So is it the real one? I asked. Flushed with the success of his story telling, Rolando came over all coy.

'That depends on your faith. If you believe, yes. If you do not believe, it will not be true.'

☧

AS FAR AS I could ascertain Helena was never actually made a saint, in the sense of being beatified according to the rules drawn up by Pope Urban VIII in the 17th century. From the beginning she had been so extolled as either 'holy' or 'blessed' that the appellation *sancta* became indissolubly linked to her name. To the earliest Christians, sainthood was the condition in which they aspired to live. St Paul referred to those who were 'sanctified in Christ' as if Godliness was conferred simply by baptism. In the Acts of the Apostles, those referred to as 'saints' are coterminous with believers, brethren, the faithful or the elect (while oddly the word 'Christian' is almost a term of reproach, employed only three times in the whole New Testament and then as a description by outsiders).

The first martyrs were automatically venerated, and by the end of the fourth century it was customary for churches to read an account of their lives on the anniversary of their deaths, the origin of the feast days in the Roman calendar. Dionysius Philocalus offered the earliest list of saints in 354, a modest catalogue of 12 popes and 24 martyrs. Their numbers expanded as clever bishops exercised their discretion to nominate local candidates for honour, with the Venerable Bede charting over 100 entries by the eighth century, shortly before Rome first intervened to try and keep some order. Even so, at the height of the popularity of the cult, the official Roman Martyrology founded by Cardinal Baronius in the 16th century contained some 4,500 names!

The problem featured high on the agenda of the second great Vatican Council, convened by John XXIII in 1962. The first such

Vatican gathering, almost a hundred years earlier, had proclaimed the infallibility of Pope Pius IX in his multiplicity of guises as 'Bishop of Rome, Vicar of Jesus Christ, successor of St Peter, prince of the apostles, supreme pastor of the universal church, patriarch of the West, primate of Italy, Archbishop and Metropolitan of the Roman province, sovereign of the state of the Vatican city.' A century later, John attempted to put the traditional dogma into a more modern context. He sought a spiritual renewal for the modern world that would reunite the rival churches of the Orthodox east and Roman west, while also making Catholic doctrine more understandable in an increasingly secular age.

Although John died before his vision could be realised, over the next three years the cardinals in their conclave bent to their tasks: reorganising the liturgical year to emphasise the life and works of Jesus, making theological doctrine more understandable to the masses, bringing canon law up to date with the swinging Sixties, and ensuring that the accounts of the lives of the saints accorded with the facts of history.

The outcome was to return to the central principle of the early church, and accord primacy to celebrating the mystery of Easter, memorialised every Sunday, over the veneration of relics and images that had been accumulated in the intervening years. 'Over the course of the centuries, more feasts of the saints were introduced than necessary,' noted John's successor, Paul VI, in an apostolic letter dated February 1969 which heralded the overdue culling of an over-crowded calendar. 'With the passage of centuries, the faithful have become accustomed to so many special religious devotions that the principal mysteries of the redemption have lost their proper place.' In the name of modernity he proposed the deletion of 'certain lesser-known saints' so that more emphasis could be put on the proper seasons of the ecclesiastical year, particularly the periods from Advent to Christmas and Lent to Pentecost.[25]

No official reasons were ever given why certain individuals or specific commemorations were dropped, for that might appear too much an admission of past error. The only clue to the new thinking came with the adumbration of the principles underlying the reformed calendar by the Constitution on Sacred Liturgy. These included geographical universality (to allow greater representation to saints from the growing Catholic populations in Latin America), and the testimony of history (to ensure that the acts of the martyrs and lives of the saints in the Roman breviary accorded with known facts). The revised arrangements came into place on 1st January 1970 and the new calendar not only lacked any reference to the finding of the cross on May 3rd (now devoted solely to the apostles Philip and James) but also left August 18th completely blank. Helena had disappeared from history without so much as an apology.

☧

'THERE IS NO body here. There were relics brought by St Helena, but not of herself.' The monk occupying a confessional-style cubicle at the Scala Sancta looked at me askance. He thought: Can't you see there's a notice up outside saying all relics were transferred to the Vatican in 1905? I thought: You're the one wearing a badge saying Jesus XPI Passio, mate. I'm not the only nutter round here. He relented. 'We have one relic of the cross and some bones of San Lorenzo, one of the first martyrs. But of Helena – no. They were brought here and then taken away.'

I was going round in circles. Having been to Santa Croce to see the relics Helena brought back, I wanted to find what remained of her. The sarcophagus at the Vatican was empty. Before being removed as a museum piece in the 18th century it had lain at St John Lateran, ever since 1153 when Pope Anastasius V seized it for his own use from the imperial mausoleum on the old Via Labicana, five kilometres out of the Porta Maggiore. I took a suburban train out to the tombs of St Peter the Exorcist and St Marcellinus the Martyr, near which the remains of a Constantinian building still dominate the skyline. It has even given its name to the district, Tor Pignattara; the tower named after the earthen pots traditionally used in vaulting to help lighten the load of the dome. The site has been locked for years and admission denied without special permit, but when I investigated I was gratified to find restoration work in progress in preparation for the Holy Year declared by Pope John Paul II for the millennium.

A catacomb was originally dug here during the second century to house the graves of the emperor's bodyguard. The land was part of the vast imperial estates subsequently granted to Helena to the south-east of the city walls, between the Via Praenestina and the Via Latina. Her name is still commemorated in the title of both a local parish and a station on the suburban railway which follows the modern Via Casilina to the site. Perhaps she donated the land to the Christians, who first began to make use of the necropolis during the Great Persecution of Diocletian towards the end of the third century?

Appropriately, a funeral was taking place in the modern church dedicated to Saints Peter and Marcellinus when I arrived, but behind it the ruined circular tower stood isolated in a windswept park serving a housing estate. It is thought Constantine built the mausoleum for his own burial but, like the sarcophagus intended for it, handed it over for his mother's remains once he moved his capital to Constantinople. Though I could not see inside, the interior was described in an inventory of Roman graveyards compiled by the Rev W H Withrow back in 1888. Steps from the entrance oratory apparently led through a sloping passageway to a vaulted gallery paved with mosaic, a construction of truly imperial magnificence, which the author believed was so far unmatched anywhere else in the Roman world. 'This catacomb is remarkable for the number of its luminari, arcosalia, and cubicula,' he enthused helpfully, referring respectively to the distinctive use of skylight-like openings in the internal ceilings, and the profusion of both individual cells and family vaults.[26]

Over the last hundred years the site has been extensively excavated by experts, and the Papal Commission for Sacred Archaeology has reconstructed an image of what the huge basilica which adjoined Helena's tower must have looked like after its construction in 320, containing many other mausolea which have not survived the ravages of time. The subterranean necropolis also contains a magnificent series of frescoes, containing scenes from both the Old and New Testament. As well as being a burial ground, the catacombs are thought to have been a place of asylum and house of prayer where the early Christians could worship free from persecution. The soft volcanic tufa of the area was easy to mine, and the network of tunnels and chambers created in it required no maintenance to prevent collapse. Mediaeval pilgrim guides to Rome indicated that the catacombs were still in use for devotional purposes in the eighth century, but shortly thereafter the relics of the martyrs were transferred with increasing frequency to the churches within the city walls, and the underground cult fell into decay. More than 30 separate cemeteries have been re-located and their treasures recovered and researched, but only a handful of these strange galleries of death, notably along the Via Appia Antica, are currently open to a curious public.[27]

☧

IN THE SEARCH for Helena's last resting place I had been directed to the Scala Santa, or church of the holy staircase. By the time I attempted to interview the monk in his cage I had been locked for an hour inside the city's biggest reliquary listening to the animated discourse of a vivacious art lecturer in polo neck blouse, slacks and high heels. Being in Italian and spoken faster than the speed of sound, I couldn't understand a word except 'Cosmati' and noted that whenever this was uttered the appreciative middle-aged audience nodded sagely. With so much time to spare it was not long before I noticed the carving in the stone by the entrance.

MAGISTER.COSMATUS.FECIT.HOC.OPUS

At first glance the Latin might look rather like 'Master Cosmatus made this work' but I already knew that Cosmati was not a man but the style adopted by a mediaeval guild of marble workers.

This was the heart of the old Lateran palace. Although the rest of the building was demolished during the Renaissance, the private chapel of the mediaeval popes was preserved in a specially constructed church. The devout called it the 'holy of holies' by analogy with the Temple at Jerusalem because of the precious relics it contained. When the gnarled woman on the door indicated that for 5,000 lire it would be the only tour of the day I had seized the chance of a closer look.

The shrine contained an image of the head of Jesus known as the Acheropita, from the Greek for 'not made by human hand.' Said to have been started by St Luke but completed by an angel, the image of Christ enthroned arrived miraculously in Rome from Constantinople some time in the eighth century. In 754 it was paraded through the city streets at the head of a procession in order to reassure the Romans that divine protection would deliver them from the threat posed by a Lombard army outside the gates. I had no comparable sanction to offer, and the mad monk outside made clear that 'not made by human hand' was not on public display either. In fact the crude face staring out from a golden halo on the far wall was a later over-painting of the original, carried out when the present silver altar was constructed in the 13th century. I wondered what else was concealed in the wooden box just visible under the altar cloth, behind bronze doors in a bolted metal cage.

The lecturer yet again flicked her long dark hair back from her face, and embarked on a detailed analysis of another bit of mosaic floor or ceiling fresco or wall decoration. The only distraction was a hole in the wall through which visitors unlucky enough to have missed the tour peered at us. It was like television in reverse, with me inside the box looking out at the viewers. These weren't just any old viewers, however. No, these people were proper pilgrims, who had hauled themselves all the way up a flight of stairs *on their knees* only to be confronted by an art tour obscuring the view of a shrine whose contents none of us could see anyway. They believed that the Scala Sancta, which they had just climbed, was brought back to Rome by Helena after her pilgrimage. It had come from the palace of Pilate in Jerusalem, and thus must have been ascended by Jesus. The actual marble is now encased in walnut, but you can just see it through slats in the wooden uprights – especially if you inspect at close quarters by going up the 28 steps on all fours.[28]

☧

EUSEBIUS RECORDED THAT Helena died 'having arrived at the eightieth year of her age' but he was so eager to note how her illustrious son was at her side, holding her hands to the last, that he failed to note when or where the tragic death-bed scene took place. We know it must be after her pilgrimage, and probably therefore in the year 329, but the confusion about the location also extended to the whereabouts of her burial. 'Her body, too, was honoured with special tokens of respect, being escorted on its way to the imperial city by a vast train of guards, and there deposited in a royal tomb,' said the bishop.[29] But by 'imperial city' did he mean Rome or Constantinople? The latter was the capital of the empire when Eusebius wrote his eulogy, and Constantine was already building it as an *altera Roma* when Helena died.[30]

Tradition has sustained the claims of Rome, buttressed by the circumstantial evidence of the sarcophagus and mausoleum. Yet logically the fact that Eusebius made perfectly plain that Helena did not actually die *in* the city must cast final doubt over the lingering claims that she personally brought any relics back to Rome at all. I suppose it was possible that her burial entourage was laden with some posthumous souvenirs, but in any case there is no contemporaneous suggestion that the tokens of the Passion gained cult status until well after Helena's death.

After drawing a blank at the Vatican, Santa Croce and the Scala Sancta, I had only one more place at which to pay homage to the patron saint of this oddball tour. Santa Maria D'Aracoeli is at the summit of the Capitoline hill, the site of the citadel of early Rome. A pagan temple once stood here, which explains why St Mary's church is also dedicated to the altar of the sky goddess. It was said that the Virgin and Child had once appeared to the Emperor Augustus in a vision after he asked the resident Sibyl whether there would one day be a greater man than himself. I particularly liked this story because its inquisitive hero died in AD 14, well before Jesus came to adulthood and thus public attention. My interest was not the church, however, nor even the elegant 17th-century domed construction inside with a familiar bronze statue on top. The importance of the Tempietto di Santa Elena Imperatrice was the older altar it housed.

'It's just a little piece of bone in a little box,' said the friar in the outer office, selling postcards and religious knick-knacks to the accompaniment of piped organ music. 'This was a pagan building dedicated to the God of Mary by Constantine. Here was the foundation stone of the Constantinian church.' He led me across uneven paving slabs and a succession of floor mosaics and jabbed his finger at the monument. 'It's the red box inside.' Beneath the statue a stone grille encircled the tomb, at the rear of which was a dark glass plate. Eventually I found a light switch, which illuminated another grille set into the marble below ground level, an internal window framed with the carving of a mystical lamb and two twisted columns forming an arch either side of it. Straining to look inside this, all I could make out was a vague reddish splodge. I turned to the church's guidebook for an explanation. 'The urn is what you see today, and inside is the preserved relics of St Helena contained in a carved sandalwood box.'

Disappointment would be an understatement. Frustration was inaccurate. I couldn't even see the blasted porphyry urn, let alone the box inside it. I sought consolation in the nearby Capitoline Museum, where I had been told that a life-size sculpture thought for generations to have depicted Agrippina, the wife of Claudius, had recently been re-labelled as Helena.[31] I found her reclining regally on a chair in the centre of a room full of busts.

I couldn't say she was pretty, or even at all attractive. The plain face was dominated by an arched yet pendulous nose. The net of hair plaited tightly and neatly like a turban gave an air of matronly sternness to otherwise boyish features. The thin lips and small mouth seemed to be both pouting and sneering at the same time. And try as I might, circling round and round with my camera, I could not meet her eyes. They were upturned to the ceiling as if Helena was used to being bored silly by such attention.

Even so, I was captivated for a good few minutes. I had never really looked at a bust so intensely before, never really considered how such cold stone could carry the imprint of a live person. Until, that is, I spotted the health warning below her chair. 'Il corpo deriva da un tip fidiacco del V sec AC,' it said, identifying the statue as conforming to a sculptural style at least a century too late to be a genuine life study. While I was feasting on the product of a fevered imagination, the sitter might as well have remained Agrippina.

CHAPTER VIII

Constantinople

If gold will tempt you more, you will find more of it at Constantinople than in the whole world, for the treasures of its basilicas alone would be sufficient to furnish all the churches of Christendom.

Emperor Alexius I Comnenus[1]

IF IT WAS disconcerting to think that my heroine's mortal remains should be scattered in several different places, it was perhaps appropriate that the woman whose activities spawned the cult of relics should herself be a prominent victim. Our culture now associates the ritual of dismemberment with punishment; particularly that of traitors and other heinous malefactors in olden days, who suffered the indignity of being hung, drawn while still alive, and then quartered before the various gory body parts were exhibited publicly as a warning to others. Even in today's secular age it is common to talk about giving someone a Christian burial, with the clear implication that the body is whole and intact when interred or cremated. The idea that Helena's head was in Trier, some of her bones in Rome, and no doubt other bits elsewhere in Europe appears ironically sacriligious to modern sensibilities.

These macabre musings were prompted by the unexpected by-product of a visit to Venice. Though the city with its famous canals was not originally on my Helena itinerary, my pulse quickened as soon as I spotted the Island of Sant'Elena on my map. It is now a working-class district, at the east end of Venice, of little interest to tourists. But a Sunday stroll along the shore became compulsory once I spied a church at the easternmost point, sandwiched between the naval academy and the football club. Especially when I heard that it was revered locally as the last resting place of the body of St Helena.

In a city of so many churches, most of them art galleries or museums in their own right, the Church of Sant'Elena is nothing to write home about. The present building is a restoration of a mediaeval original, ransacked by Napoleon's troops in 1806 and subsequently used for many years as a iron foundry. Its chief architectural treasure is the ahistorical ensemble portrayed on the façade above the doorway, featuring statues of a noted 15th-century Venetian sea-captain, Vittore Capello, kneeling before St Helena and probably praying for victory against the Turks. Inside, while about a hundred parishioners celebrated Mass, I came face to face with Helena's body in a glass coffin.

It was rather a shock at first. The Empress lay prostrate but illuminated in a specially constructed case in a side-chapel, the oldest surviving part of the church. She wore a full-length golden silk robe, edged with lace, that shimmered spookily in the lamp-light, and her head, surmounted by a high crown, lay on a pillow of red velvet. She stared peacefully up through the glass at the underside of the altar-table, hands crossed demurely on her lap. Even her skin seemed to shine like silver – which it turned out to be, of course, on closer inspection. I had been taken in by a masked metal mannequin, cleverly disguising a wooden casket containing the actual remains.

'It's probably not the whole body,' confessed the priest, Father Guiseppe Bernardo, when I collared him after the congregation had filed out. 'There are four or five places that claim to possess Helena's remains – like Ara Coeli in Rome, Haut-Villers in France, and somewhere else in Italy, Verona I think.'

The Venetian archives record that a convent was dedicated to St Helena late in the 11th Century. About a hundred years later, in 1175, the ruling Doge, Vitale Michiel II, founded a church in her honour on his return from a pilgrimage to the Holy Land. He also founded a hospital in her name, not surprisingly since he also brought the plague back with him from Constantinople. However, the tradition that the church was built to house Helena's remains did not emerge until the early years of the next century.[2] Fr Bernardo took up the tale with gusto.

'The story goes that Helena's body was brought from Constantinople in a boat bound for Venice. Unfortunately the ship got stuck on a sandbank in the lagoon. The sailors off-loaded the body along with the rest of the cargo onto the island, in order to float the vessel free. Instead of proceeding as planned the Doge decided to leave the body where it had landed, and erect a chapel over it.'

Fr Bernardo clearly relished telling his tale, but something about his demeanour suggested he didn't believe it himself. 'There's a big gap in the story. A lot happened between the 13th Century and the 19th Century,' he said. Then, Napoleon's soldiers wrought much damage to Venice, looting many of the city's treasures. They moved what purported to be Helena's relics to the nearby island of San Pietro, which was the city's cathedral for much of its history. There the remains remained until 1928 when work began on restoring the old church as part of a major public works programme to develop the area, now known as the Communità Parrocchiale di Sant'Elena Imperatrice. On October 26th the restored chapel was blessed and the first service held for more than 150 years. Two years later the church itself re-opened, and in between the relics of St Helena were transferred back again. A touching tale, although Fr Bernardo acknowledged that even with such a tradition, there were limits to local piety. 'We do have a relic of the True Cross here as well, but we don't actually celebrate Helena's feast-day on 18th August. It's not a good time, everyone is on holiday. We mark it on the first Sunday in May.'

On the face of it, the Venetian version of Helena's last journey supports the theory that the 'imperial city' where Eusebius insisted she was buried was Constantinople, and not Rome. The timing of this aspect of the legend is significant, too, coming hot on the heels of the notorious Fourth Crusade and the sack of Constantinople in 1204. This infamous episode has been described as one of the greatest crimes against humanity: not only encompassing the destruction of the capital of Christian civilisation by a nominally Christian army, but also the dispersal of countless, priceless treasures and works of art accumulated over nine centuries. Most were carried off by Venetians, who knew the value of such things, to ornament their city.

Indeed the Venetians had been commissioned to provide a fleet to transport these unruly Crusaders to the Holy Land in the first place. The forces assembled at Venice to embark, but in the event their French commanders could not raise sufficient funds to hire the ships. The Republic had by then established itself as a mercantile power on the back of the lucrative Crusader trade in providing transport for armies and supplies to the East. Its leaders increasingly sought to exploit for their own maritime advantage their strategic position between the struggling Holy Roman Empire in the West and the declining Byzantine Empire in the East. Historians are generally agreed that devious Venetian diplomacy diverted the crusaders from their original intention of recapturing Jerusalem, to intervening in the dynastic quarrels of Byzantium, under the guise of restoring the Church of Constantinople to Rome.

The Venetians were excommunicated for their part in this

fisaco, but it didn't bother them. The ruling Doges in Venice saw themselves as rivals to the Papacy, owing allegiance to St Mark in the way the Vatican derived its special role from St Peter. The magnificent basilica of San Marco in St Mark's Square, now a magnet to some 15 million tourists a year, was originally built to house the relics of the wandering evangelist. His body was stolen from its supposed tomb in Alexandria in order to fulfil a local legend that an angel appeared to Mark in a vision as he crossed the lagoon, prophesying this was where he would rest in peace. After such a start, acquiring the body of Helena, the holy mother of Constantinople, was a mere bagatelle for the tomb-robbing Venetians. The sack of Constantinople meant the booming mediaeval market in relics was flooded by a host of artifacts allegedly recovered from the imperial palace of Blachernae. Some were of genuine antiquity. Others could easily have been fabricated to take advantage of the chaos. Helena's body could have been in either category, and still be a fake. We will never know. Unfortunately for my quest, the Venetian legacy of plunder didn't hold out any great promise there would much imperial heritage left for me to see in modern-day Istanbul.

✝

THE HIPPODROME IS still colloquially known as the square of horses, At Meydanı in Turkish, but nowadays buses line the course where chariots once raced before partisan crowds decked with badges of blue or green. The custom of wearing colours to differentiate the supporters of rival teams swiftly degenerated into a political circus, in which the two sides divided into bitterly-opposed factions – the middle classes in blue, seeking to defend their privileges against the radical demands of the lower orders, wearing green. This mutual antagonism reached fever pitch during the Nike revolt in 531, so called because the riot started with one side shouting 'victory' so loud it riled the other lot. As many as 30,000 people died as the authorities put down the insurrection, but not before the revolting inhabitants had destroyed much of the city of Constantinople.[3] The story remains a salutary lesson for modern owners of Nike sportswear not to go around boasting about their designer label.

Today the same arena is witness to a less violent – though arguably no less intense – struggle between two modern factions, the tourists and the touts. As soon as a coach packed with apprehensive-looking Japanese pulls up, dozens of Turkish youths appear from every corner of the park spinning their tops, flinging their yo-yos and shuffling packs of postcards to eager cries of 'Kyoto, Kyoto'. For American and European visitors enjoying the sunshine, the diversion brings a welcome break from the incessant clamour of under-age shoe-shines forever eager to buff already gleaming toecaps. The contemporary fashion for trainers and canvass boots does not seem to have diminished the appeal of this age-old trade for youngsters on the make, but despite the shortage of business these boys remain remarkably well behaved. A polite 'no' and they go away to pester people on the next bench, who are no doubt also exercising their imagination about what Byzantium was like at the height of its glory.

Along the east side of the Hippodrome, where the emperor would sit perched above the masses in a royal enclosure known as the Kathisma, there is no longer any trace of the great palace from whose labyrinth he would emerge. Instead, the minarets of the Blue Mosque peer over walls marking the terraces where spectators lined up to cheer on their favourites. There are some exposed foundations of the original structure next to an old Ottoman house on the west side, but the mouldy stones don't offer much help towards envisaging what the scene must have been like as the chariot teams galloped down one side of the track, careered round the bend and pelted down the home straight.

Constantine enlarged the site and gave it the capacity to take 100,000 spectators. He also constructed a raised platform along the spine of the racecourse and erected a distinctive bronze column plundered from Delphi, where for 800 years previously it had graced the Temple of Apollo in gratitude for the Greek victory over the Persians. It was known as the Serpentine, because it was cast in the shape of three coiled snakes, and is still there today although the Medusa-like heads were snapped off, allegedly by drunken Polish diplomats on an 18th-century binge. The base of the column today is sunk in a pit several feet down, an interesting indication of how the ground level has risen over the intervening centuries. Its real significance, however, is that such a pagan structure should have enjoyed such a prominent position in a public place. Another column at the curved end of the track may date from the same period and have a similar function, for an inscription on the massive stones towering into the sky likens the monument to the Colossus of Rhodes.

Constantine's new capital was formally dedicated in a series of splendid ceremonies in and around the Hippodrome that lasted 40 days and culminated with high mass in the church of St Irene on 1st May 330. The celebrations ushered in an era of imperial pomp and circumstance that was to last more than 1,000 years, during which the birthday of the city was regularly marked by a procession in which a statue of Constantine was paraded around the Hippodrome by soldiers carrying lighted candles. Yet among the Byzantine ruins that abound in modern Istanbul there is tantalisingly little left to bring us into direct contact with the emperor who gave his name to the city, let alone his mother. That most of these surviving remains have important Christian connotations should not obscure the fact that, over a decade after his conversion, Constantine was still paying conspicuous homage to Rome's pagan heritage. When he marked out the boundaries of his new Rome on 4th November 328, the emperor traced the outline in person with a ploughshare, according to the ancient Roman custom. The date was decided only after much agonised consultation with augers and astrologers, and contemporary accounts indicate the pagan high priest Praetextus played an important role in the consecration rites. The planned city was over four times bigger than the existing settlement, but just like the old capital in the West which it was designed to replace, the new foundation also encompassed seven hills.

+

ROME HAD EFFECTIVELY ceased to be the political centre of the empire well before Constantine turned his back on the eternal city. Too far from the frontiers that guaranteed the imperial defences, generations of rulers had shunned it in favour of alternative military headquarters as far afield as Antioch in Syria. Under the previous regime of the Tetrarchy, or the four kings, Diocletian ruled the eastern empire from Nicomedia (now the modern Turkish industrial city of Izmit) while his deputy Galerius resided in the Balkans at Salonica (Thessalonica); and Maximian ruled the western half from Mediolanum (Milan) while *his* deputy, Chlorus, Constantine's father, was based at Trier. Despite his own victory over western rivals at the Milvian Bridge, Constantine himself faced a series of threats from the east, which forced him to leave Rome for the Danube front. This period of campaigning came to an end with a spectacular victory over his eastern rival, Licinius, on the Asian shore of the Bosphorus in 324. He would later claim it was 'on the command of God' that he chose Byzantium for his capital, just across the water from the place that gave him supreme command of the empire.[4]

The promontory overlooking the entrance to the waterway between Europe and Asia offered a natural defensive site which needed only a set of walls connecting the Golden Horn to the Sea of Marmara to protect it from landward attack. Today such fortifications are the first sight for modern travellers coming into city from the airport, though these massive defences were actually built later by Theodosius when he enlarged the city. Constantine's own boundaries, a mile beyond, are no longer visible amid the urban sprawl. Instead, a variety of pillars in the oddest locations are the only surviving monuments to the memory of the founder.

Get off the airport bus at Aksaray, for example, and walk towards the Grand Bazaar: there on the pavement you stumble on a scattering of blocks, casually left behind by the march of history, which represent the remains of the magnificent oval forum that marked the heart of the ancient city. Now it is a focal point for traders from Eastern Europe and the former Soviet Union who flock to buy cheap clothes and leather goods to flog back home. While many are of Turkic origin, the shoppers are unmistakable with their black bin-liners stuffed with potential exports. The trade has opened up the old covered market to a new lease of life, though with a touch of danger too: many Western visitors feel uneasy among the throng of short swarthy men in flat caps and leather jackets, and peroxide blonde 'Natashas' in fur coats and boots, packing the aisles in search of bargains.

The forum was the starting point of the dedication jamboree in 330, which coincided with Constantine's own silver jubilee. There, in the middle of the plaza, the emperor unveiled an enormous column. Embodying all the over-wrought artistry of the day, it paid fulsome homage to both pagan rites and Christian ritual in a riot of decorative symbolism, but chiefly it celebrated the ego of Constantine himself. A colossal statue of the emperor, arrayed in the guise of Apollo, graced the marble capital at the top of the column, a sceptre in his right hand, a globe in his left, and a glittering crown of sun-rays on his burnished helmet. The sun-god looked down on his subjects from the height of seven solid porphyry drums stacked on top of a plinth adorned with humbler representations of pagan deities, past emperors, and Christian saints.

This extraordinary monument to one man's vanity outlasted more than 50 emperors, several of whom took Constantine's name for themselves in the pathetic belief that they might benefit by association with his achievements, before literally falling victim to a hurricane. This freak storm toppled the statue and smashed it to smithereens on the ground below in 1106. Yet so important was the column as a symbol of the city that when damaged in an earthquake 600 years earlier, the municipal authorities had bound iron hoops round the junction of the drums to stabilise the structure. This kept it upright not only through the hurricane but over subsequent centuries as well, so that when the Turks captured Constantinople in 1453 they nicknamed the surviving pillar Çemberlitaş, the hooped stone. Remarkably it is still there, though the purple granite was blackened by soot from a 1770s fire, and the ancient hoops were replaced in a 1970s restoration. As a landmark for modern visitors it signals the stop on the tramway where you get off to enjoy the luxuries of one of the finest examples of a classical Turkish bath.

It has also shrunk over the years, for the bottom drum is now enclosed in a masonry casing and the original marble pedestal is buried under three metres of earth. Deep inside that base, if the legend is to be believed, were laid some of the most sacred objects of the ancient world. These were a judicious mixture of pagan and Christian artefacts: the palladium of Troy (the figure of Athene brought back by Aeneas) and the crown of Apollo, on the one hand, together with the nails of Christ's passion and fragments of the True Cross on the other. Was Constantine hedging his bets in a forerunner of Pascal's wager on the possible existence of God? Or just acknowledging that the people he wanted to impress still clung to faith in the old gods?

The act of erecting such a monument to oneself would alone appear to show traces of that religious megalomania in which Constantine became so convinced he was God's chosen instrument that he began to think he was divine. Miraculously, too, the list of buried treasure got larger over the years to match the founder's self-image, to include eventually the hatchet with which Noah built the Ark, the basket and remains of the loaves with which Jesus fed the multitude, and the jar of ointment with which Mary Magdalene washed the Saviour's feet.[5]

Who now can tell? Certainly there is evidence that the column became something of a shrine and a focal point for prayers within the next hundred years. Unfortunately the account left by an eyewitness called Philostorgius has only survived in a copy by the ninth-century patriarch Photius, who took a pretty dim view of his source and offered a running commentary on his heretical views. 'This impious enemy of God also accuses the Christians of offering sacrifice to an image of Constantine placed upon a column of porphyry, honouring it with lighted lamps and incense, offering vows to it as to God, and making supplications to ward off calamities,' reported Photius in disgust.[6]

The hapless Philostorgius was a Christian from Cappadocia who compiled a continuation of Eusebius' church history. Yet his observations were confirmed by a contemporary, Socrates Scholasticus, who commented that the practice of worshipping the pillar 'is very strange and almost incredible.' Unfortunately neither historian left any record to substantiate another tradition that Helena had her own monumental column on the Augustaeum, somewhere in the space between modern Istanbul's greatest tourist attractions, the Blue Mosque and the Haghia Sofia.

+

THE ORIGINAL Haghia Sofia, or Church of the Divine Wisdom, was completed by Constantius, son of Constantine, in 360 but was burned down in a riot the following century. Its successor suffered a similar fate on the first day of the Nike disturbances. Justinian was responsible for the splendid structure that dominates the city today, for centuries the cathedral of Byzantium before being converted into a mosque and more recently a museum. Nevertheless, its dimensions, particularly the vast dome, are generally assumed to owe something to Constantine's vision of the city as a Christian one. This contribution is recorded posthumously in a sixth-century mosaic above the doorway showing the Virgin enthroned with a child in her lap receiving homage from two crowned kings: on the left, Justinian presents her with a model of the basilica, while on the right, Constantine himself, 'the great emperor among the saints', offers Mary a miniature walled town.

The Blue Mosque of Sultan Ahmet I, the jewel of Islamic Istanbul, had no interest for my investigation other than being the contemporary location of Constantine's Great Palace. In the streets behind the 17th-century confection of domes and minarets, leading down to the Sea of Marmara, the casual stroller may come across numerous bits of Byzantine brick incorporated into later ramshackle buildings that give some clue to the size of the royal complex which descended through six terraces to the city walls. Until recently the exclusive haunt of backpackers and penny-pinchers, this dilapidated area has been transformed in the last few years and every street proudly possesses at least one former Ottoman mansion converted into upmarket tourist accommodation.

This process of demolition and renovation has at least recently enabled enthusiasts to uncover part of the Palace of Magnaura in a side street previously renowned only for possessing the Orient Youth Hostel. The excavations can be entered from the street above; down some steps in the courtyard of a carpet shop whose enterprising owners have been funding the dig according to the profits of their retailing endeavours. If they sell enough *kilimlar*, they hope to open a café under the arches. Meanwhile the only evidence of the architecture that graced these slopes at the height of the imperial era are the lonely windows of the Palace of Bucoleon, which overlook the shore from what little remained of the Constantinian sea-walls when the railway line to Europe was constructed round the coast in the 1870s.

These pitiful ruins are in sharp contrast to the solid defences of the Topkapı Saray, the palace of the Sultans, which today dominates the Marmara slopes at the entrance to the Golden Horn. Indeed the later Byzantine rulers found the area uncongenial and set up home elsewhere. When Mehmet the Conqueror rode into town he found the ruins uninhabitable and constructed his own seat of power at the top of the first hill where the ancient Roman acropolis had been. Yet tucked away in a corner of the extensive gardens, ignored by the steady stream of day-trippers making a beeline for the mysteries of the Harem, the Divan and the Treasury, is St Irene, the Church of Divine Peace. Haghia Eirene is the oldest Christian sanctuary in the city, though like its sister, Haghia Sofia, the original was destroyed by fire and rebuilt by Justinian. Unfortunately, it is invariably closed to casual visitors today.

If wisdom and peace were both characteristics of Christ with which Constantine wished to be associated, then megalomania was the emperor's attribute alone. It was expressed in the third church of the trinity he commissioned in the city, the Holy Apostles. Eusebius described a magnificent building of 'vast height' that was 'brilliantly decorated' with multi-coloured marble slabs encasing the walls, and a domed roof so 'profusely adorned' with gold that it reflected the sun's rays brightly enough to dazzle the most distant visitor. The large courtyard in which the church was set was surrounded by porticoes on all four sides, leading to a complex of chambers, baths and promenades. But it was inside that Constantine gave free reign to his extravagance, installing a dozen coffins in memory of the apostles and prudently leaving a space amongst them for his own funeral cask. 'He had in fact made choice of this spot in the prospect of his own death, anticipating with extraordinary fervour of faith that his body would share their title with the apostles themselves, and that he should thus even after death become the subject, with them, of the devotions which should be performed to their honour in this place,' reported his biographer.[7]

Constantine was duly interred here, and the church became the preferred burial place for those of his successors who also died in their beds. Several examples of the sort of huge porphyry sarcophagus used for the purpose can now be seen outside the national archaeological museum in the grounds of the Topkapı palace, but of the original building on the summit of Constantinople's fourth hill few traces remain. What masonry survived the Turkish siege was utilised as building blocks for the giant Fatih mosque, which Mehmet the Conqueror erected to celebrate the dominion of Islam. Ironically, however, the present design of the Moslem complex, with its vast domed mosque, square courtyard, colonnaded walls and network of subsidiary religious houses, still echoes that description supplied 1,600 years ago by Eusebius. And a search for remnants is not entirely futile, for the inner courtyard of the nearby *tabhane* or hospice for travelling dervishes is home to 16 distinctive columns of green granite that must have come from Constantine's church. My attempts to inspect them at close quarters, however, provoked a paroxysm of paranoia in the callow youth at the gateway. He shook his head vigorously, wagged his finger, and hopped from one foot to the other with nervous glances over his shoulder. Remaining obediently within the porch, I observed a row of shoes outside a prayer hall, heard the rhythmic chanting to Allah from within, and contented myself with the tantalising sight of half a dozen antique pillars standing out from their mediaeval surroundings like sore thumbs.

+

OTHER CONTEMPORARY columns around Istanbul are more accessible, such as the pillars which support the roof of a cistern constructed by Philoxenus, a Roman senator who was persuaded to accompany the emperor in his move east. The Turks call it Binbirdirek, the one thousand and one posts, though even when the dank and dark interior is restored into a tourist attraction complete with restaurant and boutiques and galleries the visitor will scarcely be able to count beyond a couple of hundred. Another landmark often attributed to the founder – though it may pre-date his imperial achievements – is the solitary finger of stone in Gülhane Park whose based is inscribed 'to Fortune, who returns by reason of the victory over the Goths.' Yet by far the most remarkable column is the broken marble shaft, uncovered only 30 years ago, which lies anonymously in a corner of Sultanahmet square, half-buried in a sunken pit and dwarfed by an Ottoman water-tower.

This is all that remains of the so-called golden milestone or *milion* which marked the end of the *Via Egnatia*, the great Roman road which crossed the Balkans to the Adriatic. The triumphal archway must have been a spectacular sight, four pillars bearing a cupola surmounted by statues of Constantine and Helena holding the True Cross between them. A representation of the decoration has survived in a stone relief embedded in the exterior wall of a Greek Orthodox church dedicated to the pair. The building took some finding, in the back streets of what became the Christian quarter after the Conquest, near the ruined monastery of St John the Baptist of Studius. Devotees of Byzantium regard this as the most impressive piece of unreconstructed architecture the civilisation left behind, but it's some way off the normal tourist track.

As a result my companion and I arrived too late for Sunday morning service at the church. The congregation had all disappeared but the smell of incense lingered in the gloomy interior where an anxious caretaker in an overcoat swiftly attached himself to the unexpected guests like a limpet, to ensure we took no photographs. I would have thought he would welcome the interest we offered, but perhaps centuries of survival in a hostile environment had ingrained a habit of suspicion about any outsiders. Nevertheless, we were allowed inside long enough to inspect a selection of alternative icons of the *milion* image, including another carving – in marble this time – propped up over the doorway to the nave.

Judging by its appearance this must have been the original, and a double check confirmed that the version mounted on the wall outside bore the give-away date 1805. Presumably the slab was brought indoors for protection and the location marked by a copy. Certainly the weathered writing was impossible to read without a ladder, although from below I could just make out two panels labelling Constantine and Helena. Magnificently robed, cloaked and haloed, the bas relief figures stood either side of a large cross whose beam was just above head height.

Constantine on the left sported an Orthodox beard and shouldered a staff of office: Helena on the right also brandished a wand in one hand, and with the other held the cross upright. Its top seemed to be sprouting a strange growth that after a few moments reflection I decided must have once been a cherub sitting in a cloud. No doubt an artistic fancy of the sculptor rather than an element of the *milion* statue, though from what I had seen of Constantine's grandiose imagination so far I would not put it past him to have commissioned a study showing the holy couple on their way to heaven.

At least and at last I had found something tangible to link Helena to the city. Other local connections are more tenuous, such as the legend that she founded a monastery in the district known in Byzantine times as Helenianae. From the ninth century the monks of the Gastria area revered Helena for bringing back vases of flowers from Calvary to plant in the grounds, but unfortunately no trace of their monastery existed beforehand. The octagonal Byzantine building now operating as the Sancaktar mosque, with which the foundation has been associated, is of even later origin. I was beginning to wonder whether Helena ever came to her son's new capital. After all, she could presumably have saved herself a lot of bother by boarding a ship in Rome and sailing straight across the Mediterranean to the Holy Land.

✠

ACCORDING TO LEGEND, this is precisely how she returned to Rome. Or at least started out, since the pertinent claim is that she stopped off at Cyprus in order to found a mountaintop monastery and bequeath to it two fragments of the True Cross. The story is commemorated in the Stavrovouni monastery at Ayios Chrysostomos, whose name means holy cross in Greek.[8] Travelling by sea would have been a hazardous and unpredictable undertaking, as shown by the harrowing ordeal that Paul experienced on his journey from Palestine to Rome shortly before the onset of winter. According to Acts, the apostle and 275 other people were crammed on to a small boat which spent several days at sea struggling to get as far as Crete, and then a further 14 on board after leaving the island before being shipwrecked off Malta.[9] Even an empress with all the facilities of the empire at her disposal might have second thoughts before emulating such a trip.

Nevertheless, Eusebius is unequivocal that Helena undertook an extensive circuit of the eastern provinces on her outward journey to Jerusalem. 'She bestowed abundant proofs of her liberality as well on the inhabitants of the several cities collectively, as on individuals who approached her, at the same time that she scattered largesse among the soldiery with a liberal hand,' he wrote.[10]

Eusebius does not provide an itinerary for the trip to Palestine, during which he is at pains to emphasise the piety of Helena's conduct, the gifts she makes to the poor and needy, her frequent recourse to prayer, and her generous benefactions to the churches of even the smallest cities en route. Nevertheless, his account of her progress with full imperial authority indicates that this was more than a personal pilgrimage. Tasks like paying the troops, releasing prisoners from the mines, freeing slaves and granting pardon to exiles were all official business which she conducted on behalf of the emperor, most probably at the garrison towns along the main military highway across Asia Minor. Part of the point of the exercise was for her to be seen at as many points as possible on the way. It would thus be logical for Helena to include the site already earmarked as the new imperial capital on her itinerary.

+

IF THIS IS CORRECT, what would be more natural than for the ageing empress-mother to want to pay a visit to the place of her birth, just across the Propontus, now the Sea of Marmara, in the province of Bithynia, and a major staging-post on the way east? The Roman road through Asia Minor started at Chrysopolis, the city of gold, whose ancient charms are now comprehensively obscured by the ugly Istanbul suburb of Üsküdar, on the far side of the Bosphorus. The route followed the Sea of Marmara, through Chalcedon, now Kadıköy, site of a famous Christian council, and along the northern shore of a deep coastal inlet at whose eastern end was Nicomedia, now the site of Turkey's principal naval port at Izmit. In between the ancient traveller would pass the castle of Ankyrion at Hereke, the silk carpet capital of modern Turkey, where it is reputed that Constantine breathed his last on Whit Sunday 337.

Eusebius gives a characteristically over-blown description of the deathbed scene, in which the emperor forsook the purple and 'arrayed himself in shining imperial vestments, brilliant as the light, and reclined on a couch of the purest white' as he prepared to meet his maker. The body was then placed in a golden coffin and carried to its last resting place at Constantinople where it lay in state 'for a considerable time' before being decently interred. In his biography the bishop dwells at length on Constantine's determination to be baptised before he died, summoning prelates from Nicomedia to meet him in the suburbs of that city and conduct the necessary ceremonies. 'Thus was Constantine the first of all sovereigns who was regenerated and perfected in a church dedicated to the martyrs of Christ,' he explained, clearly relieved that his patron had not delayed his formal confirmation in the Christian faith much longer.[11]

For Constantine had clearly been seriously ill that Easter. He visited the hot baths of Constantinople for a cure but when they failed to relieve his affliction, travelled instead 'to that which bore the name of his mother.'[12] Here 'he passed some time in the church of the martyrs and offered up supplications and prayers to God' and formally submitted himself for instruction as a catechumen of the church. Eusebius does not mention the name of the town but from his description we can safely assume it was Helenopolis, a short ferry-ride across the water on the southern shore of the gulf of Nicomedia.

The *Life of Constantine* offers the only remotely contemporaneous reference to Helena's traditional birthplace. Socrates Scholasticus, who brought Eusebius' church history up to date in the early fifth century, claimed Constantine renamed the settlement of Drepanum in her honour. A hundred years later Procopius, the prefect of Constantinople, included a slighting reference to this 'inconsiderable village' in his general commentary on the ambitious architectural activity of Justinian, which sought to demonstrate how his own patron either restored or improved on Constantine's pioneering Christian construction work.

'The Emperor Constantine, out of filial duty, gave this place its name and the dignity of a city, but built nothing there on an imperial or magnificent scale; for the place remained in its former condition in respect of its buildings,' he sneered.[13]

According to Procopius, Justinian repaired the omission, augmenting the town's meagre municipal facilities by the provision of public baths, churches and an aqueduct. In addition he cleared the woods around about and cut back the reeds at the mouth of the sinuous River Draco so it could discharge straight out to sea without flooding. 'For it twists about and winds from side to side, reversing its whirling course and advancing with crooked stream, now to the right and now to the left,' he noted. Procopius confirmed the importance of the harbour in another work, the secret history, where he disclosed that Justinian abolished the post relay out of Chalcedon to save the cost of four stations of horses. This move obliged travellers bound for the interior to sail direct from Constantinople by boat and disembark at Helenopolis.

A different note was struck by Philostorgius in the summary consulted earlier. 'He says that Helen, the mother of the emperor, built the city which was called Helenopolis at the entrance to the Gulf of Nicomedia,' reported Photius, 'and that the reason for her great predilection for the spot was because the body of the martyr Lucian was carried thither by a dolphin after his death by martyrdom.'[14]

Given Photius' contempt for his source, it is not clear whether we are being encouraged to believe Philostorgius or not. Certainly Eusebius acknowledged the existence of a 'church of the martyrs' at Helenopolis, and it is known that Lucian was murdered around 303, about 15 years before the traditional date for the foundation of the city. Jerome, in his *Lives of Illustrious Men* compiled around the end of the fourth century, stated that Lucian, the presbyter of a church at Antioch, was put to death at Nicomedia for confessing his beliefs and was buried at Helenopolis in Bithynia. The coincidence may be the origin of the conviction that has grown up in some quarters that Helena was influenced by Lucian.[15] It is entirely possible that the emperor decided to kill two birds with one stone, so to speak, marking both Helena's birth and Lucian's burial with a rebuilding programme. Clearly from Eusebius' account, the place had hot baths of some renown long before Justinian secured it a permanent water supply.[16]

+

WHERE ARE the ruins of Helena's birthplace today? Almost 200 years ago an intrepid Englishman, William Leake, identified the location of Helenopolis at the narrowest point in the gulf, where a narrow slip of land known locally as the Dil, or tongue, poked out from the southern shore. In the spring of 1800, Leake left Constantinople in a caravan bound for Egypt, disguised for safety as a Tartar courier. He kept a detailed journal of his adventures, the opening chapter of which recorded how the party took a ferry across the gulf, tramped along the promontory past the village of Ersek, and followed a serpentine river upstream to the pass of Kidzerwent in order to reach Iznik on the far side of a mountain range. He also took the trouble to cross-check the landscape he explored not only with Procopius but an 11th-century account of military operations in the region left by Anna Comnena, the daughter of the Byzantine emperor Alexius I.

'The river descending from Kidzerwent to the Dil can be no other than the Draco, which joined the sea at Helenopolis, a small town so named by Constantine in honour of his mother: for it seems evident, upon comparing Procopius with Anna Comnena, that Helenopolis was at or near Ersek,' he observed. 'The Dil has been formed by the alluvial deposition of the Draco, whose impetuosity has been well-described by Procopius, as well as its winding course.'[17]

Like Procopius, Leake had to cross the Draco more than 20 times: the name evidently meant 'snake' and it would not be surprising if its meandering course had changed considerably over the centuries. Nevertheless, his example spurred me to retrace as much of the route as possible. Looking up Anna Comnena's history for myself added no new information to the task other than to confirm that a small port on the Bithynian coast near the Draco was still known as Helenopolis in her day. On the largest modern map of Turkey I could obtain, covering the area between Istanbul and Iznik, I located a river descending from the mountains by the modern village of Kızderbent, which reached the coast through a projecting delta at whose tip was a tiny settlement called Hersek. The river was now called the Yalak Deresi, or stream of the drinking-trough, but the names of Leake's villages at either end were clearly recognisable, and I set off to explore.

The commuter train out of Hydarpasha station on the Asian side of Istanbul is probably the nearest modern equivalent to the ancient imperial highway. The suburban stops echoed the Roman staging posts on the excruciatingly slow *banliyo* train from Kadiköy (Chalcedon) through Pendik (Pantichion) to the terminal at Gebze (Dakibyza). A short minibus ride then connected with Eskihisar, where a ruined castle has given its name to the port from which a car ferry plies across the gulf with traffic that has raced down the expressway from Istanbul. On the far side the ferry docked in a harbour well to the west of the delta, debouching its cargo directly on to the coast road, and my companion and I took a minibus a few kilometres east to Altinova, just beyond the bridge.

It was market day with stalls selling cheap shoes, clothes and household utensils set up on the single street, but the traders were too busy to bother with a couple of Europeans striding determinedly out of the village. The path soon degenerated into a muddy track whose surface was churned up into a thick soup by a combination of winter rains and tractor tyres. The flat landscape offered no clues to the whereabouts of the village and lake marked on the map, so we followed our noses north, through orchards of peach, fig and olive trees, towards what we hoped would be the coast.

We passed the occasional deserted house, enclosed within its own yard, probably the holiday homes of wealthy Istanbullus shut up for the season. A solitary fragment of stone wall, no more than a metre long in the middle of a field, gave a momentary thrill: was this a Roman remain? Highly unlikely, of course, but it provided a psychological boost that we were going in the right direction. After an hour's steady walking the village eventually came in sight, and as we neared it became clear that the settlement had grown up on a small mound. Though only a few metres above sea level, the contrast with the surrounding plain was stark, and focussed the attention of any new arrival on the solid square stone structure perched at the highest point.

The mosque of Hersekzade Ahmet Pasha was built in 1508, according to an inscription carved over the marble doorway, but far more exciting was what it might have been built from. Like the historic buildings of Istanbul, re-fashioned over the generations through a variety of architectural styles, a conventional Islamic design had been realised out of pre-existing material which proclaimed its ancestry in a much earlier era.

The most dramatic example was the use of four large Roman-style columns to hold up a canopy sheltering a terrace of flagstones, which projected in front of the door. Though the stone of the pillars was suspiciously clean, and could even have been new, both the capitals on top and the plinths below were heavily weathered, with encrustations of green and black well settled into the recesses of their carvings. The relatively recent marble surround to the locked doorway was echoed in the clean stone lintels and ledges of a pair of windows, but these had clearly been set into a far older wall: the pattern of an archway that had been bricked up was clearly visible on the front, while the sides and rear of the building featured layers of those tell-tale thin red bricks that were unmistakably of Roman origin. Were these the last remains of Helenopolis?

'*Antik camii, beş yüz yıl,*' said a local enthusiastically after we had repaired to the teahouse across the square for refreshment.

'Ancient mosque, 500 years old.' He made room for us at a table and half a dozen men, young and old, eagerly gathered round, delighted to meet two foreigners taking such an interest in their community's piece of history. They plied us with innumerable glasses of hot, sweet tea but all our tentative efforts to probe into any local folk memory of greater antiquity than the Ottoman empire drew a blank. The nearest to a moment of enlightenment came when our host, who had been diligently scrutinising my Turkish phrase-book, seized on the translation of 'forest' and made a grand sweeping gesture as if to indicate the landscape had once upon a time been noted for its woodland. But it was too much to hope that he had heard of Procopius and his patron's tree-clearance scheme: I couldn't even get him to recognise 'Roman' or 'Bizant' in a variety of pronunciations.

Our efforts were interrupted by the arrival of a wizened gent with a magnificent moustache who spoke a few words of English. Unfortunately he was more interested in boasting about how he used to work at the former American naval base just down the coast. As if on cue, an official limousine flying the Turkish flag on its bonnet and stuffed with senior officers appeared from nowhere and sped through the village, a military escort in a minibus trailing behind. Reluctantly, we took our leave of the tea-house and retraced our steps, casting wistful glances back at the mound that might once have been Helena's home town.

CHAPTER IX

The Pilgrims' Road

She did not shrink from the fatigue of the journey on account of her extreme old age, but undertook it a little before her death, which occurred in her 80th year.

Theodoretus[1]

THE CAPPADOCIAN BISHOP Gregory of Nyssa once complained that he could not talk to shopkeepers in the market place or attendants at the public baths without being engaged in intense debate about the finer points of Christianity. It is hard to imagine such a situation today, and more difficult still from our perspective to understand the arcane terms in which the doctrinal disputes of the fourth century were conducted. The nearest contemporary equivalent that comes immediately to mind might be the argument over whether Britain should join a European single currency, the prospect of which stirs deep atavistic feelings about national sovereignty in the popular psyche while also generating a highly specialised discussion about the economics of exchange rates and an interminable political row over timing. One thousand seven hundred years ago, the chattering classes of the Roman empire were furiously debating the merits of replacing the melange of competing pagan cults and personal household idols with a single imperial religion.

As Gregory himself put it, 'If you ask a man for change, he will give you a piece of philosophy concerning the Begotten and the Unbegotten. If you enquire the price of a loaf, he replies, "The Father is greater and the son inferior." Or if you ask whether the bath is ready, the answer you receive is that the Son was made out of nothing.'[2]

Stripped to its core, however, and denuded of the confusing theological terminology, the issue that plagued the thinkers of the emerging state religion was the precise relationship of Jesus to God. The New Testament repeatedly stated that Jesus of Nazareth was the Son of God. John the evangelist sought to explain this in that beautiful but baffling opening passage to the fourth gospel where he wrote, 'In the beginning was the Word, and the Word was with God, and the Word was God.'[3]

The Greek word *logos* was traditionally translated as Word in this context, partly because it implies the Word of God, as in the Ten Commandments, but also because it carried an even deeper implication as the meaning, or rationale, of the universe. John went on to identify Jesus Christ directly as the human agent of God's creation: 'And the Word became flesh, and dwelt among us (and we beheld his glory, glory as of the only begotten from the Father), full of grace and truth.'

So he was the only Son of the Father? Not so fast. It soon occurred to a number of budding theologians that this particular father-son relationship was complicated by the divinity of the former and the humanity of the latter. Arius, a Libyan presbyter based in Alexandria in 318, took issue with his bishop, Alexander, on the subject and ended up effectively questioning the divinity of Christ altogether. He threw the Christian world into turmoil for generations by suggesting that the so-called Son of

God could not have the same attributes as his Father because he was also a man. Or put it another way, if God was the first cause, his Son must have been inferior.

In 320 Arius was summoned before the massed bishops of North Africa and excommunicated as a heretic. However, in that fevered intellectual climate on which Gregory of Nyssa was shortly to remark, his teachings spread like wildfire. They were aided by his reputation as a pupil of the respected teacher Lucian of Antioch, one of the editors of the Septuagint, the earliest Greek version of the Old Testament, who was martyred during the great persecution of Diocletian's time. And Arius himself was not slow to harness his own genius for self-publicity in order to propagate his ideas, turning his talents to composing popular songs and jingles for ordinary folk to hum or whistle during the course of their daily business.[4] Having been drummed out of Egypt, he travelled to Palestine where Eusebius was bishop at Caesarea and gave him a sympathetic hearing. Subsequently he also visited the eastern capital of Nicomedia, where he caused a small stir. By the time Constantine assumed full control over the empire in 324, the so-called Arian heresy was the chief talking point of the Greek-speaking world.

The emperor was no great intellectual, by all accounts, but he could see the threat posed to his secular dominion by an idea that was subversive of the received wisdom of the church. 'You ought not to have raised such questions at all, and if they were raised, not to have answered,' he wrote testily in a letter to the warring parties in an attempt to mediate between them.[5] Constantine deputed his then adviser in church matters, Bishop Hosius of Cordoba, to investigate further, and the outcome was the first ecumenical church council, convened in 325 at Nicea on the shores of an inland lake not far to the south of Helenopolis.

THE PLEASANT WALLED town of Iznik is a sleepy place today, especially out of season when a chill wind whipping over the lake deters all but the most hardened tourists. However, it was the nearest obvious source of hotels after our excursion in search of Helena's birthplace, and we reached it by *dolmuş*, the ubiquitous Turkish shared taxi, in a spectacular drive over the mountains from the coast that culminated in a grand entrance through the crumbling remains of one of the four great gates of the former Roman capital of the Bithynia province.

Nicea was originally a Greek foundation, said by some to have been named after the wife of a general who served under Alexander the Great, but subsequently by others to be a further derivation of the concept of *nike* that bore witness to Constantine's more recent military victories. Although it had prospered under Roman rule, the city lost some of its early prominence following the founding of the rival capital of Nicomedia at modern Izmit, about 50 kilometres away, and by the beginning of the fourth century had been brought to the brink of ruin through successive invasions by the Goths and the Persians. However, it still possessed a serviceable palace, where Constantine briefly took up residence while waiting for the completion of his new imperial capital at Constantinople. As a staging post on the military itinerary through Asia Minor, Nicea also offered a convenient location for convening a council of more than 300 bishops, who were granted the privilege of using the imperial post-horse system to get there.

It must have been an impressive gathering, even though (aside from Hosius) hardly any bishops from the Latin-speaking west bothered to attend, and Pope Sylvester could not be bothered to do more than send a couple of legates from Rome to stand in for him. However, in recognising Christianity as the official religion, Constantine had effectively created a new clerical class. The bishops were no longer just pastors of their flocks but had become bureaucrats in the state machine, enjoying extensive privileges such as relief from the burdens of undertaking public office in the towns and exemption from district taxes in rural areas. Men of ambition were increasingly attracted into the Church by the prospect of material advancement and the opportunity to wield wide discretionary powers to enforce and exploit the law. The worldliness of this profession was reflected in episcopal garb, in which bishops dressed like wealthy noblemen of the period. In fact the distinctive cassock, cope and mitre which bishops still wear on ceremonial occasions to this day is merely a fossilised version of standard senatorial issue in the late Roman empire. What we regard as quaint ceremonial attire that sets the clergy apart from ordinary folk was originally intended to perform the opposite function and reinforce the wearer's place within civil society.[6]

Nevertheless, my imagination failed me as we searched out the side street where the Kaynarca Pansiyon catered for the few backpackers who bother visiting Iznik nowadays. The town's chief claim to tourist fame is as a centre for the Ottoman art of baking coloured tiles, an industry that flourished under the Seljuk Turks and is celebrated in the glazed bricks of the eponymous Green Mosque. The pretence that I was following in the footsteps of an episcopal arrival at an imperial summit quickly collapsed in surroundings that were implacably Turkish, and provincial to boot. This is not at all to disparage the hospitality of the tea-houses and kebap restaurants along the main thoroughfare, Ataturk Avenue, where we spent many happy hours in convivial company, but simply an acknowledgement that – unfortunately – modern Iznik is a shadow of its former self.

We attempted a bit of mental reconstruction by walking the circuit of the ancient city walls, which is virtually complete and boasts more than a hundred towers overlooking a protective moat. However, it soon transpired that these fortifications largely dated from late Byzantine times, when the deposed emperor Theodore Lascaris established his court here because the Fourth

Crusade had kicked him out of his capital. Only an inscription above the eastern gate that proclaimed it was constructed in the year 123 offered a link to an earlier era.

Similarly the historic remains of Sancta Sofia, the church of divine wisdom, in a sunken garden just off the main square, were also a disappointment: the oldest bits, a mosaic floor and mural, went back no further than the sixth century when the emperor Justinian refurbished and embellished the place that Constantine had put back on the map. That original church had been destroyed by an earthquake a couple of centuries after it had been used as the venue for a later ecumenical council in 787 – which incidentally solved the problem of iconoclasm, by ruling that images and icons were not prohibited by the Bible – yet of that earlier pioneering gathering of Catholic eminences there was no sign.

⚓

NICEA GAVE ITS name to the first agreed Christian creed, the declaration of basic beliefs that in its various amended versions is chanted aloud by the congregation and still forms the kernel of most church services. Constantine insisted on taking the chair at the council, but was easily exasperated by the theological disputations in which the other participants excelled and pressed for an early result to the argument set in train by Arius. Eusebius of Caesarea crafted the compromise that eventually emerged, under which Jesus was held to be 'of one substance' with the Father. The deal hinged on a single word, *homoöusion* in Greek, sometimes translated via the Latin as 'consubstantial' in English, which did not appear anywhere in scripture and whose meaning was deliberately vague. Arius himself did not accept the definition, and fresh arguments over the nature of the Trinity would rage on long after these protagonists had passed away. Ultimately Athanasius, a deacon from Alexandria who succeeded

Alexander as patriarch of the east, was successful in a long campaign against the confusing doctrine of consubstantiality, and by reasserting the essential divinity of Christ gained a place in ecclesiastical history as the father of orthodoxy.

Nevertheless, all bar a couple of the representatives at Nicea backed the formula that was enshrined in the Nicene Creed. It meant that Christians would thenceforth affirm their belief not only in God but also in Jesus as 'begotten not made, being of one substance with the Father, through whom all things came into existence.' The success of the conference was further enhanced with a deal over the date of Easter, discussions on the canon of the New Testament, and new rules on church discipline. The latter ensured that power was concentrated in the hands of the metropolitans in Rome, Alexandria, Antioch, Jerusalem and subsequently Constantinople as well, an outcome that particularly pleased Bishop Macarius of Jerusalem because it granted his city recognition as the spiritual capital of Palestine ahead of the rival claims of Eusebius at Caesarea Palestina.

It was later suggested that Constantine had been thinking of going on a pilgrimage to the Holy Land himself, but postponed his travel plans to deal with the bickering bishops. One can imagine the appeal of such a grand gesture to an emperor determined to unify the church as well as the state. According to Eusebius, the emperor was pretty pleased with the outcome of Nicea and was determined to build on it – literally – with a monument to the accord in Jerusalem. 'He judged it incumbent upon him to render the blessed location of our Saviour's resurrection an object of attraction and veneration to all. He issued immediate instructions, therefore, for the erection in that spot of a house of prayer.'[7] Within two years of the council, Constantine had dispatched his elderly mother on a state visit to Palestine instead.

In his fulsome and wordy *Life of Constantine,* the church historian gave his patron the personal credit for discovering the holy places. Constantine's thoughts had been concentrated on the east ever since he defeated Licinius at the battle of Chrysopolis, on the eastern shore of the Bosphorus, in 324. He had already been to Palestine as a young man serving under Diocletian, the notorious persecutor of Christians. He had later expressed a wish to be baptised in the Jordan. On assuming control over the reunited empire he immediately announced an end to persecution in the east – but as far as we know never travelled further than Nicea. It was Helena who 'had hastened with youthful alacrity to survey this venerable land' on his behalf, her pious devotion overcoming the advancing years, in order to give thanks for the commemorative building her son had authorised. 'And while he thus nobly testified his reverence for these places,' said Eusebius, 'he at the same time eternised the memory of his mother, who had been the instrument of conferring so valuable a benefit on mankind.'[8]

⚓

THE LATIN WORD *peregrinatio* simply meant 'going abroad' before it took on the specific associations of pilgrimage. There had been visitors to the Holy Land before, like Melito of Sardis and Alexander of Cappadocia, but the records of their travels were not invested with the quality of a spiritual quest. Many early Christians actually thought of Jerusalem as a heavenly destination, confounding the secular authorities. Pamphilius the martyr was once interrogated at Caesarea as to the whereabouts of Jerusalem, the poor magistrate not realising his prisoner was talking about a spiritual home and fearing the Christians had established a hostile base in his territory.[9] But, according to Eusebius, Helena had from the start a purpose to her journey aside from personal considerations. 'As soon, then, as she had rendered due reverence to the ground which the Saviour's feet had trodden, according to the prophetic words which says "let us

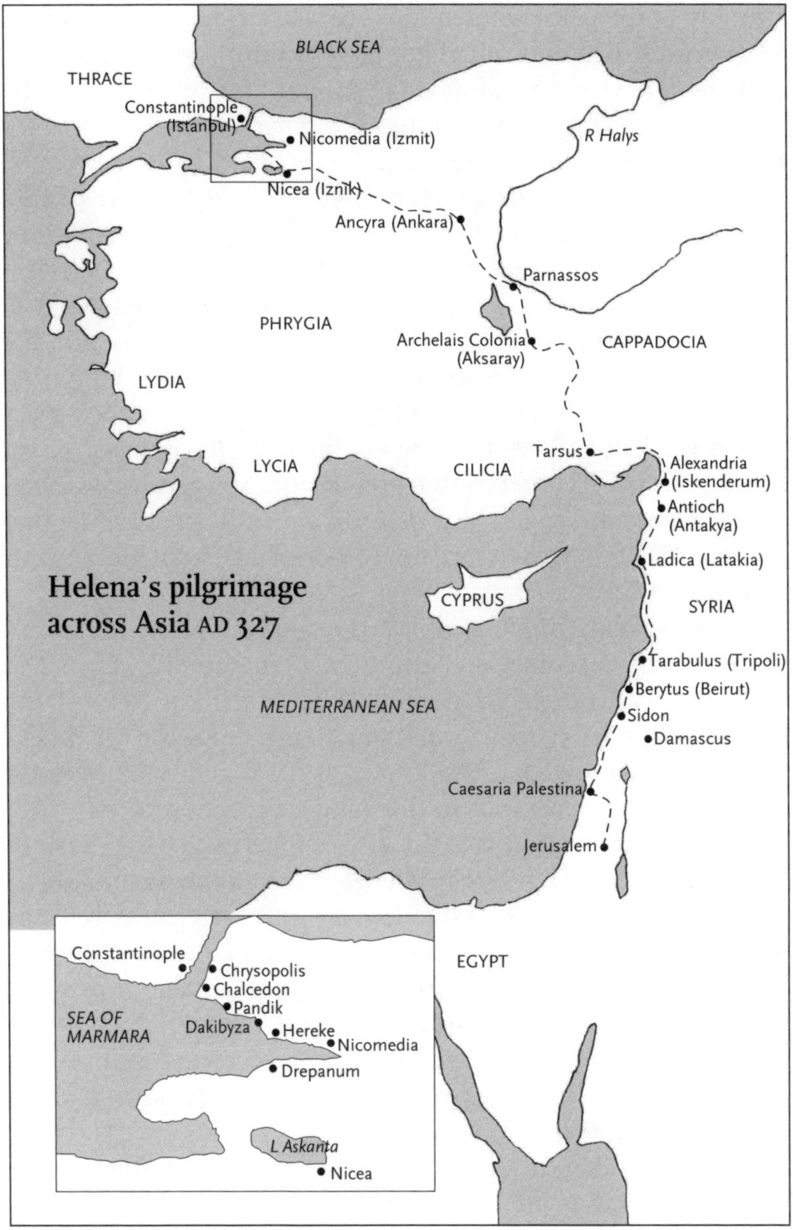
BLACK SEA
THRACE
Constantinople (Istanbul)
Nicomedia (Izmit)
R Halys
Nicea (Iznik)
Ancyra (Ankara)
Parnassos
PHRYGIA
Archelais Colonia (Aksaray)
CAPPADOCIA
LYDIA
Tarsus
LYCIA
CILICIA
Alexandria (Iskenderum)
Antioch (Antakya)
Ladica (Latakia)
Helena's pilgrimage across Asia AD 327
CYPRUS
SYRIA
Tarabulus (Tripoli)
Berytus (Beirut)
MEDITERRANEAN SEA
Sidon
Damascus
Caesaria Palestina
Jerusalem
Constantinople
Chrysopolis
Chalcedon
Pandik
SEA OF MARMARA
Dakibyza
Hereke
Nicomedia
Drepanum
L Askanta
Nicea
EGYPT

worship at the place whereon his feet have stood," she immediately bequeathed the fruit of her piety to future generations.'[10]

Although we have no information about the precise route she followed, probably in the spring of 327, we can reconstruct her most likely path from the itinerary recorded by an unnamed pilgrim from Bordeaux six years later.[11] This is the first written account of a pilgrimage to survive, recording a circular journey from France to Jerusalem via Milan, the Balkans, and Constantinople. He or she – or more probably they – crossed the Bosphorus to Chalcedon, and then headed inland through the province of Bithynia to Ancyra, now respelled Ankara as the modern capital of Turkey. The Bordeaux pilgrim recorded every over-night halt and every change of horse on his journey, so we know the party passed through both Nicomedia and Nicea. Then they struck more or less due east, on a cross-country route that can still be followed today on minor roads into the ancient province of Galatia.

After Ankara, identifying all the ancient place-names on modern maps becomes something of a hit-and-miss affair. The 19th-century historical geographer William Ramsay believed the old Roman military road struck south-east, following the line of the mighty Halys River (now known as the Kızılırmak) yet never daring to cross it because of the danger of winter floods.[12] The immediate destination was the city of Parnassos, just north of Gregory's bishopric at Nyssa, and whose location was the subject of fierce debate to Professor Ramsay and his chums but has almost certainly been lost to posterity anyway since the construction of a series of modern barrages flooding the valley upstream from Kesikköprü, the quaintly-named 'broken bridge'.

From Parnassos, wherever it was, the road swung south to one of many places called Caesarea, this one being also known to the ancients as Archelais Colonia or today as Aksaray, the 'white palace' in Turkish. It is now one of the gateways to the popular tourist destination of Cappadocia, though the road probably skirted this area altogether as it was still heading south-east for the strategic mountain gap called Pylae, or the Cicilian Gates, the entrance to the coastal province of Cilicia. The approach was marked by a castle at Tyana, whose defensive function is still preserved in the name of the Turkish settlement of Kemerhisar, literally 'the fortress of the arch', and the exit from the hills was at Tarsus, the birthplace of Paul the apostle near modern-day Adana.

The road then followed the curve of the coast to the principal city on the journey at Antioch, modern Antakya. Here in this important regional centre of Christianity it was said that Helena was somehow insulted by the local bishop, Eustatius, who was later exiled by Constantine. The circumstances of this apparent snub are conjectural: one suggestion is that the bishop cast aspersions on the lowly upbringing of his distinguished visitor, another that he might have made some disrespectful remark about having to provide the imperial train with board and lodging. Ecclesiastical historians have seen Eustatius' deposition in terms of a doctrinal argument, with the loyal bishop being suspicious of Helena's supposed links with Arianism through her revered teacher, Lucian. The episode is only recorded in Athanasius' history of Arianism, in which the author had an axe to grind against the heresy.[13]

Meanwhile Helena moved on, along the Mediterranean littoral of Lebanon. There local legend preserves the tradition of a series of watchtowers she built on the road linking the great ancient towns of Tripoli, Beyrut, Sidon and Tyre, ostensibly to signal her discovery of the cross back to Constantinople by means of lighted beacons.[14] This must be a myth because it implies she knew before she set out what she was going to find – unless she returned the same way before taking ship across the Mediterranean. Finally the exhausted pilgrim entered Palestine at the regional Roman capital of Caesarea Palestina, near the present-day Israeli port of Haifa.

The Bordeaux pilgrim was no literary genius and provided only a matter-of-fact list of staging posts and the mileage between them. The 50 miles from Constantinople to Nicomedia, for example, took three days and necessitated as many changes of horse. Clearly the route was well-organised, and probably closely followed the *cursus publicus*, the official transport system that provided pit-stops, stables and fresh mounts at convenient points along the way to enable officials to pass to and fro on the business of the empire.

Yet in 333 the pilgrim was introducing it to a new audience for an unusual purpose. On his calculations, hardy travellers could make the thousand-odd miles from Constantinople to Jerusalem in about eight weeks if they stayed only one night at each hostel along the way and didn't need to rest their horses. Even on arrival in the holy city, however, this pragmatic character failed to exhibit any sense of awe at his achievement. Before describing the return journey – via the Adriatic and Rome – the itinerary gave a Cook's Tour of Old and New Testament locations in the tone of a practical guide to an experience it was now possible for others to undertake.

⚓

MY ORIGINAL PLAN had been to recreate Helena's pilgrimage across Asia Minor by making the whole overland journey from Istanbul to Jerusalem myself. My heroine left no published or manuscript account to guide me, in the manner beloved by many travel writers, but the idea nevertheless sought to embody one of these classic devices of the travel genre in which each of the experiences through which I lived on the way would somehow illuminate aspects of her story. There was always going to be a practical problem with this scenario, however, and that was the Middle East peace process. Without a diplomatic breakthrough that never seemed on the cards during the entire time I was researching and writing this book, I knew all along that it would be impossible to cross the border between Lebanon and Israel.

A further complication set in when I considered how in fact I had already undertaken several other elements of the proposed route, though not necessarily in the proper order. The long trip that included that first eye-opening visit to Bethlehem and Jerusalem, for example, also incorporated a segment that inadvertently was the reverse of Helena's route: crossing from Syria into Turkey by the border-post nearest the coast, and making our way via Antakya to Adana. As an adventure it had its own story to tell, but in such a different context that doing it backwards purely for literary purposes seemed perverse.

A little later on during the same expedition, having traversed a lot else of Turkey in the meantime, we also explored the strange fairy-chimney landscape of Cappadocia. Presciently, perhaps, one entry in my diary at the time noted a fresco featuring St Helena and the True Cross in the so-called Church of the Snake as one of the highlights of the Göreme open-air museum. Yet whether Helena came this way was debatable, if the Bordeaux pilgrim followed her itinerary. In any case the rock-cut monastery chapels and underground cities of this curious area, which provided a troglodyte refuge for generations of Christians, were not carved out of the volcanic tufa before the fifth century, and most of the surviving murals dated from later mediaeval times. On reflection, I feared there would be little of direct relevance to my quest to be uncovered by undertaking another expedition, albeit in a different direction.

In the spirit of those subsequent excursions to Trier, Rome and Istanbul, however, I did at one point undertake a brief reconnaissance to Lebanon, in the hope of uncovering evidence of those watch-towers lining the coast-road that allegedly Helena had built. I actually spotted one possible site from a fast-moving bus on the autoroute between Beirut and Tripoli, too, but in the process concluded that there was no point trying to pretend I could somehow do bits of the journey and fit them together later like a jigsaw. As avidly as I consume travel books, as a reader I also abhor the artifice employed by some authors who never let logistical obstacles get in the way of a good story. It had to be all or nothing, from beginning to end, or a different project altogether.

The experience of visiting Iznik confirmed my worst suspicions, when I finally admitted to myself that there was almost certainly not enough extant Roman material from the relevant period to illustrate the undertaking in the way I had originally hoped. Since I didn't want to write a travelogue about Turkey, even though I love the country and its culture, I feared I would be following in Helena's footsteps for the sake of it, rather than for enlightenment. How frustrating, I thought, to have to abandon my dream now, considering how much effort I had already put into it.

Until it struck me that all the reading and research had not been in vain at all. In fact it had become an integral part of my personal pilgrimage, for which the journey had only ever been a pretext. While investigating Iznik itself had drawn a blank, for example, the process of inquiring into the Council of Nicea had been intellectually productive. The answer was not to cancel the quest but divert on to a different path, following a train of thought rather than taking a Turkish bus.

⚓

CONSTANTINE RECKONED he had solved the problem of Arianism and sent his mother to Palestine to bestow the imperial seal of approval on the monuments he was erecting to doctrinal unity. Yet in Eusebius' history of the preceding three centuries, amid all the heroic accounts of the early martyrs and the deeds of the saints, there is curiously little written about those places associated with the birth, death and ascension of Jesus. At one point the historian refers in passing to the 'historic sites' as if their location was self-evident to contemporaries, but there is no sense in which the execution of Jesus or the whereabouts of his relics were a relevant issue. At one level, I suppose, Christian belief in the resurrection meant there were self-evidently no bones left behind to worry about. Yet it struck me as odd that Eusebius should go into such great detail about the death and burial of many important figures in the early church without making any link with the guy who started it all. Especially as the whole point of the Arian controversy was over whether Jesus was a man or a God.

What Eusebius did do, however, was balance his blood-curdling account of the persecution by outsiders of early believers with a fearsome onslaught on the heresies that threatened to undermine the church from within. Although oddly reticent about the subversive role played by Arius in his own day, Eusebius devoted a great deal of space to charting how in previous years the church fathers had overcome a number of ideological and theological challenges to the authority of the emerging institution. In particular he attacked the 'knowledge so-called' of unscrupulous impostors who did the devil's work to corrupt and destroy the true Word of God: 'that impostors and cheats, by cloaking themselves with the same name as our religion, should at one and the same time bring to the abyss of destruction every believer they could entrap.'[15]

As well as being a scholar writing for posterity, Eusebius was also Bishop of Caesarea and for the quarter-century until his death in 340 he contributed greatly to the business of weeding out heretical writings in order to assemble a canon of authoritative scriptural works. The process began in the second century and it was not until 367 that Athanasius first proposed the final version of 27 New Testament books we know today. Yet Eusebius anticipated the victory of orthodoxy by listing 22 books that were universally acknowledged, alongside a number that he definitely rejected, and an indeterminate category about which he had not made up his mind. This interim version was formalised when in 322 Constantine ordered that 50 accurate copies of the scriptures should be made on parchment, so that the dioceses of the empire were all singing from the same hymn-sheet.[16]

Until recently the heretical ideas which Eusebius and his forbears spent so much energy refuting were only known through the distorting prism of their condemnation. Figures like Irenaeus, Tertullian, Origen and later Epiphanius, bishop of Salamis in the late fourth century and author of a massive refutation of all heresies, made their reputations slagging off the bad boys who got it wrong. History is written by the winners, and since the heresies were by definition impure, inadequate, or incorrect, the church itself had little interest in exploring them further. The losers were called Gnostics, from the Greek *gnosis* meaning knowledge, of which they claimed to be in special possession, but their religious speculations were routinely dismissed as distinctly unchristian, if not downright wacky. They did not constitute a single coherent corpus of thought, but an anarchic collection of sub-sects united only by the common belief that the world was divided into rival powers of good and evil.

The existence of an evil demiurge naturally represented a direct threat to Christian teaching about the supremacy of God. Other characteristic Gnostic ideas, such as belief in a secret teaching passed on by a teacher, or faith in a redeemer who brought salvation, appeared as corruptions of the truth preached in the gospels. It was not until the discovery in 1945 of a cache of scrolls at Nag Hammadi, in Upper Egypt, that a proper reassessment of the phenomenon was possible.

A passing Arab peasant uncovered by accident a series of fourth-century Coptic translations of earlier Greek writings in their original form, before they had the chance to be re-interpreted or simply written out of history by the heretic-hunters. This new evidence presented scholars with the prospect that Gnosticism not only flourished alongside the beliefs of Christians for 400 years, but also was so inextricably intertwined with the development of Christianity that some of its exponents even called themselves Christians. It also indicated that the row associated with Arius was only the most recent outbreak of a continuing controversy that went right back to Jesus' own days on earth.

⚓

THE GNOSTIC GOSPELS purported to fill gaps in the orthodox narratives, with which they were probably contemporary. The Infancy of Jesus contained the story of the baby boy's foreskin being preserved after the circumcision, for example, while the Protevangelicum of James identified the brothers of Jesus as sons of Joseph by a former wife. However, the emphasis was on events after Jesus' death, particularly the period between the resurrection and the ascension – traditionally 40 days long but extended by some Gnostic sources to more than a year. The Gospel of Nicodemus, later known as the Acts of Pilate, sought to explain what had happened when Jesus descended into hell between Good Friday and Easter Sunday. The Apochryphon of James contained secret sayings of the resurrected Christ, while the Epistle of Peter to Philip featured a dialogue between him and the disciples.[17]

Between them all they fuelled a common theme, a general confusion over whether Jesus was a divine visitor or a mortal prophet. The danger posed by the Gnostics for orthodox Christians was that they too readily queried the literal truth of the resurrection. Many of the free-thinkers preferred a metaphorical interpretation based on their own charismatic experiences of the risen Christ through dreams, visions or ecstatic trances.

Basilides, for example, who taught in Alexandria during Hadrian's reign, denied that Jesus had suffered on the cross at all. He claimed Jesus had been impersonated by Simon the

Cyrene, who not only gave him a hand by picking up the cross when Jesus stumbled on the way to his execution, but was crucified in his stead. This version of events was hinted at in the Gnostic Apocalypse of Peter and made explicit in the Second Treatise on the Great Seth. In the latter account, Jesus openly boasted of his triumph – 'I did not die in reality but in appearance' – and said that Simon not only bore the cross but wore the crown of thorns as well. 'And I was laughing at their ignorance,' he added.[18]

Despite the scorn of the heretic-hunters, this startling idea remained remarkably persistent over the centuries. It was picked up and promulgated by Mani, the instigator of Manichaeanism who was actually dubbed the New Jesus by his followers, and whose teachings on the universal conflict of light versus darkness permeated the early Christian world. Mani also maintained that Jesus did not die on the cross but was replaced by a substitute.

The notion is echoed in the Koran, the holy book of Islam compiled in the seventh century. One passage, citing Jesus as one of the Jewish prophets who preceded Muhammad, observed: 'They did not kill him, nor did they crucify him, but they thought they did.' The common English translation of that final phrase hides an even greater ambiguity in the original Arabic, which literally reads, 'he was made to resemble another for them.'[19]

Another influential Gnostic thinker, Valentinus, took the opposite view: that Jesus did not inhabit a real human body and so did not suffer on the cross. His followers were sometimes called Docetists, the name coming from the Greek word *dokein*, to seem, because they argued that Jesus only 'seemed' to be a corporeal person. The Gnostic Acts of John, for example, suggested that Jesus was not a material being at all. The author complained at one point: 'I often wished, as I walked with him, to see his footprint, whether it appeared on the ground (for I saw him as it were raised up from the earth) and I never saw it.'[20]

The challenge presented by such Gnostic heresies went right

back to the Bible itself, which described a seminal incident in which Peter, the first apostle, clashed with and overcame the first heretic. The story as told in the Acts of the Apostles portrays this rival to the rock on which the church was built in a bad light. Simon Magus was identified as a magician from Samaria who was reputed to hold people spellbound with his sorcery. Significantly, however, he started out as a convert, baptised by the apostle Philip on a missionary journey to the city after witnessing 'signs and great miracles wrought' by him. So fertile was this territory that Peter turned up as well to bestow further spiritual powers on the new recruits. But Simon was too eager to get in on the act.

'Now when Simon saw that through the laying on of the apostles' hands the Holy Ghost was given he offered them money, saying, give me also this power that on whomsoever I lay my hands, he may receive the Holy Ghost,' said Acts.[21] Peter promptly chastised Simon for his impudence, and the first heretic went down in history as the author of the offence of simony, or bribery to obtain ecclesiastical office.

Eusebius condemned Simon for duping his followers into believing he exercised the great power of God. He was accused of presiding over a sort of first-century travelling circus, being worshipped as a god with incense, sacrifices and libations. He was also, incidentally, accompanied by a woman called Helen who was said to be a prostitute from Tyre. 'Their more secret rites, which they claim will so amaze a man when he first hears them that, in their official jargon, he will be wonderstruck, are indeed something to wonder at, brimful of frenzy and lunacy, and of such a kind that not only can they not be put down in writing,' fulminated the bishop, tantalisingly. 'They involve such appalling degradation, such unspeakable conduct, that no decent man would let a mention of them pass his lips. For whatever could be imagined more disgusting than the foulest crime known has been outstripped by the utterly revolting heresy of these men, who make sport of wretched women, burdened indeed with vices of every kind.'[22]

Later in his *History* Eusebius went on to deliver a similar warning against the followers of another Samaritan, Menander, who succeeded Simon as 'tool of the devil's ingenuity' and claimed to be a saviour sent down from earth. Apparently one of their beliefs was that they would not die. Eusebius noted with distaste that they usurped the name Christian, making a mockery of the Church's teaching on the resurrection of the dead. He also vilified Basilides as another impostor who invented 'monstrous fictions', and blamed Gnostics in general for not only transmitting Simon's magic arts – whether spells cast by sorcery or the evocation of familiar spirits – but also practising 'unspeakable rites' which by association gave the Christians a bad name. 'This was the reason why that wicked and outrageous suspicion regarding us was current among the unbelievers of that time – the suspicion that we practised unlawful intercourse with mothers and sisters and took part in unhallowed feasts,' he complained.[23]

The passion that the good bishop put into his invective may have been fuelled by genuine outrage. Yet it also serves to disguise the possibility that the real problem with Simon Magus was that he was extremely popular. Interestingly enough, he was credited with abilities uncannily similar to those of Jesus – walking on water, turning water into wine, feeding 5,000 people from five loaves and two fishes, or raising the dead. The Gnostic Acts of Peter and Paul, for example, both portrayed Simon engaged in a contest to raise a dead body back to life.

Hegesippus, a Christianised Jew of the second century who devoted his scholarly energies to exposing heretics, identified Simonians as one of the original seven sects that perverted the teaching of the apostles. 'From these in turn came false Christs, false prophets, false apostles, who split the unity of the Church by poisonous suggestions against God and against his Christ,' he warned.[24] The sheer venom deployed by Eusebius himself in his account indicated that his real fear was that followers of Simon's 'disgusting sect' continued to exert influence in the bishop's own day. 'Following in their progenitors footsteps they slip into the Church like a pestilential and scabby disease, and do the utmost damage to all whom they succeed in smearing with the horrible, deadly poison concealed on them,' he wrote.

Epiphanius, bishop of Constantia (whose see served the port of Salamis on Cyprus), was even more explicit about the continuing threat later in the fourth century. Simon was not only the first sectarian to start up after Christ, he noted, but his followers were still disturbing the peace of God – and Epiphanius was not so shy about detailing the 'dreadful things' they got up to. In the *Panarion*, or medicine box (a collection of essays prescribing holy remedies against the poisons of the sectarians) he accused Simon of concocting a sexually depraved ceremony in which semen and menstrual blood were utilised in a corruption of the Eucharist. 'He instituted rites of shamefulness and of fluxes from bodies, to speak with some decency: of men through effluence, and from women through the usual menses, which were collected for the rites, a most shameful collection. And these he said were rites of life, knowledge and perfection,' spluttered the bishop.[25] Historians believe that Epiphanius, who hailed from Eleutheropolis in Gaza, had a close encounter with a sexually-orientated group early in his own ministry and became paranoid lest he lose his chastity thereafter. Nevertheless he was influential in the early Christian world, and travelled to Rome with his friend Jerome in 382. There the pair stayed with the wealthy widow Paula and were instrumental in persuading her to abandon a life of aristocratic luxury for the cloister and a pilgrimage to Palestine, where she founded a convent at Bethlehem.

So in the intellectual and spiritual ferment of the later Roman Empire, before Constantine gave Christianity a special place as the state religion or his bishops established a canon of Christian doctrine, it would appear that there was considerable fluidity about the content of Jesus' message. Some scholars have even speculated that gnosticism in its broadest sense was the majority view in those troubled times among the mass of people who followed revivalist sects based on charismatic figures, some of whom called themselves Christians.

Tertullian, for example, eventually rejected orthodoxy and became a follower of the Gnostic sage Montanus, who preached an ascetic movement which claimed that God spoke through the ecstatic utterances of prophets. Even Origen, the great ascetic theologian of the third century, was himself retrospectively condemned as a heretic in the sixth century as Catholicism sorted itself out from the mixture of primitive Christianity, Greek philosophy and Roman government in which it was born.

In some ways the Gnostics were the first Protestants. They challenged the institutional hierarchy that was developing in the early Church, through which spiritual authority was exercised according to the principles of the apostolic succession. In place of the priest, mediating between God and man, they promoted alternative religious experiences through self-discovery and enlightenment. What mattered to them was the inner spiritual vision available to initiates, who could encounter the risen Christ in the present for themselves. Ultimately they were defeated by the imposition of the creed and the organisation of church membership, with its objective criteria of baptism, worship through a liturgy, and obedience to the clergy. Yet what gradually became clear to me was how the legend of Helena's finding of the True Cross fitted precisely with this larger purpose, too.

Nowhere in all the books and documents and treatises I had studied had this suggestion been made before, but it seemed obvious once you accepted as a fact what the Church always suppressed, which was the extent of Gnostic beliefs at the time. The appearance of relics of the cross in the fourth century represented far more than sacred archaeological remains or props for church consecrations. Here was proof positive that Jesus had been crucified after all. It was the final refutation of those subversive ideas promulgated by the Gnostics, and one whose credibility was buttressed by the authority of the state.[26]

Traditionally Catholic historians gave prominence to the significance of establishing the scriptural canon because they tended to see the development of the early Church in terms of a doctrinal argument. Yet surely for the mass of ordinary believers, the recovery of the wood of the cross would have been a far more potent symbol of the literal reality of the resurrection. Whether it actually happened or not was a subsidiary question to its value as an instrument of propaganda, to reinforce the victory of orthodox theology against popular superstition. Such was the climate of the times that it is surely possible to say, if the True Cross had not been discovered, it would have had to have been invented.

⚓

THINKING FURTHER ALONG these lines, the potency of the Gnostic alternatives to the gospel message also provided me with a clue as to why Helena herself should have been credited with the discovery. One of the oddities about her story is how little is known about her life before the pilgrimage she made at the end of it. One of the few facts we do know, however obvious it may seem, is that she was a woman. Was this significant?

Despite the old feminist joke, that when God created man she made a terrible mistake, the God of the Old Testament is irredeemably masculine, a Jewish tradition carried on in the New Testament and perpetuated today in the hostility of the Catholic church towards women priests. Yet there is much circumstantial material in the Bible that suggests the fledgling religion either encouraged women or had a special appeal for them. In Acts and some of the epistles are mentions of women deacons such as Phoebe in Rome, apostles such as Junia, and missionaries such as Priscilla and Aquila who, like Paul, were tent-makers by trade.

Of course the 12 disciples were all men, chosen to symbolise the 12 tribes of Israel at the time but interpreted as the origins of an all-male priesthood ever since. But it has been noted that Jesus violated Jewish convention by talking openly with women during his ministry and included them among his companions. Most notably, they were the first witnesses of the resurrection.

The women who followed Jesus in Galilee rated little coverage in the gospels until the crucifixion scene, when Mark described them 'looking on afar off.' He named Mary Magdalene, Mary the mother of James the Less and of Joses, and Salome among 'many other women which came with him unto Jerusalem.' These three key players see him laid in the tomb, whither they return on the morning after the Sabbath to perform the traditional task of anointing the body with spices in preparation for burial. They see a young man in a long white garment – an angel, according to Luke – who tells them Christ has risen and they should inform the disciples. Matthew adds that they meet Jesus himself on the way, and they fall to the ground worshipping him.

John's account makes no mention of mourners off-stage but identifies 'his mother, and his mother's sister Mary the wife of Cleopas, and Mary Magdalene' in the crucifixion party. The latter returns alone to the tomb, discovers the stone has been rolled away, and runs to tell Peter and 'the disciple whom Jesus loved' – traditionally assumed to have been the author himself. They rush to check, and see the clothes but no body. The grieving Mary is left alone to keep vigil by the tomb, and when Jesus appears to her she mistakes him for the gardener. When Jesus calls her name, she recognised him – calling him *rabboni,* which means 'teacher' in Hebrew – and tried to embrace him, but he warned her not to touch him. It is a poignant scene, which suggests Mary Magdalene had a key role as one of Jesus' female followers, possibly the only witness to the resurrection, and probably the first to be charged with proclaiming the ministry of Christ.[27]

Looking back on Jesus' travels round the countryside in the

light of what took place at his death, there has been an attempt to rehabilitate Mary Magdalene as more important than the repentant sinner that she became to Christian tradition. She is mentioned earlier in the gospels as one of three women – the others being Joanna, the wife of Chuza, steward to Herod, and one Susannah – who 'ministered unto him.' The Greek word in this case, *diakonein,* is the one from which we derive deacon, and implies rather more than domestic tasks. Luke adds that they 'ministered unto him of their substance' which implies even more, perhaps that they provided the means for Jesus and his itinerant preachers to carry out their work. Jewish custom seated women apart in the synagogue gallery and they exercised no liturgical role. Yet Mary is the only female character in the gospels identified by her place of birth – probably el Mejdel, a fishing village on the lakeshore north of Tiberias – which suggests she was financially independent of a husband or son.

The possibilities raised by such an interesting character are crushed in the western Christian tradition, where Mary Magdalene became confused with the 'sinner' whom Luke described as washing Jesus' feet with her tears, wiping them with her hair, and anointing them with unguent from an alabaster box. By mediaeval times she had become typecast as the weeping woman, and also conflated with Mary of Bethany, the sister of Martha whose brother Lazarus was raised from the dead, because Luke introduced her as sitting at Jesus' feet when he preached.[28]

Yet in the Gnostic writings, which incidentally contain a wealth of feminine imagery, Mary Magdalene remained something of a heroine. The Gospel of Mary built on the story of her seeing Jesus in a vision before the rest of the disciples to portray her as standing up to Peter and the others when they try to ridicule her. And most controversially, the Gospel of Philip suggested she possessed more intimate knowledge of Jesus than all the rest. 'The companion of the Saviour is Mary Magdalene,' it observed. 'But Christ loved her more than all the disciples, and used to kiss her often on the mouth. The rest of the disciples were offended . . . They said unto him: why do you love her more than all of us? The Saviour answered and said unto them: why do I not love you as I love her?'[29]

Much wild speculation has been prompted by this passage that goes far beyond my purpose,[30] which is simply to suggest that, hidden in the gospels but explicitly on offer in the Gnostic alternatives, are potent female characters and a potential appeal to women that was subsequently and ruthlessly excised by the church fathers, who either marginalised women or wrote them out of scripture altogether. They took their lead from Paul, who quoted Genesis to assert man's authority over women. Eve was the second sex because she was created after (and from) Adam, and for her disobedience she was not formed in the image of God. Paul followed the Jewish tradition in advising Christians at Corinth: 'The women should keep silence in the churches. For they are not permitted to speak, but should be subordinate . . . It is shameful for a woman to speak in church.'[31]

Critics argue that such strictures point to the existence of contrary practices, otherwise prohibition would not be necessary. And indeed there is evidence that early Christianity had a peculiarly feminine appeal, not least judging by the number of women who followed Helena's lead and went on pilgrimages in the fourth century and beyond. Jerome's writings record that his feminine circle in Rome contained not only Paula and her daughters Blesilla and Paulina, but a host of other devout women who spent their time praying, singing Hebrew psalms, and studying the scriptures – Julia Eustochium, Marcella and Principia, Asella, Lea, Furia, Titiana, Marcellina, Felicitas and Fabiola. Under Roman law women were denied the benefits of citizenship and therefore participation in public life. The church offered some of them an acceptable outlet for social activities outside the home.[32]

Classical society had been dominated by the *paterfamilias*, the male head of the household, and traditionally women were bound in subjection either to their fathers or, after marriage, to their husbands. However, this rigid social structure was breaking down during the imperial period with the development of a form of 'free marriage' in which a women remained attached to her former family, retained her own property, and had the freedom to divorce. The emergence of Christianity as a popular force, allied to the cult of celibacy among its adherents, gave a new respect to virgins and widows, and allowed wealthy single women to live outside the family for the first time.

Indeed, the creation of specific orders of widows in some early Christian communities allowed women to opt out of marriage and the family altogether, giving them the ability to move freely in the service of God and avoid sexual harassment or unwelcome attention.[33] So worried did the emperor Augustus become by the phenomenon that he introduced a law to halt the alarming drop in the birth-rate, which had implications for maintaining numbers in the militia. This decreed that widows could only remain unmarried after the age of 50, or past childbearing age.

The strong eschatological element in early Christianity, in which believers were convinced of the imminent return of Christ, may also have had a liberating effect on its followers. Social conventions probably seemed less relevant when the world was about to come to an end and usher in the 1,000-year reign of the saints. But as the millennium failed to materialise, and the organisation of the church developed, the bishops sought to re-establish the patriarchal principle in line with the society it mirrored. They upheld the teaching of the pastoral epistles, such as the Letter of Timothy which gave instructions for proper household behaviour: women should be subject to men, and both to the priest.[34]

The heretic-hunters played their part in suppressing those Gnostic ideas that encouraged women. Irenaeus noted that 'many foolish women' from his congregation were attracted to heretical groups, such as one run in his Rhone Valley bishopric by Marcus the magician, who spoke about the feminine side of God and allowed women to celebrate the Eucharist. Tertullian, before his defection to the Gnostic cause, raged at the heretic Marcion for treating women equally.

'These heretical women, how audacious they are! They have no modesty, they are bold enough to teach, to engage in argument, to enact exorcisms, to undertake cures; and, it may be, even to baptise!' he complained. 'It is not permitted for a women to speak in the church, not is it permitted for her to teach, to baptise, nor to offer (the Eucharist), nor to claim for herself a share in any masculine function – not to mention any priestly office.'[35]

In these circumstances, therefore, the fact that a woman found the True Cross appears rather more than a coincidence. I suspect Helena represented an unthreatening role model for a male-oriented organisation that knew women were especially attracted to the message of Christianity yet did not want them using it to upset the natural order of things. She was the loyal wife and mother who also became the pious pilgrim, a prototype for the cloistered nun devoting her life to the worship of Christ. The fruits of her piety earned her world-wide renown, yet the discovery with which she was credited also served to reinforce doctrinal orthodoxy at a critical point in the fortunes of the church. Her life's work, or at least what little was to be known about her later years, would come to be extolled to future generations as a practical exemplar of female faith. This Helena of legend practised what the gospels preached, illustrating by her personal conduct the value of those homilies delivered by Jesus during his ministry: seek and ye shall find; what was lost is found; labour brings its own reward.

CHAPTER X

Palestine

The preoccupation of some practising Christians with the most minute and gory details of the crucifixion has always seemed rather morbid and unhealthy to me.

Colin Brewer[1]

THE TROUBLE WITH embarking on a quest is that you do not know where it will take you, let alone how it will finish. Having started out to tell what I thought would be a simple story, following in the footsteps of Helena, it gradually dawned on me that I was being shadowed too. Increasingly a dark cloud seemed to hang over the whole enterprise, lurking in the background but growing bigger all the time. The more I travelled and thought about my chosen subject, the more I had to keep looking over my shoulder to dispel the intruder.

Initially I endeavoured to avoid a confrontation, largely out of fear of being accused of penning some sort of awful religious tract full of gawkish personal testimony about how I finally found the faith. Eventually, however, like the earlier decision to re-route my inquiries on the pilgrim's road in the last chapter, it had to be done for literary and historical reasons. I could no longer continue to research and write about an obscure fourth-century saint without tackling the object of her own devotions.

If the thesis I put forward was correct, and the real significance of the discovery of the True Cross was the mixture of contemporary scepticism and competing stories about what had allegedly happened on it, then the mysterious first-century figure with whom the symbol was indissolubly linked warranted some investigation too. I could not make sense of Helena without coming to a position on Jesus.

T

THE NAME OF Jesus with which we are so familiar is the Greek form of the Hebrew name Joshua, as in he of Old Testament fame who brought the walls of Jericho crashing down to the sound of the trumpet. Joshua or Yeshua, in turn, means, 'Jehovah is his help' and thus carries connotations of a saviour acting on behalf of God. When you see those signs outside evangelically-minded churches nowadays proclaiming 'Jesus Saves!' therefore, the phrase is really a tautology.

The Jesus of the New Testament, moreover, was hailed by his followers as the Messiah, which means, 'anointed one' in Hebrew. This ancient Jewish term itself carried connotations of kingship, though not necessarily divinity, and was rendered into Greek as *Christos*. The figure we should properly, albeit cumbersomely, refer to as 'Jesus the Christ' was thus from the beginning identified as both a saviour and the anointed one, an individual who first became known to history by a functional title rather than a personal name.

It is a common misconception that Jesus founded Christianity. Biblical scholars now generally acknowledge that the itinerant Galilean holy man whose exotic adventures were recorded in the gospels was a charismatic Jew whose own theological imagination was limited to the self-imposed task of reforming Judaism. His brother James, and the other followers of what they themselves called The Way, did not see themselves as establishing a new religion, but advocated a Jewish heresy.[2]

Their inspiration was the man we now know, thanks to a distinction made famous by the 20th-century German commentator Rudolf Bultman, as the 'Jesus of History'. All trace of this elusive character effectively disappeared from view with the disbandment of the Jerusalem church in AD 70, 40 years after the crucifixion and four after the Jewish revolt, when the city was sacked by the Romans and its native inhabitants forcibly dispersed.

By that time, however, the process had already begun by which this character was to be replaced by what Bultman called the 'Christ of Faith' – an inspirational, mystic figure in whom followers could at least believe, even if they knew nothing about the real man behind it. This idea of Christ was effectively invented by the apostle Paul, who peddled his spiritual vision up and down the cities of Asia Minor and Greece before being arrested and sent in chains to Rome for his pains. He rejected the rigid Judaic law of his own upbringing, symbolised by that unholy trinity of ritual requirements – male circumcision, a strict diet, and respecting the Sabbath.

Instead, he upheld a faith that was based on his own spiritual encounter with God on the road to Damascus. Almost single-handedly Paul developed the concept of the resurrection as mankind's salvation, which became the guiding light of the New Testament and the foundation of Christian doctrine. In sceptical terms, what Paul did was to construct a theology which successfully promulgated the worship of Jesus Christ as a moral rival to the pagan figure of the demi-god who dies and comes back to life, an ethical version of the popular Mediterranean mystery cults of the time personified by Adonis, Tammuz or Attis.

Christians often describe their religion as a uniquely historical phenomenon, rooted in places that existed and events that happened. This is true up to a point, since this is the justification Christianity has made for itself over the centuries. Yet for all that the New Testament books are bursting with biographical details and records of missionary journeys, they are not and were never intended to be works of history. Instead they represented the testimony of a group of believers who saw in the drama of Jesus' death a theological meaning that was never available to contemporaries during his lifetime. The facts about the characters and their exploits were selected for the purpose of instruction: the miraculous elements of the story, from the virgin birth at the beginning to the resurrection at the end, were devised or depicted for a reason. When John's gospel told the famous story of Doubting Thomas, the disciple who demanded proof of Jesus' injuries on the cross, for example, the author added the rider: 'These are written that ye might believe.'[3]

Although 300 years separated the events to which the evangelists bore witness and Helena's journey to Palestine in homage to them, the gap was in some ways a lot smaller than it might seem. For the intervening period was one in which the story had to be told to gain a wider acceptance. Initially it was transmitted by the apostles through word of mouth, and thus was no doubt both embellished and refined as the preachers sought to win over their audiences. Probably other elements were either recovered or pruned as this oral record was eventually committed to parchment, but not necessarily before the memory of those who propagated it became muddled with time and their recollection of the past confused with their purpose for the future. History was literally made, as the gospels, acts and epistles took shape in a literary fashion and became literature, as much as a literal account. As we have seen, it was not until Constantine's time that the church first agreed on a canon which separated out the orthodox version of the New Testament from the mass of rival stories and interpretations which had circulated in that intervening period.

The earliest Christian documents about which we can be at all certain are actually Paul's letters, beginning in about the year 50 with an epistle to followers in Thessalonika, almost 20 years after Jesus' death. The gospels themselves are all dated even later, and reflect in varying degrees the Pauline theology that had already been established before their composition. They contained, as the Greek title 'gospel' would have it, the 'good news' that the Messiah predicted by the Old Testament prophets had come and offered salvation to all who embraced him. The teaching of Jesus put forward in these documents may or may not have had an authentic basis, yet each incident recorded therein also served as a parable in itself, with a higher theological meaning. Matthew, Mark, Luke and John, whoever they might have been, were so determined to demonstrate that Jesus' ministry was the fulfilment of scripture that we cannot be sure their prior reading of scripture did not suggest some of the ingredients of the story for them.[4]

Most authorities now agree that Mark, the shortest gospel, was the core on which the other synoptic gospels were built, dating from shortly before the Jewish revolt of AD 66, although some believe there was an even earlier common original that is now lost. We call the first three 'synoptic' from the Greek *synoptikos* meaning from the same point of view, because they share so much material. Yet there was probably 20 years between them, with Matthew written in Antioch around AD 85 and Luke in Corinth a few years earlier, possibly by the physician friend who accompanied Paul on some of his missionary journeys, and composed the Acts of the Apostles as well. The dating process is significant because it explodes the lingering myth that the gospels were a contemporary record. Had Jesus lived to the typical Biblical span of three score years and ten, for example, he would still have died before the three longest accounts of his life were published.

The chronological gap between the events and the record of

them is also telling because it highlights the contemporary intentions of the authors, who were not simply – or even – recalling someone they knew. Luke, for example, writing in the wake of the siege and destruction of Jerusalem, is constantly anxious to reassure any Roman readers that his radical message represents no threat to the imperial authority, and that the characters in his story have no political connection with any Jewish malcontents of the time. The 'kingdom' preached by his Jesus was therefore strictly portrayed as a spiritual and not a civil goal. Another consequence of this approach, with enormous social and religious ramifications down the years, was that the blame for Jesus' death was firmly fixed on the Jews themselves, exonerating the Roman proconsul, Pontius Pilate, of any responsibility. From such partisan motives, Luke unwittingly unleashed official sanction for the stain of anti-Semitism that disfigured the church down the centuries.

The fourth gospel adopted a more pronounced theological tone than the others and largely for this reason has traditionally been presumed to have been the last, written about the turn of the century. However, it does also contain a mass of additional quasi-historical detail, often contradicting the synoptics and confusing the efforts of subsequent chroniclers to put together a coherent chronology of Jesus' life and times. This is most crucially the case with the crucifixion, which John places the week before the Passover festival. Although the other evangelists all assert it was carried out during the feast, scholars have come down on the side of John on the grounds it was inherently unlikely that the Jewish authorities would interrupt such an important religious occasion to conduct a trial. They argue that the alternative timing of the synoptics was a retrospective insertion into the narrative, determined chiefly to substantiate Paul's subsequent assertion that the Eucharist tradition of taking bread and wine at holy communion was inspired by the final meal Jesus took with his disciples the night he was betrayed.

John's text is also punctuated by regular claims to have been an eyewitness to the events, particularly the crucifixion. 'He that saw it bare record, and his record is true, and he knoweth that he saith true, that ye might believe,' declared the evangelist.[5] Such personal touches convinced early Christians that this gospel was based on the memories of the disciple John, one of the sons of Zebedee recruited in Galilee. Such a view was first put forward in 170 by Theophilus of Antioch and subsequently endorsed by Irenaeus, bishop of Lyons and one of the early pillars of orthodoxy. It explained the frequent references to a haunting figure called 'the disciple that Jesus loved' who was never named yet was a close enough companion to boast that he lay his head against Jesus's breast at the last supper.

On the other hand, if the author John was this self-same contemporary, it was odd he never mentioned the fortunes of the organised Jerusalem church, which sought to preserve Jesus' teaching under the leadership of his brother James. The Acts of the Apostles painted a fascinating portrait of this community struggling to conform to Jewish requirements while remaining faithful to Jesus's ideals. 'The faithful all lived together and owned everything in common; they sold their possessions and shared out the proceeds among themselves according to what each one needed. They went as a body to the Temple every day but met in their houses for the breaking of bread,' it reported.[6]

Yet the fourth gospel had quite a different view of Jesus' legacy, wrapping up its factual account of his life in a distinctive theology, in which the followers of Christ were a community of individual believers, each seeking their own personal relationship with God. It was a vision that caused some anxieties among those whose self-imposed task it was in the early centuries to define Christian doctrine. John's favourite image of the division of the world into light and darkness was a disturbing echo of the dualism preached by the Gnostics, that disparate band of heretics whose dramatic claim to be themselves the beneficiaries of a special revealed knowledge was rapidly condemned by church elders.

All four gospels are therefore poetic and devotional texts rather than chronicles like the Acts, which acts as the second half of Luke's good news for the gentiles (or non-Jews) to whom Paul's ministry was directed. While they cannot be relied on as the first draft of history, these documents are nevertheless virtually all we have got. For independent evidence of the existence of Jesus is limited to a handful of brief classical references. Josephus, the Jewish historian, refers to 'Jesus, the so-called Christ' in a passage in the *Antiquities* about his brother James being killed on the orders of the high priest. Tacitus, the Roman historian, noted that the founder of the Christian movement had been executed in the reign of Tiberias by the procurator Pontius Pilate. And Suetonius, the Roman writer, recorded that Claudius expelled the Jews from Rome in AD 41 because they were 'at the instigation of Chrestus, repeatedly rioting.'[7] If we want to know any more we are stuck with the Biblical texts, in the certain knowledge that they are an imperfect historical vehicle yet in the vague hope that nevertheless they can still provide tantalising glimpses of a long-gone era, 'like driftwood left behind on the tide of events.'

T

THE DISCOVERY IN 1947 of a cache of scrolls in the cave complex at Qumran, overlooking the Dead Sea, irrevocably changed the way scholars looked at the scriptures. The documents described the practices and rituals of the ascetic sect known as the Essenes, who had withdrawn from Jerusalem to purify themselves in the desert. These threw new light upon the world of the New Testament and pronounced the death knell of the conventional view that Christianity simply emerged as an updated and revised version of Judaism with a universal appeal to the pagan world. Instead the scrolls were instrumental in promoting an alternative picture in which contemporary Judaism was convulsed by a credibility crisis that spawned a myriad of reforming movements. The Essenes were one such, but the Pharisees and Sadducees familiar from the gospels were part of the argument too. Though portrayed by the evangelists as almost identical guardians of Judaic orthodoxy against the challenge posed by Jesus, in fact we now know that the former was a radical middle-class group devoted to improving the people's adherence to the principles of the Law, while the latter were defenders of the traditions and primacy of the Temple.

Into this internal turmoil stepped John the Baptist, preaching a simple call to repentance from the banks of the River Jordan. His promise of salvation through immersion evidently attracted many followers, combining as it did the wild-man image of the Old Testament prophet with an echo of the ritual purity of the Essenes. He may well have been a Nazarite or Nazorean, someone who had taken a vow of asceticism in protest at the moral decline of the times. This was usually a temporary thing, and both Samuel and Samson went down this path in the Old Testament, abstaining from intoxicants, allowing their hair to grow long, and avoiding any contact with the dead. The persistence of the practice is attested in the New Testament, too, where Paul pays the expenses of four men completing similar vows in the Acts, and it is even hinted that the apostle may have joined them.[8] There is also a body of opinion which suspects that Jesus, too, first came to public attention as a Nazarite or Nazorean, and that the folk memory of this description is the origin of the tradition that he hailed from Nazareth.

For this particular Galilean town is not mentioned in the Old Testament at all, and is described in the New Testament as the residence of Joseph and Mary only by Luke, whose authority for the quaint tales of Jesus' infancy has already been queried. The popular assumption that Jesus learned his trade here as a humble carpenter is equally suspect: the Aramaic word *naggar*, translated into the Greek as *ho tekton*, can either mean craftsman or scholar, and the latter makes much more sense not only in view of his subsequent calling but even in terms of the tradition; for example, the tale of the adolescent Jesus disputing with the scribes in the synagogue. Matthew inadvertently gave the game away by arguing that the young Jesus went to live in Nazareth 'that it might be fulfilled which was spoken by the prophets, that he should be called a Nazarene.'[9]

The name of the town came from the Hebrew *netzer*, meaning a branch or shoot, and thus something separated from the main body, the same derivation as the description of those Israelites who closeted themselves away from others for religious reasons. On the same basis, the early Christians were known in Hebrew as *ha-nozrim* to signify their difference from Jews. Mark described Jesus being called 'the Nazarene' when Peter was challenged at cockcrow on the morning of the crucifixion and denied he was a follower, to his subsequent shame. Later on the morning of the resurrection, an angel in the tomb told the first witnesses: 'Be not amazed: ye seek Jesus the Nazarene, which hath been crucified.'[10]

The use of the Greek *Nazaraios* in these contexts is ambiguous enough to signify either Nazarite or Nazorean, rather than necessarily meaning Nazarene as an inhabitant of Nazareth.[11] Even where the gospels refer specifically to Jesus of Nazareth the label appears to be as much a term of reproach as an attribute of residence. And later when the Acts records the arrest of Paul, he is arraigned before Felix, the Roman governor of Caesarea, on charges drawn up by the high priest which echo the earlier trial of Jesus: 'for we have found this man a pestilent fellow and a mover of insurrections among all the Jews throughout the world, and a ringleader of the sect of the Nazarenes.'[12]

So where the gospels would like to have us believe that they record the foundation of a new religion, what they actually offer is a descriptive gloss on the development of a Jewish renewal movement, which for shorthand purposes some have called the Jesus sect. Its leader was one of a number of wise men, or *hasidim*, who wandered the hills of Galilee, an independent territory at the time which was fertile enough to be prosperous while yet earning a reputation further south in the Roman jurisdiction as a refuge for brigands. This Jesus was portrayed alternately as an exorcist who drove out devils, a miracle-worker who healed the sick, a preacher offering hope to the poor, and a shaman controlling the weather.[13] Yet his message also posed a political threat, implicit not only in the millenarian aspect of his teachings, predicting an imminent end to the world, but through the personalities who jumped on the bandwagon as well.

For all Luke's efforts to cover up any evidence that insurrection was on the agenda, the disciples clearly included known political activists as well as simple fishers of men. Simon the Zealot was a deserter from a militant Jewish sect devoted to upholding the law by force, for example, while Judas Iscariot's surname signified membership of the *sicarii*, the terrorist arm of the Zealots who specialised in mixing among the crowds to assassinate their enemies with a short curved dagger known as a *sicari*.

The endorsement of these two activists does not necessarily mean that Jesus himself was a revolutionary, determined to overthrow a state in which the Jewish leaders were collaborating with the Roman rulers, though some have maintained this view. My point is only to highlight how much of the original factual landscape of first-century Palestine, so painstakingly reconstructed or reinterpreted by scholars in recent times, was lost to view so soon after the events themselves took place. It is hard to imagine the emperor Constantine giving his imperial blessing to a religion that contained even the merest hint of such radical roots. The apostles and the evangelists did their work well, not only proselytising their new faith across the Gentile world but also rewriting history for generations of believers that came after.

T

THE TRADITIONAL CHRISTIAN portrayal of the crucifixion shows Jesus with his arms outstretched, pinned to the wood of the Latin † or *crux imissa* by nails driven through his hands and feet. Yet the evangelists themselves said nothing about the precise procedure undertaken by his executioners. Many of the details of the image that appears so familiar to our culture were inferred by posterity from related gospel references. For example, the actual shape of the cross is based on the reference by Matthew to the title-plate being fixed above Jesus' head: it was therefore assumed the upright projected beyond the cross-beam.[14] Modern research suggests it was more likely the Romans used a short T-bar (known as a Tau cross after the Greek letter of that name) with a mortise and tenon joint so that the victim could be easily lifted into place after being fixed to the crossbar.

The use of nails is not mentioned in the brief descriptions of the crucifixion either, but is implied from the subsequent gospel incident in which the doubting disciple Thomas demanded proof of the resurrection by inspecting the holes in Jesus' body. 'Except I shall see in his hands the print of the nails, and put my finger into the print of the nails, and put my hand into his side, I shall not believe,' declared Thomas.[15] The poor chap had to wait over a week before Jesus appeared to his followers again and his wish was fulfilled; though the proof was restricted to an inspection of Jesus' hands and the wound in his side, not the feet. The point of the incident, however, was that the details did not matter. 'Blessed are they that have *not* seen, and *yet* have believed,' said Jesus – a moot theological point the early Christian fathers ignored completely in their eagerness to credit Helena with discovering the nails as well as the True Cross.

The Doubting Thomas encounter was recorded by John alone. Luke has a variation, in which Jesus terrified the remaining disciples by appearing amongst them like a ghost when they were debating what had happened to him. 'See my hands and my feet that it is I myself,' he said,[16] though in the context of this passage it is clear that Jesus's aim is to reassure the disciples that he is flesh and bone rather than demonstrate the marks of the passion. Other New Testament references to the use of nails either echo sayings from the Old Testament, such as Psalm 22 ('They have pierced my hands and my feet')[17] or are more like figures of speech in themselves. For example, in Paul's letter to the Colossians, the apostle employs rhetorical language in explaining how Jesus had cancelled the debt mankind had to pay by 'nailing it to the cross.'[18] The Acts of the Apostles only ever refers to Jesus 'hanging on a tree.'[19] To my mind it is quite feasible that Jesus was bound to the cross by cords.

This would have achieved the same purpose, and been a lot less messy, than using nails. Given the shape of the human frame, stretched against a hard wooden frame, it would have been far easier to tie the victim's arms, pulling them backward over the crossbar so it ran under the armpits. The early church fathers also suspected, correctly, that hammering nails through Jesus' palms and feet would have been counter-productive to the purposes of his executioners. The weight of the body would simply have torn the pierced flesh and failed to keep the victim in place. A quaint solution to this dilemma, first proposed by Irenaeus, bishop of Lyons in the late second century, was that there must have been a little seat or shelf projecting from the upright to support the sufferer until he died. This carefully positioned prop, the *sedula*, subsequently made frequent appearances in Christian art, as did a similar block lower down the upright on which the feet could rest.

The development of modern medicine has spawned a cottage industry into the grisly matter of how Jesus died. Research has come a long way since the Edinburgh physician, William Stroud, diagnosed a ruptured heart in his 1874 *Treatise on the Physical Cause of the Death of Jesus Christ.* In the 1950s Dr Pierre Barbet performed experiments on freshly amputated arms hung with weights in order to prove that nails would have torn through the flesh of the hands. Subsequent research has suggested that the most effective, albeit brutal, way of carrying out the punishment would actually have been to drive a six-inch iron spike through each wrist and ankle instead. If strategically placed, these would allow the bones to support the weight of the body, and avoid severing the arteries so that the victim remained alive, while also ensuring that any attempted movement of the arms and legs to relieve the relentless pressure on the chest would only antagonise the nerves and therefore deliver more pain. This was the conclusion reached by an American pathologist, Dr William Edwards of the Mayo Clinic in Rochester, Minnesota, and collaborators from the United Methodist Church who analysed the crucifixion from a medical point of view in order to counter claims that Jesus did not die on the cross.

In the process they also argued that the events of Jesus' last day on earth would have put him in a particularly vulnerable state, especially after a scourging with multi-tailed whips into whose tendrils were customarily embedded metal studs and animal bones for greater effect. 'As the Roman soldiers repeatedly struck the victim's back with full force, the iron balls would cause deep contusions, and the leather thongs and sheep bones would cut into the skin and subcutaneous tissues. Then, as the flogging continued, the lacerations would tear into the underlying skeletal muscles and produce quivering ribbons of bleeding flesh. Pain and blood loss generally set the stage for circulatory shock,' said Dr Edwards' report.[20] Already effectively on the critical list from this beating, physically exhausted by being up all night, and emotionally wrecked after being abandoned by his companions, Jesus would not have survived long on the cross, struggling to lift his chest in order to breathe, by pushing up on his cruelly pinioned feet and flexing his cramped elbows. 'Each respiratory effort would become agonising and tiring and lead, eventually, to asphyxia.' As to the specific Biblical references to the stigmata in Jesus' hands: advocates of the wrist theory like Dr Edwards and his fellow worshippers pointed out that the ancients did not make a distinction between two parts of the body so close together. The Greek word *cheir* could mean either arm or hand.

Whatever the merits of this debate, asphyxia was the accepted cause of death for a generation of modern medics until the arrival on the scene of another American, Frederick Zugibe, a professor of pathology and the chief medical examiner of Rockland County, New York. He decided in the best interests of scientific accuracy to conduct an experimental crucifixion. A succession of fit young male volunteers stripped down and stepped up to be fixed by leather gauntlets to a cross contraption erected in Prof Zugibe's laboratory, and were wired to a variety of meters and machines. Sweating copiuosly throughout their ordeal, the poor guinea-pigs provided readings that showed rising blood pressure and an increased heart rate that Prof Zugibe attributed to an adrenalin rush. However, none displayed evidence of breathing difficulty, even when suspended only by their arms without any foot support. In fact, the experiment showed that to relieve the strain on the shoulders, each body arched so the crown of the head touched the upright of the cross. This instinctive reaction actually increased the oxygen supply to the lungs as the victim hyperventilated.

Fortunately for the students, complaining of muscle cramps in both the shoulders and arms, the experiments were terminated after about 45 minutes. Nevertheless, the results enabled Prof Zugibe to argue that hanging on the cross was only fatal for Jesus in that it was the last straw in a day of horrific physical and mental stress, each element of which would subject the body to degrees of physiological shock. The agony began in the Garden of Gethsemane when the gospels recorded Jesus sweating blood – or hematidosis, a condition brought on by acute anxiety. The brutal beating and scourging of the flagellation would have had a traumatic effect on the body, probably causing pleural effusion (an accumulation of fluid around the lungs) as well as hypervolemic shock (reducing the blood supply to the tissues). This would be compounded by the nerve-wracking pain of the crown of thorns, the burden of carrying the crosspiece to the execution site in the intense heat of the midday sun, and the strain of being nailed to the cross until the heart simply stopped pumping. If Dr Zugibe had written the death certificate, it would have recorded cardiac and respiratory arrest, due to severe pulmonary edema (or water on the lungs) combined with cardiogenic, traumatic and hypervolemic shock.[21] In lay terms, the circulatory system shut down in protest at treatment no human body could stand.

T

ONE OF THE PROBLEMS in resolving these issues is that archaeological evidence of an actual crucifixion is limited to a single example found in 1968 at the Giv'at Ha-Mivtar graves in north Jerusalem. The fate of the first-century occupant, Jehohanan, has been the subject of fierce scholarly debate, with the original excavators accused by later researchers of being mislead by Christian assumptions about what they were looking for. Among the bones one large nail survived, apparently transfixing the heel of a man whose shins had been broken. The initial reconstruction suggested that the victim had been pinioned into a peculiarly contorted pose, with a nail through each outstretched forearm yet his trunk twisted and knees bent together by a single nail through both feet. A later reassessment disputed whether the shins were broken at all or whether the feet were fixed by the same nail. This posited a completely different technique in which the crucified man straddled the upright, facing towards the cross rather than hanging from it. Either way the wristbones of Jehohanan appeared completely undamaged.[22]

The significance of the argument over the shin bones was that accounts have come down to us from non-religious sources indicating that the Romans sometimes broke the legs of crucifixion victims in order to put them out of their misery. This was not necessarily an act of clemency: John's gospel disclosed that the Jews asked Pontius Pilate for permission to do just that, to avoid the embarrassment of any bodies remaining on their crosses for the whole of the next day, the Sabbath, when the work of disposal or burial would have been forbidden under Hebrew law. According to John the soldiers duly broke the legs of the two thieves, but found Jesus already dead so did not need to bother with him. Instead one of the guards, fancifully christened Longinus by mediaeval spin-doctors many years later, double-checked his mortality by thrusting a spear into the side of the corpse, from which gushed a mixture of blood and water.[23]

The verisimilitude of this account is undermined by its obvious theological purpose, to which John himself readily admitted in suggesting that both incidents were predicted in the Old Testament. 'For these things came to pass that the scripture might be fulfilled: "a bone of him shall not be broken" – and again another scripture saith: "they shall look on him whom they have pierced",' he said.[24] None of the four gospellers assumed their readers needed footnotes, but for the record the latter text is a quotation from Zechariah while the former is to be found in Exodus, where Moses is leading the children of Israel out of Egypt. In this case God advises him to keep the Passover in memory of the escape, but not to break the bones of the sacrificial lamb before consuming it.

Yet if indeed Jesus was already dead, then why poke a spear into him? Perhaps, in such a symbolically charged narrative, the shedding of blood was a necessary ingredient to highlight the nature of the sacrifice. And perhaps there was no blood on his hands because there were no nails? Was he in fact dead? For if blood and water flowed from the wound in the side, might that not indicate the heart was still pumping and he was still alive? Mark, reporting how Joseph of Arimathea asked for permission to take the body for burial, said Pilate was astonished that Jesus had died so soon and asked the centurion in charge of the execution squad for confirmation of the fact.[25] The whole sordid business was over within a few hours. Matthew, Mark and Luke each noted the darkness that came over the land between the sixth hour and the ninth hour, a midday eclipse of the sun that has enabled scholars to date the episode to Friday 3rd April AD 33. If the trial of Jesus ended at noon, this agreement of the evangelists limits Jesus' torment on the cross to a rather short struggle in the unaccustomed darkness of early afternoon.[26]

According to the synoptic gospels, the two robbers crucified alongside Jesus reportedly harangued him throughout, picking up on the mocking comments of a crowd that had come to watch the so-called 'saviour' fail to save himself from an earthly fate. I imagine them rabbiting away on either side, like extras from Monty Python's *Life of Brian* singing 'Always look on the bright side of life.' By the time their legs were broken to hasten death, Jesus was apparently already dead on his perch. 'What a wimp, this so-called Son of God,' might Gestas on one side have called out to Dismas on the other. 'We mere mortals easily outlasted him, when surely it would have been a sign of his divinity if he was difficult to kill off?' In Luke, the presence of these malefactors is used to draw a comparison between their guilt and Jesus' innocence. Yet in all the accounts, the matter of fact way in which they are disposed of as common criminals contrasts sharply with the detail of his trial, torture and travails. Were they similarly scourged and humiliated beforehand? Did they go through the ordeal by flogging which modern medical evidence indicates was a crucial component in Jesus' death? It is almost as if Jesus was singled out for special treatment, to ensure that he was seen to suffer so much that he could not possibly survive. And talking of films, isn't it interesting how that flagellation scene was milked for every drop of blood and guts in Mel Gibson's powerful epic *The Passion of the Christ*. Methinks the celebrated Old Catholic actor-turned-director protests too much.

One of the oddest images of the crucifixion story is of Jesus being offered a sponge soaked in vinegar to drink. John suggested this happened shortly before Jesus breathed his last, after he complained of thirst, and explained the incident as yet another fulfilment of scripture, like an anointment in reverse. Luke just said the offer was made by the soldiers on guard, who were mocking him at the time. In both cases there would be no particular significance in the liquid being vinegar, which was probably just the sour red wine available to the soldiers, although John says it was served 'upon hyssop', a plant used for sprinkling water in ritual purification. However, both Matthew and Mark timed the offer before the actual crucifixion, and specified that the wine was flavoured with gall and myrrh respectively. Such a beverage mixed with bitter herbs would be consistent with a medicated drink designed to deaden the pain – although Jesus apparently refused it.[27]

He died not through thirst, however, or hunger, or even a heart attack, but simply 'yielded up his spirit' when it was time to go. According to Mark and Matthew, Jesus finally gave up the ghost with a haunting Aramaic cry that two millennia later still has the power to chill the blood: *Eli, eli, lama sabachthani* – 'My God, my God, why hast thou forsaken me?' Since the phrase came from the opening words of Psalm 22, this represented yet another prophecy successfully fulfilled, although one whose impact was undermined by Luke's insistence on a completely different version, taken from Psalm 31: 'Into thy hands I commend my spirit.' Nevertheless, the departure, according to all the synoptics, was the occasion for a celestial demonstration of fire and brimstone: the earth quaked, rocks were rent, and the veil of the Temple, which hid the Jewish 'holy of holies' from public view, was torn in half. John eschewed the histrionics in favour of a simple exit, in which Jesus bowed his head with the final words: 'It is finished.'[28]

The discrepancies in the conventional accounts offer a field day to conspiracy theorists who want to believe Jesus never died on the cross at all. Perhaps the event was stage-managed in order to persuade the gullible that the scriptures were fulfilled and demonstrate that Jesus was the Messiah? Maybe the star of the show was given a narcotic to numb the pain and taken down alive but apparently lifeless, like those fanatics in the Philippines who voluntarily get themselves nailed to crosses on Good Friday to fulfil a religious vow? Possibly he was not nailed to the cross, but simply tied up there until he could be taken down under convenient cover of darkness and spirited away? Did the Romans deliberately misread the signs of his sorry state, and report prematurely the 'death' to a Pilate who was only too happy to accept it because he had already washed his hands of the whole embarrassing business? And just who was the mysterious Joseph of Arimathea, who appears out of nowhere in the gospel narrative to claim the body and take it away for burial – and equally suddenly disappears, never to be heard of again? For most of Christian history any of these questions would have been blasphemous, inviting the most severe penalties on those who dared entertain or promulgate anything other than orthodoxy.[29]

Yet with the wisdom of hindsight, looking at the evidence from a more dispassionate contemporary viewpoint, the gnostics might have been on to something after all. The kernel of the heretical idea that the resurrection story was not quite what it seemed even has Biblical foundations. Matthew's gospel ends with a strange passage about a clumsy attempt by the chief priests to bribe the soldiers who had stood guard over the empty tomb. 'Say ye his disciples came by night, and stole him away while we slept,' they suggested. The soldiers took the money on the promise that the priests would square it with the governor, if word reached him of their negligence. So they did as they were told: 'and this saying was spread abroad among the Jews, and continueth until this day.'[30] At face value, it would appear that even as Matthew was putting quill to parchment, rival versions were already doing the rounds suggesting the crucifixion was a charade and this author at least was rather anxious to nip them in the bud.

T

IF JESUS DID NOT die, it stands to reason he could not be resurrected and the chief pillar of Christianity would therefore collapse. 'If Christ be not risen, our faith is in vain,' Paul wrote to the people of Corinth about 20 years later.[31] The resurrection represented public testimony that Jesus was the Son of God and proof that his sacrifice had been accepted in atonement for our sins. In his epistle to the Corinthians, one of the earliest Christian documents, Paul summarised the authorised version of events as follows: Jesus died, was buried, rose again on the third day, manifested himself to a number of apostles on several different occasions before ascending into heaven, and finally revealed himself to Paul on the road to Damascus.

Leaving aside Paul's conversion, which probably took place some years later, the New Testament recorded at least ten separate appearances by Jesus between the resurrection, when his body miraculously disappeared from the tomb, and the ascension, when his bodily form conveniently disappeared off the face of the earth. The time-lag is described in Acts as 40 days, and although this is a symbolic figure that frequently features in the Bible, it indicates that over a significant period the risen Jesus was not with his former disciples all the time.

During this otherwise unexplained limbo, he made himself known to his followers either clandestinely or unexpectedly. As apostles they were supposed to be witnesses of the resurrection, yet often they failed to recognise Jesus amongst them – as when he accompanied some on the road to Emmaus, or manifested himself as others were fishing in Tiberias. He possessed magical qualities that enabled him to materialise in a locked room (the doors were shut so the Jews could not find out what was going on) or vanish from their sight at will. Yet apparently he continued to give teachings about the kingdom of God as he had during his ministry. He also allowed them to examine his hands and feet to prove he was flesh and blood, and at one point ate a piece of broiled fish with them to demonstrate he was not an apparition. It is not surprising Luke described the apostles reacting with a mixture of astonishment and terror, though he could also be referring to a form of religious ecstasy whose participants had started seeing things.[32]

On the most charitable view, the discrepancies in the gospel accounts probably reflected the disciples' own confusion about what on earth was going on. If Jesus had indeed risen from the dead, he had not simply returned to normal life, like Lazarus when raised from his deathbed. John claimed that when Mary Magdalene saw Jesus in the garden, outside the empty tomb, he shied away from her outstretched hand, saying famously *noli tangere*: 'touch me not, for I am not yet ascended to the Father.' Yet Luke recorded an appearance, shortly before the ascension near Bethany, when Jesus deliberately confronted them with the physical evidence of his humanity: 'See my hands and feet that it is I myself.'[33] Being carried up into heaven was probably a huge relief all round because it provided a respite from the frightening and baffling visitations with which this ghostly man-god haunted his former associates.

The conundrum was resolved by Paul's theology, but that did not come until some time later. In any case Paul's own encounter with the risen Christ, in a vision which temporarily blinded him and caused him to renounce his career as Saul the persecutor, was qualitatively different from the befuddled experiences of the apostles, occasionally bumping into what purported to be the bodily presence of their teacher. Paul had faith: he had no need for other evidence of the resurrection, and never mentioned the empty tomb in his own writings. The evangelists subsequently employed his theology to provide a meaningful explanation after the event, but in their underlying muddle the gospels carry an authentic sense of the confusion that must have reigned at the time.

Shaken by the outcome of a trial and crucifixion that they did not or could not prevent, the disciples looked for leadership to Peter, already marked down as the foundation stone on which the church would be built. Like Paul, he underwent a symbolic name-change – the former fisherman was originally known as Simon until Jesus dubbed him Cephas, the Syriac for 'rock', translated as *petrus* in Latin. Yet until Paul redefined the mission, the so-called First Apostle was rudderless. His first act in the Acts was to summon the brethren to choose a replacement for the traitor Judas Iscariot. 'There was a multitude of persons gathered together, about a hundred and twenty,' and they elected Matthias from among those who had accompanied Jesus 'to become a witness with us of his resurrection.'[34] It sounded more like keeping a football team up to strength in memory of the manager than a bid for new trophies.

T

APOLOGISTS HAVE OFTEN argued that it would have been unthinkable for the earliest Christians to forget the locations where their Saviour had been executed, buried and discovered risen from the dead. Yet it is all too easy to make such assumptions in retrospect, peering back into the past at the hazy events of first-century Palestine with all the accumulated baggage of a creed weighed down by its own sense of history. For what have since become articles of faith were contentious assertions at the time, and not even obvious to all those who called themselves Christians. Many arguments over the finer points of doctrine were not clarified until Constantine's day and, although many continued bitterly to divide the church long afterwards, the parameters of what could be safely said (and even thought) were for a long time sharply constrained. Ironically the mass of conspiracy theories, revisionist histories and sensationalist claims about Jesus – so popular in the field of Biblical studies these days[35] – probably better reflects the intellectual and ideological ferment of those early centuries than the rigid certainty of Christian orthodoxy which was soon imposed to hide these challenges from view.

Undoubtedly there were doubts from the start – about the circumstances of Jesus' birth, life, death and resurrection. Identifying locations for these events would have been a natural part of the process of reinforcing belief and combating scepticism in which the early church was engaged, not least for its own protection and self-preservation against the populist appeal of the gnostic heresies. Yet there is no indication in any of Paul's letters that physical relics mattered one jot to the real founder of Christianity. Faith was a living thing: what was important to him was the state of mind of its adherents, and their conduct in the world. After all, the essential Christian rite of communion could be celebrated anywhere there was a table for an altar, and some bread and wine to represent the body and blood of Christ. The whole point of the Acts of the Apostles, the epistles to the embryonic church community across Asia Minor, and the Pauline theology which so imperfectly infected the gospels, was to encourage believers to go out and spread the universal message beyond the narrow confines of Jerusalem. This central concept of 'witness' involved the active testimony of individuals who had seen the light for themselves, not the commemoration of places or things that had been passive participants in the drama. As

Peter put it in his second epistle: 'For we did not follow cunningly devised fables, when we made known unto you the power and coming of our Lord Jesus Christ, but we were eyewitnesses of his majesty.'[36]

The change in attitude must have come as these original witnesses died out. In his first letter to the Corinthians, Paul listed those to whom the risen Jesus had appeared: first Peter, then the 12 disciples; James and all the sundry other apostles; a mass meeting of more than 500 brethren 'of whom the greater part remain until now, but some are fallen asleep;' and finally himself, 'as unto one born out of due time.'[37] The acknowledgement that Paul was a special case, who uniquely on the road to Damascus experienced a vision of Christ *after* his ascension into heaven, is of a part with his passing observation that already some of the original witnesses had passed on, or 'fallen asleep.' It was in those circumstances that empirical evidence of sites which could be visited and objects which could be touched came into their own. As the memories of eyewitnesses faded and their numbers shrank, they left only the oral – and later written – records of their experiences with which to convince the sceptical.

Gradually the gap would be filled for later generations by an emphasis on more practical, physical representations of the faith. By the time Constantine was ready to adopt Christianity as the state religion, putting his money where his mouth was through the construction of huge church buildings and ecclesiastical edifices, the founder of modern Christendom had to be sure that the historical basis of the creed was sound. What better way to seal that project than finding hard evidence of the crucifixion at the suspected site of Jesus' tomb? The miraculous recovery of the True Cross would have posed an enormous temptation.

EPILOGUE
Jerusalem

Now whether these pieces of wood which Helena found were ingeniously prepared by the Christian residents of Jerusalem to deceive her and Constantine; or whether the Emperor himself, having in view his favourite sign of the cross, and a determination to make use of the Christian faith, had arranged the whole spectacle of this discovery; or whether the simple fact was that the cross had lain buried there and was found where the Christians said it was – every reader must decide for himself.

William Cowper Prime[1]

SHE LAID ON the tears and tantrums a bit thick, but it was still an arresting sight. From underneath her white shawl the pretty blonde interpreter pleaded and prayed on behalf of her party of pilgrims, but to no avail. The Russians had arrived at the holiest shrine of Christendom just as it prepared to close for the most solemn event of the Christian year, and the gatekeeper just shrugged his shoulders.

'The door will open for five minutes. If you want to go in you must stay all night. This is the same for all people.'

She turned to me. 'But we are flying to Moscow tomorrow. We

want to go inside, the last thing before we leave. Surely you can help us?'

It was late in the afternoon of Maundy Thursday as we gathered in the courtyard outside the church of the Holy Sepulchre at Jerusalem.[2] The unfortunate Orthodox visitors from Nizhni Novgorod had failed to appreciate that the Catholic year operated one week in advance of their own religious calendar. There was nothing I, just another casual visitor, could do. In consolation the Russian pilgrims queued up to kiss the fire-cracked stone pillar supporting the great arch, as the heavy wooden doors clanged shut and the official custodian locked 40 Franciscan friars inside the church for the annual Easter vigil.

'This post has been in my family, passed down from father to son, since we received a *firman* from the Sultan Saladin,' said 67-year-old Abed Joudah proudly as he pocketed the key. 'I will retire after my funeral and the job will be passed immediately to my son Ahab.'

It transpired the boy had a PhD in communications from Texas, so I wondered whether the tradition would be preserved. Mr Joudah puffed himself up again and introduced his colleague Wajeeh Nuseibeh, the doorkeeper. 'He gets paid every time the door opens. I don't receive anything: it is an honour and a duty for me.'

The two Arab families entrusted with the guardianship of the Crusader church since mediaeval times used to collect fees from Christian pilgrims to the Holy Land and distribute the proceeds to the Moslem poor of the city. Today their representatives boast they keep the peace between the different denominations that vie for the use of the building on the spot Helena identified as the site of the execution of Jesus. The task has become fossilised into an elaborate twice-daily ceremony when a square hole opens in the great door and a wooden ladder is poked through. Once set in place, the portly Mr Joudah flourishes the huge key, and the wiry Mr Nuseibeh climbs the ladder to insert it in the lock. The solemnity with which this odd couple perform their historic task, clad in sober black suits offset by shiny shoes and oiled hair, only compounds the resemblance to a carefully choreographed Laurel and Hardy routine.

Early the following morning the custodians rehearsed their opening comedy, releasing a rush of cold air from the Holy Sepulchre. 'Like a tomb,' shuddered one bystander presciently, as dozens of waiting worshippers shuffled inside for the Good Friday solemnity on the site of Calvary. They milled around the two chapels, Greek on the left, Latin on the right, whose upstairs floor is level with the summit of the original rock. Down behind the stairway visitors can see the block itself, protected by a glass plate. But the most devout lined up on top to kneel under a marble table and kiss the hole in the floor of the Greek section where Jesus' cross was said to have been planted. Among them was a thirty-something American woman I had briefly chatted to in the queue outside, who had confided she was no longer sure about the Christian beliefs with which she had been brought up but hoped some of the atmosphere here would aid her search for inner peace.

The intensity of such personal piety on public display contrasted sharply with the perfunctory responses of the professionals for whom the Celebration of the Passion was just one of dozens of scheduled services during Holy Week. Some of the friars were giggling, larking about like schoolboys at the back of morning assembly. A handful of barefoot black Ethiopians, wrapped from top to toe in gleaming white robes, arranged themselves elegantly in a corner like a chequered tableau and took no further part in proceedings. A photographer whose video camera had its own searching spotlight gatecrashed a pulpit with a commanding view over the scene, acting like he had exclusive recording rights. The celebrant's voice quavered, the choir sounded off-key, and half the congregation seemed uncertain how to behave in such an intimate commemoration of the crucifixion.

Taking advantage of being locked in for at least two hours without any tourists, I wandered off to explore the recesses of a building that is really several churches in one. Beyond the apse I found (as I hoped) the stairs leading down to St Helena's crypt, the way marked by small crosses carved into the sandstone wall by generations of pilgrims. This chapel, run by the Armenians whose gloomy paintings of venerable patriarchs grace the walls, dates from the 12th century but its brickwork corresponds with the foundations of Constantine's basilica. And in the corner is a stairwell leading down to the cistern of the quarry in which Helena is said to have discovered the cross. This element of the legend was first developed in the sixth-century Breviarius of Hierosolyma. Yet excavations by the Franciscans in 1965 confirmed that the zone was once a quarry for *malaki* stone, outside the ancient gates of Jerusalem.[3]

That morning the subterranean chapel was a place of quiet contemplation for at least four other people. A young man and three women squatted on the floor under the overhang of pinkish rock which formed the ceiling, their eyes on the plain altar table behind which a pillar bore a bronze statue of Helena, leaning on the fruit of her labours. Did she or didn't she? If it happened, was it here? For a moment, awed by the presence of stones 2,000 years old, I was inclined to believe. I wanted to touch the bare rock, in case it transmitted some energy from the past that would establish a connection to dispel scepticism forever. I stretched out a hand to explore but every time I moved, my sandals squeaked hideously on the polished marble floor, stabbing into the silence. Feeling that by my fumbling I was desecrating a private space to which others had a prior claim, I withdrew and promptly bumped into the bustle of the back end of the Franciscan service. The friars were getting ready to walk the way of the cross.

☦

TO SPEND EASTER in Jerusalem is to cross the narrow bridge between pilgrimage and tourism and see religion bring history to life. On Good Friday the sublime meets the ridiculous along the Via Dolorosa, with an endless series of processions along the route revered for centuries as Jesus' final footsteps. Western visitors equipped with sticks, sunhats, and shorts rubbed shoulders with monks bearing backpacks, nuns wearing baseball caps, and priests carrying mobile phones. At each of the Stations of the Cross, tour-guides could be found leading their party in prayers and a hymn, the devotees perhaps touching the pictorial representation carved in stone before they moved on to the next. Never mind that even Catholic authorities accept that the well-worn path bears little resemblance to the reality uncovered by the archaeologists.[4] The devotional walk first put on the map by the Franciscans in the 14th century followed a quite different route and had fewer stops, but the idea so impressed the imagination of mediaeval pilgrims that they took it back to Europe. There the tradition developed of marking as many as 14 separate incidents around the walls of every church, The Stations of the Cross, starting with Jesus being condemned and ending with his death. The whole package was then exported back to Palestine because later pilgrims expected to find in Jerusalem what they had been accustomed to following at home. The modern route of the Way of Sorrows was not in fact fixed until the 18th century, and some of the points on it are even more recent than that.

Near the beginning I watched a cheerful party of Indians from Dubai taking snaps of themselves as they prayed before the altar of the flagellation, and marvelled at the symbiotic relationship between faith and photography. The Anglican tradition in which I was brought up would have frowned at the idea of taking pictures in church, except perhaps surreptitiously at weddings. Here it was not simply tolerated as a natural part of what tourists did, but almost encouraged as a way of fixing the minds of Christian pilgrims on the process in which they were engaged. Just as the way everyone jostled together in the crowded narrow lanes of the Old City, causing chaos amongst the Arab street vendors and Palestinians promenading on the Moslem day off, not to mention Jews out celebrating Passover the same weekend. Pausing for breath at the Fourth-Station souvenir shop, proprietor Mohammad Ali confided to me that, despite all the T-shirts, stuffed camels, painted icons and olive wood sculptures of the Last Supper on display, his most popular product was still a Jewish menorah, the seven-branched candelabra of the Hebrews.

Round the corner a sudden commotion heralded the most histrionic of the day's dramas. A half-naked man wearing only a crown of thorns and a loincloth, his face and torso streaked with red gore, was bent double under the weight of a wooden cross. Over a chorus of shouts, cries and groans cracked the gut-churning snap of a whip. The sight and sound was momentarily shocking, until you realised the lashes were being wielded by an actor dressed up as a Roman centurion, complete with plastic-moulded breastplate and helmet with a red nylon plume. An authentic Palestinian woman, crouched on a cloth laid out with piles of olives and coriander for sale, was almost trampled underneath the accompanying scrum of television cameras.

'For Gaaad's sake, have mercy,' wailed the leading lady of this walking soap opera, her broad American accent amplified by a portable microphone and both features at odds with her oriental costume. 'Will saaamebody pleeeze wipe his faaace?' On cue a female accomplice stepped forward with a cloth. 'Oh thaaank you, Veronica!' shrieked the grande dame, displaying with a clumsy sleight of hand an instamatic imprint of the suffering man's face on a cloth, as the portable PA pumped out its lachrymose pomp-rock. I laughed out loud, for the story of Veronica's veil is a classic case of mediaeval wish-fulfilment.

Like several other Stations of the Cross there is no justification for the episode in any of the Gospels, though Luke mentions the presence of women in the crowd who 'bewailed and lamented'

Jesus on his long march to the place of execution.[5] The idea that one of them engaged in a simple act of charity to mop his brow had such popular appeal that she became a saint, and eager hagiographers sought retrospectively to identify her with someone who had been touched by Jesus' teaching or healing earlier in his career. In their enthusiasm to construct a biography, however, admirers of Veronica somehow lost sight of the origin of the name in the Latin phase *vera icon* – which referred not to an individual but the 'true image' left on the cloth that wiped the face of Jesus.[6]

'The Americans do this every year but we forbid them to come into the church. Once they brought their Jesus show into the courtyard but acting Christ upset the Christians,' Mr Joudeh told me later. The travelling players had performed the climax to their cod crucifixion in the street outside the Holy Sepulchre before the sun reached its peak, but a steady stream of other less attention-seeking groups kept arriving at the complex throughout the blisteringly hot day. 'There are maybe thirty or forty other processions and they all have to leave their crosses in the courtyard,' added the custodian, despairing at the task of trying to marshal the crowds. A CNN crew was interviewing two Spanish girls about the Middle East peace process for a broadcast about why Western visitors were staying away from Jerusalem for fear of political unrest. If this was a bad year for religious tourism, I thought, God only knows what normality would be like.

Inside, busloads of Greek women in black dresses and headscarves were arriving for the start of their own Holy Week; each equipped with a collapsible stool for the long hours of waiting. At the entrance they prostrated themselves over the unction stone marking where Jesus' body was washed before burial. This particular marble slab had only been there since 1810 but that did not deter them from sloshing water over it and mopping up the now-blessed liquid with sponges to squeeze it back into glass jars and plastic bottles. One enterprising supplicant had brought a syringe to suck up every drop. Another hitched up her skirt and rolled down her stockings without a trace of embarrassment to swab her painfully swollen legs.

Then they advanced on the Treasury, which the Orthodox priests open once a year so that pilgrims can kiss the glass case preserving a fragment of the True Cross in a 17th-century reliquary from Poland. A black-robed clerk laboriously taking down names in a ledger told me that prayers would be said for the families of each named individual that night. I followed one of the faithful into a side room where the sacred splinters were barely visible, enclosed in a cross-shaped receptacle an inch or so in diameter, which was itself sunk into a larger wooden cross set in a simple wooden frame. Having paid their respects the pilgrims toured the musty room to peer at cases full of anatomical specimens and decayed tissue. I spotted the left hand of St Basil, the right arm of St Michael Synadon, the cranium of St Parascene the Samaritan, and other 'divers reliques' once attached to saints of whom I had never heard. Selected portions of Mary Magdalene, fortunately unidentified, were neatly arrayed in one silver casket; the golden-tongued St John Chrysostom, however, was divided between two boxes, one of which mixed the mortal remains of the good bishop with those of eight rivals. In morbid fascination I explored a blackened and wizened array of assorted femurs, digits and pates – until elbowed out of the way by a black-clad granny who had urgent business with a bit of bone.

‡

THE HOLY SEPULCHRE today is as different from the structure that Constantine built as that fourth-century edifice was itself unrecognisable as the place where Jesus was crucified. The Constantinian church was destroyed by the Caliph Hakim in 1009 and its contents reduced to rubble; the modern building is essentially what was rebuilt by the Crusaders. The Jerusalem of

Jesus fell foul of the Jewish insurrection in AD 66–70 and the ill-fated Bar Cochba revolt 60 years later, after which the Temple was destroyed by the Romans in revenge and the Jews themselves expelled. Then the emperor Hadrian completely refashioned the city, naming it *Aelia Capitolina* in honour of his own family and the gods, and raised a temple to Aphrodite on the site where local tradition was said to remember Jesus' death.[7] Whether this was a deliberate act of desecration against the Christians has long been disputed by those who believe this emperor was not particularly ill-disposed towards what was still an obscure sect during his day. Nevertheless, the dedication to the pagan goddess of love and all the associated activities, including ritual prostitution, no doubt helped fix the place in the collective memory of the early Christian community.

According to John's gospel, the crucifixion occurred just outside the old city walls near a grave at Golgotha, traditionally known as the place of the skull.[8] (Golgotha is actually the Aramaic version in Greek letters of the Hebrew word *gûlgoleth,* which means skull. The Greek translation, *kranion,* was the inspiration for the Latin *calvaria*, or bald place, which gives us our traditional name for the site, Calvary.) Even before Hadrian's municipal reconstruction, Herod Agrippa had extended the circuit of the city to include the site. It was probably impractical for the early Christians to venerate the location, even if they were inclined to do so. The community appears to have shunned the site of the resurrection, congregating instead in a house of prayer on Mount Sion, outside even the expanded boundaries of the new Roman city. In an upper room of that building on the first Pentecost, the apostles were inspired by the Holy Spirit to go out and spread the word to the Gentiles. As the centre of gravity of the Christian world shifted to Rome, the remnants of the Jerusalem church perhaps also tried to look forwards and outwards, rather than backwards and inwards to remember ruins now rendered inaccessible by the conquerors.

The Bordeaux pilgrim confirmed the evidence of Eusebius by specifically noting that Constantine had commanded the construction of churches at the Holy Sepulchre, the Mount of Olives, and Bethlehem. 'On your left is the hillock Golgotha where the Lord was crucified, and about a stone's throw from it the vault wherein his body was laid and rose again on the third day,' he noted in his prosaic travel guide style. 'By order of the emperor Constantine there has now been built there a basilica – that is to say, a church of wondrous beauty – which has beside it reservoirs from which water is raised, and a bath behind where infants are washed.'[9] However, the pilgrim's tedious account of how he found scripture mapped out in the Holy Land in the year 333 had nothing to say either about the visit of Helena only five years' earlier, or the presence of any sacred relics like the wood of the cross. To sceptics, this omission casts fatal doubt on the legend that the empress-mother discovered the True Cross, as for that matter does the absence of any direct connection with Helena in the description of the relic being displayed given by the Spanish nun Egeria in 384. Neither of these two first-hand accounts of the burgeoning tourist trade, compiled within 50 years of each other, demonstrate more than passing awareness that Helena had travelled to the Holy Land at all.

They leave Eusebius looking rather exposed as the single original source for the whole story – and of course he never mentioned the discovery of the cross either. As Edward Gibbon put it, 'The silence of Eusebius and the Bordeaux pilgrim, which satisfies those who think, perplexes those who believe.'[10] The *Life of Constantine* was written several years after the Bordeaux pilgrim's visit, too. Reading it closely, there is an ambiguity in the way Eusebius said Helena dedicated two churches, at the grotto of Jesus' birth and the cave marking his ascension, yet described in detail the building of the Holy Sepulchre without any reference to her at all. Perhaps the crucial task of identifying the holy places and commemorating them in stone had started before she arrived, bearing the imperial purse to pay for it all?[11]

If so, she would have encountered in Jerusalem a major civil engineering programme which would never be allowed today. The aim was to isolate the central feature of Jesus' tomb, effectively removing it from its context by destroying the surrounding area, and organising around it a structure for worship. The plan was based on the assumption there would be visitors, and the imperial architect envisaged generous access, opportunities for refreshment, even the provision of shade, in a gradual ascent from the entrance in the Roman market place towards the shrine. 'He realised that he ought to display the most blessed place of the Saviour's resurrection in Jerusalem in a worthy and conspicuous manner,' said Eusebius.[12]

The task involved substantial excavation, not only razing the 'gloomy shrine of lifeless idols dedicated to the impure demon Aphrodite' but digging into the foundations of the temple to clear the rubble which Eusebius believed had been deliberately carted in to bury the site of the resurrection.The tomb was transformed from a cave in a slope into a free-standing structure, the exterior rock carved away into the resemblance of a small building with columns, henceforth known as the *edicule*, or little house. The entrance appeared as a small porch on the east side, and the whole probably resembled Absalom's tomb which one can still see today in the Kidron Valley: similar shapes were found embossed on the flasks in which pilgrims carried home quantities of holy oil.[13]

Bishop Cyril of Jerusalem, a young man at the time, recalled the original 'cleft in the rock' in his lectures in 348. 'You cannot see it now, because the outer cave has been hewn away for the sake of the present decoration, but before His Majesty zealously decorated the tomb there used to be a cave in the face of the rock,' he said.[14] The labour involved in literally cutting away the cliff meant it might not have been finished by time the church itself was dedicated in 335. The Bordeaux pilgrim's description of the vault near Golgotha two years' earlier implied the site was then still in the open air. At some stage the tomb was enclosed by a more elaborate rotunda, called the Anastasis, or place of resurrection, which dominated the western end of the complex by the time Egeria visited.

At some point also the mound of Golgotha was reshaped into a tall stump of rock, about 12 feet high, situated in the southeast corner of the colonnaded courtyard, with a chapel behind. Eusebius himself did not record this because his chief concern was the tomb, the 'holy of holies' which he believed was 'by its very existence bearing clearer testimony to the resurrection of the Saviour than any words.' Yet the site of the crucifixion, now renamed Calvary, was clearly a key feature for Egeria's generation, perhaps because it had become more important in the wake of the discovery of the remains of the cross.

Nevertheless, Eusebius was unstinting in his praise for the Martyrium, or place of witness, which faced the tomb across the open space. He quoted a letter Constantine wrote to Macarius, the Bishop of Jerusalem, in which the emperor ordered the construction of a basilica 'finer than any other.' The inner walls of this New Jerusalem were lined with polychrome marble panels, the exterior surface veneered with polished stones. The roof was of lead to protect against winter rains, but inside the ceiling was carved, coffered and gilded to make the church 'sparkle and shine.' The hemispherical apse at the western end was lined with 12 pillars rescued from the pagan temple, symbolising the apostles, their capitals adorned with silver bowls. The building was two storeys high, supported by double columns, with three large doors opening on to an atrium which adjoined the forum through 'a marvellously ornate entrance, which allowed a breathtaking view of the interior to those passing by.'[15]

‡

SO EXTENSIVE IS the description given by Eusebius of the building programme, that it would be only logical to conclude he would have mentioned the cross if it had been found. Recently some modern scholars have challenged this assumption and suggested that the wily church historian may not have been telling the whole truth.[16] They argue that while it is true that the *Life of Constantine* is silent on the subject, there are contradictory hints elsewhere in rival panegyrics; notably the oration delivered on the occasion of the emperor's 30th Jubilee in 336, and a further speech tagged on to the back of it in later compilations, known as *On Christ's Sepulchre*, which was probably given at the dedication of the Jerusalem basilica a year earlier. No one in their right mind would now want to read these ghastly specimens of pompous imperial verbiage for pleasure, but those who have undertaken close textual analysis of the original Greek point out that there is a subtle difference between what Constantine wanted to hear about himself while he was alive, and what Eusebius was prepared to say publicly about his patron after his death.

On their view, the gap is evidence of a disagreement between the emperor and his biographer about the theological significance of the cross. To Constantine, it was clearly a symbol of power with a military function, the 'saving sign' which had been revealed to him at the Milvian Bridge outside Rome and secured victory over his enemies. Yet as a bishop Eusebius would have been uneasy about the implications of such crude, muscular Christianity. While eager to idealise the first Christian emperor as the instrument of promulgating the unity of the church, he would not want to prejudice the purity of the faith that was behind it. As a result he never referred directly to the cross in all his writings, preferring curious codewords like 'trophy' or 'token' of the Passion or indeed phases like 'the saving sign' – just as if he was embarrassed by its very existence.

Take a key passage from the Jubilee oration hailing Constantine's construction activities, for example. 'In the Palestinian nation, in the heart of the Hebrew kingdom, on the very site of the evidence for salvation, he outfitted with many and abundant distinctions an enormous house of prayer and temple sacred to the saving sign,' declaimed Eusebius. 'And he honoured a memorial full of eternal significance and the Great Saviour's own trophies over death with ornaments beyond all description.'[17] Is there a reluctant reference to Golgotha here that Eusebius subsequently dropped from his descriptions of the Anastasis and Martyrium in the funeral oration, once the emperor himself was no longer listening? In the section immediately following he goes on to list the 'three mystical caves' recovered by Constantine in the region, which were revered with appropriate memorials marking the birth at Bethlehem, the ascension on the Mount of Olives, and 'between these, at the scene of the great struggle, signs of salvation and victory.' Are these 'signs' in fact a tacit admission of discoveries the author does not want to publicise?

I confess that on its own this argument seemed to be stretching a point. Yet it remains odd that Eusebius never mentioned the cross as such, and ingenious to suggest that the absence might have been a reflection of his adverse reaction to a contemporary discovery. It assumes that as an historian he would naturally have doubts about its authenticity, and as a theologian he would in any case believe the resurrection of Jesus to be more important than his death. The theory also suggests that as the Metropolitan of Palestine, Eusebius might have been anxious about the way in which Macarius, the bishop of Jerusalem, could use such a find – whether true or not – for his own episcopal ends.

The rivalry between the two is implicit in much of Eusebius' writings about events in Palestine, in which he frequently emphasises the significance of the region in general at the expense of the holy city in particular. While we look back on him as the father of church history and the confidant of the first Christian emperor, his position at the time was not so secure. As recently as

325 he had been provisionally excommunicated for holding Arian sympathies, on the recommendation of Constantine's chief adviser, Hosius of Cordoba. Although this proved only a temporary hiccup, and Eusebius was swiftly reinstated at the Council of Nicea later that year, the interval would have been enough to allow Macarius to obtain the ear of the emperor and obtain permission to raze the temple of Aphrodite in the first place.[18]

In the *Life of Constantine*, the emperor's decision to order the building of a church in Jerusalem comes right out of the blue. 'He judged it incumbent upon him to render the blessed locality of our Saviour's resurrection an object of attraction and veneration to all,' wrote Eusebius.[19] Just like that. Mind you, Eusebius himself already knew about the tradition locating the site of Jesus' death, since he had listed it in a Biblical gazetteer compiled a few years earlier, probably during the last decade of the previous century. 'Golgotha, the place of the skull where Christ was crucified: this is pointed out in Aelia to the north of Mount Sion,' he noted in the so-called *Onomasticon* of the Holy Land.[20] Yet subsequently in the *Life* Eusebius admitted some surprise at the results of the archaeology his patron had commissioned on the spot. 'As soon as the original surface of the ground, beneath the covering of earth, appeared, immediately, and contrary to all expectation, the venerable and hallowed monument of our Saviour's resurrection was discovered.'[21]

Eusebius made clear he was referring to the emergence of Jesus' tomb, which he regarded as 'clear and visible proof' of the resurrection. At this juncture in the narrative, however, he inserted a copy of the letter written by Constantine to Macarius with detailed instructions for commemorating the find. If genuine, this document represents not only the most contemporary evidence we have, but also one that gives expression to the personal views of the emperor at the time rather than as recalled by his biographer some years later. And within it, those who suspect that Eusbius has been hiding something from his readers see further evidence of his cunning inadvertently exposed, hailing as it does the 'miracle' which has brought to light 'a clear assurance of our Saviour's Passion' – in other words his suffering on the cross rather than his return from death.[22]

It is enough to make the revisionists wonder whether the word traditionally translated as 'monument' in this context, with all the implications that carries for us of a structure, is not better given as 'sign' or 'token' with all the ambiguity that carries for Eusebius. And that, in turn, gives a whole new meaning to the 'wondrous circumstance' which Constantine described in his own words as he gave Macarius free rein to hire all the craftsmen and labourers necessary in order to decorate 'the most marvellous place in the world' to a standard that exceeded any other city in the empire. How galling for Eusebius, who regarded Macarius as merely 'the bishop who presided over the church at Jerusalem' and barely condescended to mention him by name! Yet by including this letter, Eusebius could not disguise the enthusiasm exhibited by the emperor himself for the project, thereby offering a tantalising glimpse of the true nature of the discovery which Constantine believed had been granted him by the grace of the Saviour. For as he told Macarius: 'That the monument of his most holy Passion, so long ago buried beneath the ground, should have remained unknown for so long a series of years, until its reappearance to his servants . . . is a fact which truly surpasses all admiration.'[23]

☦

ON GOOD FRIDAY evening the Latin patriarch, Monsigneur Michel Sabbah, rehearsed the burial of Jesus in an official piece of play-acting, during which the altar on Calvary was demolished, and the pint-sized plaster body of a bleeding Christ taken down from the cross and wrapped in a shroud, to be anointed and borne off to the tomb. I secured a ringside view of the unction stone, perched on a temporary scaffolding put up to service the electric lamps. No one seemed bothered by my intrusion, and like earlier in the day there was no attempt to manage the crowd inside the church, which swirled around the Franciscans as they enacted their ritual under the clicking of camera shutters and flickering of flashbulbs. I felt sorry for those pilgrims who could be seen standing on the fringes, holding lighted candles as if they expected somehow to be part of the sound and light show. Unable to see over the heads of those nearer the action, they were forced into private meditation instead.

Father Enrique Bermejo, the friar in charge of liturgy, had earlier told me the pattern of Easter services was based as closely as possible on the fourth-century model. I had been introduced to him because I was asking questions about the Franciscans' own relic of the True Cross that no one else was able to answer. It had been brought out for the morning service, and put on display in a side chapel for a couple of hours while the friars walked the Via Dolorosa. Once again I was amazed at the ease with which I was allowed access, able to photograph the bejewelled reliquary from close up, and continue taking pictures while a couple of elderly women were given permission to kiss the artefact. I later discovered that the gold and silver-plated container, encrusted with 243 diamonds, 39 rubies, 20 amethysts, ten emeralds, four sapphires, one opal, a topaz and 700 pearls, was less than half a century old.[24] Without a better grasp of Spanish I could not extract as much information as I wanted about the history of its contents, but Fr Enrique assured me the practice of veneration was firmly based on the unique record provided by his countrywoman Egeria.

She described how on Good Friday morning in the year 384 a chair was placed on Golgotha, behind a table covered with a cloth. The priests brought out a gold and silver box, from which they lifted the wood of the cross, together with its title-plate identifying Jesus of Nazareth, King of the Jews, and laid it out before the bishop. Speaking Greek that was simultaneously translated by a presbyter into Aramaic for local consumption, he then invited the penitents to come forward. They were allowed to touch the sacred object with forehead, eyes or lips, but sternly injuncted to keep their hands off.

'As long as the holy wood is on the table, the bishop sits with his hands resting on either end of it and holds it down, and the deacons round him keep watch over it,' said Egeria.

'They guard it like this because what happens now is that all the people, catechumens as well as the faithful, come up one by one to the table. They stoop down over it, kiss the wood, and move on. But on one occasion (I don't know when) one of them bit off a piece of the holy wood and stole it away, and for this reason the deacons stand round and keep watch in case anyone dares to do the same again.'[25]

Egeria's account of her pilgrimage was only discovered in 1887, was for years wrongly attributed to Silvia of Aquitaine, and is unfortunately incomplete. Nevertheless, it exudes innocent enthusiasm for the way in which psalms and lessons are chosen to fit the time and the place. As our first witness to the liturgy used by the early Jerusalem church for ceremonies from Epiphany through to Pentecost, her description suggests worship was a full-time activity at the holy places, from first light to dusk. The Easter cycle was particularly intense, with eight weeks of fasting and daily instruction for baptismal candidates, culminating in an almost continuous replay of the Biblical events during the Great Week. On Palm Sunday the crowds would gather on the Mount of Olives for a procession into the city led by the bishop.

'All the people go before him with psalms and antiphons, all the time repeating "Blessed is he that cometh in the name of the Lord." The babies and the ones too young to walk are carried on their parents' shoulders. Everyone is carrying branches, either palm or olive, and they accompany the bishop in the way the people did when they once went down with the Lord. They go on foot but they have to go pretty gently, on account of the older women and men among them who might get tired.'

The most magnificent feast of all was the anniversary of the day back in 335 when Constantine's new basilica in Jerusalem was consecrated. Fifty years after that event, the so-called *encaenia* was linked to the discovery of the cross in a double celebration. 'So they arranged that this day should be observed with all possible joy by making the original dedication of these holy churches coincide with the very day when the cross had been found,' said Egeria. The Holy Sepulchre itself was resplendent in gold, mosaic and precious marble. Lamps burned day and night over Jesus' tomb for the occasion, while choirboys intoned the *Kyrie eleison*. Although signally failing to mention Helena in the context of the discovery of the cross, however, Egeria did attribute decorations 'too marvellous for words' to the feminine touch of the emperor's mother. 'All you can see is gold and jewels and silk: the hangings are entirely silk with gold stripes, the curtains the same, and everything they use for services at the festival is made of gold and jewels. You simply cannot imagine the number, and the sheer weight of candles and the tapers and the lamps and everything else they use for the services.'

‡

I SOUGHT A BREAK from the intensity of the Holy Sepulchre on Saturday, walking to the Mount of Olives overlooking the City in search of the 'stately structure' that Eusebius said Helena raised on the summit of the hill. The historian refers to the site as encompassing both a commemorative temple on the spot from whence Jesus ascended into heaven, and the original cave in the mountainside where he taught his disciples. The latter is marked today by the Eleona church, which is not a misprint for Helena but the Greek word for olives, and was first recorded in this context by Egeria. The Bordeaux pilgrim saw it, too, but the original building was destroyed by the Persians. Its modern successor, the Pater Noster church, reflects the unsubstantiated Crusader tradition that this was where Jesus taught his followers the Lord's Prayer, whose verses are now inscribed on the walls in (so far) 78 world languages. However, there is a cave dating back to the fourth century beneath the courtyard.

Luke, the only evangelist to mention the ascension, failed to give enough details to enable that site to be located by subsequent generations. In the Acts of the Apostles he said only that it took place 40 days after the resurrection about a Sabbath's day journey from the city.[26] A church was built a few hundred yards up the hill from the Eleona cave in 392 by one Poimenia, one of many female members of the imperial family to follow in Helena's footsteps. Nothing now remains of it, and the Crusader reconstruction was converted into a small mosque by Saladin in 1198. Since Islam regards Jesus as a prophet, the Moslems continued a tradition that venerated marks in the flagstones as his footprints, carting the left one off to the El Aqsa mosque on the Temple Mount. The remaining mark looks nothing like a footprint, let alone a right one, and the two surly Arab guardians demanded an entry fee to see it, which to my mind just about summed up the point where pilgrimage ended and tourism began. The unwelcome attentions of these particular ticket-sellers were underlined by a tatty notice posted on the wall by the gateway: 'Holy place – keep out.'

I made my way down to the viewpoint outside the Seven Arches Hotel where Jerusalem is spread about before you in all its glory, the sun glinting on the Dome of the Rock. Other pilgrims had the same idea, and I couldn't help overhearing. 'Those of you attending "New Life" meetings will know that we believe events in this land are connected with the return of Jesus Christ,' declared their leader. I surreptitiously asked him later what 'New Life' was, only to discover it was a Baptist group from Woking. The members had done the Holy Sepulchre but were sceptical of its historical claims, preferring the Protestant ethic of the Garden Tomb. So that afternoon I paid a return visit, more than five years after first being enticed by its charms, and found the volunteer guides sent out from England still doing brisk business to record crowds – but rather wary of preaching the exclusive message put out by their predecessors.

'We don't know whether Jesus died here or at the Holy Sepulchre, or where he died, that is not important: what matters is that we know he died for you and me,' said Tony Hyland, a florid-faced man in a Panama hat who looked as if he had stepped out of the cast-list at a church fete back home.

'When Queen Helena came and discovered what she thought was the tomb, they destroyed everything by building a church. Why did Helena want to establish these sites anyway, when they were not important to the early Christians? The key thing is that when the disciples entered the tomb that Easter morning it was empty. He had risen! We can all say Hallelujah to that.'

The subtle change of tone, from the ever-so-slightly-patronising superiority about the Protestant claims I encountered on my previous visit, to almost unashamed agnosticism now about the rival Catholic tradition, appeared to reflect a reluctant acceptance of archaeological orthodoxy. For it is now generally agreed that General Gordon's enthusiasm to find an alternative site for the crucifixion in 1883 was based on a fundamental flaw. Carried away by the gospel hints that Jesus was put to death outside the city, he failed to appreciate that the walls which stood at the beginning of the first century ran on rather different lines to the impressive fortifications put up 1,500 years later by the Ottoman sultan Suleyman the Magnificent, and which still stand today.

In fact the Romans under Herod Agrippa I expanded the city defences about a decade after Jesus' death, effectively enclosing the Golgotha district and its old tombs within the ramparts. Although these walls were themselves razed to the ground after the Jewish revolt, their plan formed the basis for Hadrian's new city, Aelia Capitolina, and the later Muslim conquerors followed much the same layout.[27] Nowadays modern visitors can climb Suleyman's magnificent construction to look out across a busy thoroughfare at Skull Hill, half-hidden by the Arab bus station of East Jerusalem, but the death's head that General Gordon saw so vividly in the stony outcrop opposite is difficult to pick out today. Comparisons with 19th-century photographs show it has become the victim of erosion and pollution, a process so rapid and cumulative over the last century that one is forced to wonder whether 2,000 years ago the knoll would have looked anything like the shape of a skull at all. Significantly, the old pictures are played down in the latest glossily-produced guidebook to the renamed 'Resurrection Garden', which skates carefully round the whole controversy, referring instead to the qualities of 'this special place' as simply a 'reminder' of the risen Saviour in a harsh, uncaring world. The many tourists who each year regard their visit to the garden as the spiritual high-point of their time in Israel, it says, love the sacredness of this quiet spot as lives are changed and faith renewed.[28]

More than 1,500 people turned up at the Garden Tomb for a sunrise service that Easter Sunday. I was taken aback by the numbers, but also put off by their behaviour. The queue that wound patiently round the block lost its inhibitions once it had filed inside, and personally I found the happy-clappy atmosphere cloying. All those self-conscious yet apparently spontaneous 'Alleluias!' being exchanged between participants grated on my nerves. I recalled reading somewhere that although the Hebrew shout of *hallelujah* literally meant 'praise the Lord', it was also akin to the ululation uttered by Moslem women at times of great emotion. Like the survival of Amen, from the Hebrew exclamation 'so be it', such anachronistic acclamations struck a jarring note in the mouths of Western pilgrims. I felt far more of an outsider among those of my own kind than I ever had among the exotic otherness of the inhabitants at the Holy Sepulchre. The experience was made more uncomfortable by the sight of a tubby middle-aged steward in an old-fashioned blue blazer and tie jiving to Chuck King and his Worship Choir. Not to mention the embarrassingly unrestrained activities of two women repeatedly hugging, kissing and caressing each other on a park bench in a display of religious ecstasy that bordered on exhibitionism. In protest against the Protestants, I gratefully returned to the smells and bells of the traditional ceremonies.

‡

THE AIR IN the Holy Sepulchre was already thick with incense and a cacophony of competing sounds from an event that must rate as the original multi-media festival. The Copts, clothed in bright white robes with golden sashes, set the tone with an eerie wailing round the back of Jesus' tomb. The monument once aptly described as a 'hideous kiosk' was built after the great fire of 1808 destroyed the previous edifice; itself erected in the 11th century after the Constantinian rock-tomb was destroyed by Caliph Hakim. A section of the fourth-century original is visible at the base of the Coptic shrine at the rear, though inside the tiny chamber itself an altar slab conveniently covers what is left of the rubble. The interior is disappointing because there is nothing to see except a few candles and bunches of flowers in a cupboard you have to crouch to get inside. Pilgrims place religious objects to be blessed by contact through several inches of red marble, beneath a wall adorned by three depictions of the resurrection which only proved that Latins, Greeks and Armenians possessed equally poor taste in kitsch.

There was no chance of even a glimpse inside the *edicule* that morning. In front of the entrance, the purple-clad Catholic pontiff presided over High Mass to the accompaniment of swirling organ chords that reached a crescendo with the ethereal sound of the Agnus Dei. 'They think the Lamb of God is dead, so they are trying to make him hear more,' quipped a grinning Mr Nuseibeh in passing, before scurrying off to co-ordinate the imminent arrival of the Syrians.

Each denomination was ushered in by a posse of guards, the *kuwass*, in Ottoman costumes of red fez, gold-embroidered waistcoat and baggy blue trousers, their authority signified by banging heavy silver-tipped staves on the ground. The Syrian Orthodox contingent carried giant palm-leaves over their shoulders on their way to mark the start of Holy Week with a service in their private chapel. The Armenians in their black cowls had already turned up, and were trying to raise the roof by chanting in an upper gallery they had made their own. But the most melodramatic entrance of all was heralded by the deep booming of bass bells as the Greek bishop, Jacobus, headed a delegation of black-bearded monks. Every inch of the Katholicon, the Greek choir of the Crusader church, was already jam packed with Palm Sunday worshippers who had been patiently waiting for their priests.

I scurried from one spectacle to another, absorbed and entranced by the infinite variety brought together in one place. There were still others indulging their own rites elsewhere in the complex. A wraith of ebony Ethiopian women wrapped in thin white sheets stood silently for hours in a side-chapel leading to the roof, praying until it was time for their own ritual. Over the years the Ethiopian colony was gradually forced out of the main building into huts on the roof, but they retain some of the most colourful of all the ceremonies. Little girls in white chiffon dresses edged with green, yellow and red stripes scampered across the flagstones while the grizzled patriarch, swathed in a white gown embroidered with gold crosses, and shaded from the sun by a stately blue palanquin, heard readings from the scriptures as he slowly led a motley procession three times round the dome which allowed light into St Helena's chapel below.

On the stairs leading down from the Armenian gallery I found a refuge to escape the press of the crowds that also gave a clear view of the front of the tomb, between two huge pillars. Despite – or perhaps because of – the sweet smoky haze, my vantage-point offered an unexpected moment of illumination – the realisation that perhaps Constantine had been quite sensible after all to construct buildings to protect these holy places.

Maybe he guessed that once unleashed, the magnetic power which first drew him to unmask the physical sites where Christianity began also held within it the potential for their destruction. Put such places on a metaphorical pedestal and you make them vulnerable to the human need to kiss relics, touch stones, bless water, or even snatch a lump of rock to take home with them as a memento of a unique experience. Quietly, I gave thanks to Helena for her part in trying to preserve something for posterity out of the process her pilgrimage had set in train. And I thanked her also for inspiring me to undertake a voyage of discovery that had culminated in the greatest free show on earth. I believed no more than when I started out, but felt I understood a little better.

That a holy relic called the True Cross existed in Jerusalem in the latter half of the fourth century seemed indisputable, whether or not it was genuine, and whether or not pieces have survived to this day. Helena was not credited with its discovery until some years later, but oddly, neither was anyone else in the meantime. The more I reflected on what I had learned, the more that silence appeared suspicious. Surely the recovery of such a significant religious artefact would have been trumpeted from the rooftops of Christendom? Unless, that is, there was something dodgy about its provenance from the start, and all the characters in my quest were implicated.

Eusebius appeared to acknowledge that something happened during the excavations for Constantine's ambitious building programme in the Holy Land but was reluctant to admit to it in public – perhaps out of envy of his episcopal rival, Macarius, whose idea it might have been to undertake some creative digging. The bishop of Jerusalem has kept a low profile in history, and little is known about him aside from his receipt of Constantine's letter authorising the construction of the Holy Sepulchre. However, the role attributed to him a century later, in the legend of the finding of the cross popularised by Rufinus, may reflect a folk memory of his importance in events at the time. Was Macarius deliberately written out of the script because Eusebius disapproved of his unscrupulous methods?

Undoubtedly there was a powerful motive for the early church to invent a tradition in which the True Cross was revealed, as proof positive of the historical fact of the crucifixion in the face of the challenge presented by popular Gnostic and heretical interpretations of scripture. The success of the Helena legend in succeeding centuries demonstrated its value as a propaganda instrument for disseminating orthodoxy. Yet ironically Helena herself may have had only an incidental role in the drama, her arrival in the Holy Land with the imperial train providing a convenient cover story for an ecclesiastical confidence trick that embarrassed contemporaries but was subsequently extremely successful.

All we can be certain about is that we will never know for certain, I thought, gazing down on the communion of celebrants, choristers, and congregation gathered outside the tomb of Jesus. The concealed contents represented the only tangible link back to that far-off time. As the Latins concluded their rites with a rousing chorus and tried to depart, the Greeks emerged from the Katholicon and began trundling in the other direction, intent on circling three times round the tomb behind a gold cross in a forest of burgundy banners. The impending clash of ecclesiastical cultures had the makings of an almighty traffic jam, as if that unholy encounter I witnessed between Franciscan friar and Orthodox monk at Jesus' birthplace on Christmas Day, which set me on my journey five years earlier, had now come full circle on Easter Sunday in a splendid inter-denominational confrontation right outside his last earthly resting-place. In the confusion it was time to make my excuses and leave. Exhausted yet exhilarated, I stumbled out through the seething mass of humanity into the mid-day sun. And then the first tourists started coming in.

Notes

Prologue: Bethlehem

1 Mark 8.34.
2 See *Israel and the Palestinian Territories – a travel survival kit*, Lonely Planet 1996. This and other LP guidebooks provided an invaluable starting point for my researches in the field. Paschal Baldi, *The Question of the Holy Places*, Rome 1918, puts a Franciscan perspective on the centuries-old rivalry with the Greeks.
3 Mgr Michel Sabbah presided at the Christmas Day service in 1992 and was still in post at Easter 1998. Some of the descriptions in this chapter first appeared in a travel article, 'A Time of Bedlam in Bethlehem', in *The Daily Telegraph*, 24th December 1994.
4 Quoted in E D Hunt, *Holy Land Pilgrimage in the Later Roman Empire* AD *312–460*, Oxford 1982.
5 Robin Lane Fox, *The Unauthorized Version: Truth and Fiction in the Bible*, London 1991.
6 Matthew 2.1.
7 Luke 2.1.
8 Matthew 2.5–6.
9 Fr Jerome Murphy-O'Connor, *The Holy Land: an Archaelogical Guide from Earliest Times to 1700*, Oxford 1980.
10 The nativity of Jesus is celebrated in the Orthodox churches on January 6th, the festival of Epiphany that is traditionally associated in the West with the baptism of Jesus. The Eastern Orthodox split with the Roman Catholics in 1054 and still use the Julian calendar (introduced by Julius Caesar) rather than the reformed version proclaimed by Pope Gregory XIII in 1582.
11 From Hunt, see note 4.
12 Quoted in Wendy Pullan, 'Mapping Time and Salvation: Early Christian Pilgrimage to Jerusalem', in G D Flood (ed), *Mapping Invisible Worlds*, Edinburgh 1993.
13 From an anonymous *Life of Constantine* that is one of several extant versions of the original guide by Epiphanius the Monk, *The Breviarius, or short account of the Holy City*. 'It provides us with the earliest known statement of the belief, still stoutly maintained by many local Christians in the Holy Land, that St Helena was personally responsible for building almost all the churches in the

country.' John Wilkinson, *Jerusalem Pilgrims before the Crusades*, Warminster 1977.

14 The fallacy that Helena not only founded the Church of the Annunciation in Nazareth, but also the Basilica of the Young Jesus on the site of the family home and the Church of St Joseph over the remains of his earthly father's carpentry workshop, is perpetuated in Graham Phillips, *The Marian Conspiracy*, London 2000.

15 Steven Runciman, *A History of the Crusades*, Cambridge 1951.

16 Naomi Shepherd, *The Zealous Intruders – The Western Rediscovery of Palestine*, London 1987.

17 Quoted in Lane Fox, see note 5.

18 This is probably a local confusion with Egeria, the Spanish nun, who visited Sinai as part of her pilgrimage to the Holy Land in 381–4. Epiphanius the Monk also included it in his itineray. See John Wilkinson, *Egeria's Travels*, SPCK 1971.

Chapter I: St Helens

1 William Cowper Prime, *A History of the Invention, Preservation and Disappearance of the wood known as the True Cross*, London 1877.

2 St Helens Metropolitan Council Official Guide. I visited on Thursday 20th July 1995.

3 May 21st is the joint feast day of Constantine and Helen in the Orthodox calendar.

4 Tom Henderson, *A Short History of St Helens Parish*, St Helens, 1976. J F Giblin, *The Churches of St Helens – A Brief Historical and Architectural Note*, St Helens 1995.

5 Martin Hengel, *Crucifixion in the Ancient World*, SCM Press 1977; see also Paul Vallely, 'Why we cling to the cross', *Independent on Sunday*, 5th April 1995.

6 Deuteronomy 21.22–23. 'If a man have committed a sin worthy of death, and be put to death, and thou hang him on a tree: his body shall not remain all night upon the tree, but thou shalt surely bury him the same day: for he that is hanged is accursed of God: that thou defile not the land which the Lord thy God giveth thee for an inheritance.' This book of the Old Testament also contains Moses' account of the Ten Commandments and the Ark of the Covenant.

7 Josephus, *The Jewish War*, trans G A Williamson, Penguin 1959.

8 Hengel, see note 5.

9 Hengel, see note 5.

Chapter II: The Invention of the Cross

1 J H Newman, *Essay on Miracles*, Oxford 1842.

2 *Catholic Encyclopaedia*, Appleton, New York 1907, entry on Bollandists. The older editions of this multi-volume encyclopaedia are a mine of fascinating and

colourful snippets about what Roman Catholicism used to be about, though the modern version is pale and pruned by comparison.

3 Veronica's veil: official showings of this holy relic are recorded as recently as 1933 and 1950, but no photograph of it exists, its precise location remains a secret, and much doubt surrounds what (if anything) is actually displayed. See also Chapter VII, note 15 and Epilogue, note 6.

4 *Catholic Encyclopaedia* (note 2), entry on relics. The author of this entry, Fr Herbert Thurston, said: 'Neither has the Church ever pronounced that any particular relic, not even that venerated as the wood of the Cross, is authentic.'

5 Eusebius, *The History of the Church*, trans G A Wilkinson, Penguin 1965. Eusebius, bishop of Caesarea in Palestine, is known as the father of Church history. He was trained by the scholar Pamphilius, and took his mentor's name after he was martyred in the Diocletian persecution, so he was known as Eusebius Phamphilii. The *History* includes verbatim chunks of earlier works by other authors, often no longer extant. One such is the description of Polycarp's martyrdom in Book 4, chapter 15, taken from a newsletter sent out by his local church.

6 Fr Herbert Thurston, article in the Jesuit magazine *The Month*, May 1930.

7 Robert de Clari, The Conquest of Constantinople, trans E H McNeal, New York 1936.

8 Canon Law 1983.

9 Telephone conversation with Fr Patrick Casserly. The legend of the relics of Jesus' circumcision comes from a second-century document known as *The First Gospel of the Infancy of Christ*. It relates how an old Hebrew midwife took the foreskin and preserved it in an alabaster box containing old oil of spikenard. See *The Lost Books of the Bible*, Testament Books, New York 1926 (reprint 1979).

10 T J Willcock, *The Church of Holy Cross and St Helens centenary*, St Helens 1962. Anon, *A walk around Lowe House church*, 1993. Fr Reginald Riley, *St Mary's, Lowe House*, St Helens 1940.

11 Private correspondence with Fr F J Turner, 27th June 1996.

12 Fr John Morris, article in *The Month*, March 1882.

13 Mgr Charles Rohault de Fleury, *Memoire sur les Instruments de la Passion*, Paris 1870.

14 The Rev James Bellord, *Relics of the True Cross*, Catholic Truth Society 1898. The relic at Slindon is kept at the back of a filing cabinet in the vestry and the parish authorities are unsure what to make of it, I discovered on a visit to the Sussex village. The three-inch sliver housed in a pewter reliquary was part of a hoard of religious artefacts retrieved from the big house opposite St Richard's Church, the most revered item of which is now in the Arundel museum – the cope of Cardinal Morton, Henry VIII's Chancellor.

15 *ΙΧΘΥΣ – Iesos Christus Theou Yios Soster*. See Henry Chadwick, *The Early Church*, Penguin 1967.

16 Quoted in *Catholic Encyclopaedia* (note 2), entry on the cross.

17 Quoted in Wilkinson, *Egeria's Travels*, see Prologue, note 18.

18 Paulinus of Nola, letter 31 to Sulpicius Severus. Ancient Christian Writers

series no 35, trans P G Walsh, London 1967. Paulinus lived at the monastery he founded between 395 and 431 but this letter was probably written around 402.

19 Eusebius of Caesarea, *The Life of Constantine the Great*, in *Select Library of the Nicene and post-Nicene Fathers of the Christian Church*, New Series Vol I, ed Henry Wace and Philip Schaff, Oxford and New York 1890. Ironically we know little about Eusebius' own life, apart from the fact he was a prolific author. Though he portrayed himself as the confidant of Constantine, he first came to prominence as one of those condemned for Arian tendencies in the run-up to the Council of Nicea. After encountering Constantine at this gathering, he had second thoughts and emerged from the controversy as an upholder of the orthodox majority. As a major source for the setting of the Helena story, Eusebius should not be confused with Eusebius of Nicomedia, another contemporary bishop with Arian sympathies, who was a pupil of the martyr Lucian.

20 Ambrose of Milan, *Oration on the death of Theodosius*, in *Select Library of the Nicene Fathers*, Vol X, 1896.

21 Helena is regarded as the patron saint of nailsmiths and needlemakers. Mary Sharp, *Saints in Europe*, 1964.

22 Quoted in Paul Johnson, *A History of Christianity*, London 1976.

23 Jan Willem Drivjers, *Helena Augusta*, Leiden and New York 1992, is the most comprehensive and scholarly modern account of Helena's life and times. He dismisses the story of the cross as historical fiction on the basis that it emerged 50 years after Helena's death. This traditional Protestant view is challenged from a Catholic perspective by Stephan Borgehammer, *How the Holy Cross was found: from event to mediaeval legend*, Bibliotheca Theologicae Practicae 47, Uppsala 1991. He attempts to reconstruct the missing history of Gelasius on the basis that an oral account was probably circulating decades before it was written down.

24 *Catholic Encyclopaedia* (note 2), entry on the cross.

25 The first Vatican Council in 1869 proclaimed the infallibility of the Pope.

Chapter III: The English Connection

1 Bede, *Ecclesiastical History of the English Nation*, trans A M Sellar, London 1917.

2 Cynewulf, 'Elene' and 'The Dream of the Rood', in *Anglo-Saxon Poetry*, trans R K Gordon, Everyman 1926.

3 Drivjers, see Chapter II, note 23.

4 Bede, see note 1.

5 Mrs Jameson, *Legends of the Monastic Orders*, London 1863. The author believed Helena's remains were carried off from Rome in 863 and deposited in the Benedictine abbey of Hautvillers in France. See also Clemens Jöckle, *Encyclopaedia of Saints*, 1995.

6 One of the earliest dedications to St Helen was a Saxon nunnery in Abingdon. No traces remain of the original seventh-century church, but its 14th-century successor became famous for the painted ceiling of its Lady Chapel. Meanwhile the parish church of Ashton-under-Lyne, near Manchester, has four celebrated

15th-century stained glass windows commemorating episodes in Helena's life, from her birth to Cole to her building of the Holy Sepulchre in Jerusalem. Featured in E Tasker, *Encyclopaedia of Mediaeval Church Art*, 1993.

7 Evelyn Waugh, *Helena*, London 1950.

8 John Giblin has researched and written extensively about the Catholic families of the North-West and the history of the churches in the St Helens area. We met on 9th October 1995.

9 The first mention of Old King Cole occurred in a humourous article on *The Art of Writing Unintelligibly*, in which the author took up a challenge to write a poem that would confound the critics. His chosen subject matter was sourced to the alleged poet laureate to the mythical British king Lud – 'this was the prince who built Colchester, whose real name was Coil,' he explained.

> Good King Cole
> And he called for his bowle
> And he called for his fiddlers three;
> And there was fiddle-fiddle
> And twice fiddle-fiddle
> For 'twas my Lady's birth-day
> Therefore we keep holy day
> And come to be merry.

From the magazine, *Useful Transactions in Philosophy and Other Learning*, Jan/Feb 1709.

10 William Camden, *Brittania*, 2nd edition 1806. While Chlorus served in Britain 'he married Helena, daughter of Coel or Caelius, a petty prince of Britain, and by her had Constantine the Great, born in Britain.'

11 The Rev Alban Butler, *The Lives of the Fathers, Martyrs and other Principal Saints*, London 1847.

12 *The Town Hall, Colchester*, Colchester Borough Council & Jarrolds Publishing, 1997. See also *Colchester Castle Museum Souvenir Guide* and *Colchester, a Jarrold Guide to Britain's Oldest Recorded Town.*

13 Henry of Huntingdon, *Chronicle*, trans Thomas Forrester, 1853.

14 The Rev Isaac Taylor, *Words and Places*, London 1864.

15 Louis de Ludwig von Wohl, *St Helena and the True Cross*, New York 1958, assumed Helena was the daughter of Cole of the Trinovantes. 'There is no doubt she was one of the greatest women of all time.' His work is a fictional account for children with a religious slant.

16 Edward Gibbon, *The History of the Decline and Fall of the Roman Empire*, 1776–88 (Folio Society, London 1983). The references to Helena and the story of the cross are relegated to footnotes in the grand sweep of imperial events.

17 Geoffrey of Monmouth, *The History of the Kings of Britain*, translated with an introduction by Lewis Thorpe, Penguin 1966.

18 Quoted by Thorpe, see note 17.

19 Geoffrey of Monmouth, see note 17.

20 James Tatlock, *The Legendary History of Britain*, Berkeley 1950.

21 Lane Fox, see Prologue, note 5.

22 See S T R O d'Ardenne, 'The Old English Inscription on the Brussels Cross', in *English Studies* vol 21 no 4, 1939.

Chapter IV: The British Emperor

1 Thomas Babington Macaulay, *History of England*, London 1873.
2 Frances Arnold Forster, *Studies in Church Dedications: England's Patron Saints*, 1899.
3 Eutropius, *The Abridgement of Roman History*, Liverpool 1993.
4 See Shephard Frere, *Brittania*, London 1967. Also Geoffrey Ashe, *The Quest for Arthur's Britain*, London 1971. In putting down the rebellion of Marcus Aurelius Carausius and re-establishing Roman rule, Constantius Chlorus ironically set the stage for the powerful idea that was to be attached to first to his son Constantine (and later to Arthur) of a Romanised, Christianised and independent Britain existing before the arrival of the barbarian pagans from northern Europe.
5 Richard of Cirencester, 'On the Ancient State of Britain', in *Six Old English Chronicles*, trans J A Giles, London 1848. This volume also contains a version of Geoffrey of Monmouth's *History*, and the works of Gildas and Nennius.
6 Gibbon, see Chapter III, note 16.
7 Thorpe, see Chapter III, note 17.
8 This was established by Acton Griscom in 1929 when he produced the first authoritative Latin version of the *History* alongside a Welsh translation.
9 See William F Skene, *The Four Ancient Books of Wales*, Edinburgh 1868.
10 Thorpe (Chapter III, note 17) explores four theories about Geoffrey's source: that the source-book was genuine but has disappeared; that evidence of its existence can be traced back through Old Welsh documents; that the source was actually oral tradition; or that Geoffrey fell for a hoax. He concluded, 'We are free to accept any of these theories, to attempt a combination of two or more of them, to try to discover some intermediary position between some pair of them, or indeed to reject them all.'
11 Skene, see note 9.
12 Chris Barber and David Pykitt, *Journey to Avalon*, Abergavenny 1993.
13 *Roman Life at the Yorkshire Museum*, York 1985.
14 Francis Drake, *Antiquities of York*, London 1736.
15 *Walking the Walls, A Tourist Guide*, York 1994.
16 Quoted in the Rev Sabine Baring-Gould, *Lives of the Saints*, London 1896.
17 Winifred Joy Mulligan, 'The British Constantine – an English historical myth', in *Journal of Mediaeval and Renaissance Studies* 8, 1978.

Chapter V: The Welsh Princess

1 Giraldus Cambrensis, *The Description of Wales*, 1194, trans Lewis Thorpe, Penguin 1978.

2 Tomen-y-mur means 'mound on the wall.'
3 Helen Livingston, *In the Footsteps of Caesar: walking Roman Roads in Britain*, Shepperton 1995. See also Ivan D Margary, *Roman Roads in Britain*, London 1995 and David E Johnston, *Discovering Roman Britain*, Shire 1983.
4 Camden (Chapter III, note 10) said 'it is reasonable to suppose that they were made by Helena, mother of Constantine the Great, whose works were many and magnificent over the Roman Empire.'
5 M Maples, *Sarn Helen*, Welsh Outlook Press 1939.
6 *The Mabinogion*, trans Gwyn Jones and Thomas Jones, Everyman 1974.
7 Baring-Gould, see Chapter IV, note 16. Also S Baring-Gould, *Curious Myths of the Middle Ages*, London 1897, and S Baring-Gould and J Fisher, *Lives of the British Saints*, London 1907–13.
8 Geoffrey of Monmouth, see Chapter III, note 17.
9 See Gwyn Alf Williams, *When was Wales?* Penguin 1985.
10 Gildas ap Caw, 'Concerning the Ruin and Conquest of Britain', in Giles, see Chapter IV, note 5.
11 Gildas was educated at the monastery of Llaniltyd Fawr in south Wales but emigrated to Rhuys in Armorica (Brittany) and wrote a book of lamentations about his exile in about 546.
12 On deals, see Lesley Alcock, *Arthur's Britain*, Penguin 1971; on dragons see Barber and Pykitt (Chapter IV, note 12).
13 Nennius, a disciple of Elfod, Bishop of Bangor, gave the first recorded mention of King Arthur. His *History of the Britons* opens: 'I bore about with me an inward wound, and I was indignant, that the name of my own people – formerly famous and distinguished – should sink into oblivion and like smoke be dissipated.' See Giles, see Chapter IV, note 5.
14 John Morris, *The Age of Arthur – A History of the British Isles from 350 to 650*. London 1993. Also Ashe, see Chapter IV, note 4, and Alcock, see note 12.
15 Zosimus, *New History*, quoted in Morris, see note 14.
16 Nennius, see note 13. Caer Segont was the Welsh version of Segontium, as the Romans knew Caernarfon. According to Matthew of Westminster, when Edward I captured the town in 1283 he found the remains of 'that great prince, the father of the noble emperor Constantine.' See Jennifer Westwood, *Albion, a guide to legendary Britain*, London 1985.
17 Barber and Pykitt, see Chapter IV, note 12.
18 See Arthur Wade-Evans, *Vitae Santorum Britanniae et Genealogiae*, Cardiff 1944. He points out that 'Britannia' was to Welsh writers of Latin in Norman times what we now call Wales.
19 Quoted in *Archaeologia Cambrensis*, Cardiff 1846.
20 Quoted in Rachel Bromwich, *The Welsh Triads*, Cardiff 1961.
21 Quoted in Barber and Pykitt, see Chapter IV, note 12.
22 See Gwyn Alf Williams (note 9).
23 See Taylor (Chapter III, note 14).
24 The best-preserved northern stretch of the Sarn Helen is marked on the Ordnance Survey landranger map 124 between SH727318 and SH722337.
25 Members of the Cambrian Archaeological Association published their researches

and speculations annually in the *Archaeologia Cambrensis*. Contributors to these volumes all took the Helena legend seriously, with some believing that she brought relics from her travels in Palestine to Segontium. In 1867 one J G Williams wrote in to ask: 'Can you or any of your correspondents inform me of the strength of the escort which accompanied the Empress Helena when en route from Llanio in Cardiganshire to the Emperor at Tomen-y-Mur? And if she visited any of the chieftains, or avoided them?'

26 Prof John Rhys, the first serious student of Celtic mythology, claimed Elen was not only daughter of Cole but wife of Merlin (Myrddin) and the prototype of Elaine, daughter of Pelles, in the Arthurian romances. See *The Origin and Growth of Religion as illustrated by Celtic Heathendom*, London 1888.
27 *Dolwyddelan Castle*, Cadw: Welsh Historic Monuments, Cardiff 1994.
28 J R Green, *A Short History of the English People*, London 1907.
29 Quoted in Westwood, see note 16.
30 M E James, Catholic Truth Society 1901.
31 Cited in *Archaelogica Cambrensis*, 1846. See also the 1848 and 1877 editions.
32 Edward Wedlake Brayley, *History and Antiquities of the Abbey Church of St Peter*, Westminster 1818.
33 *The Inventories of St George's Chapel, Windsor Castle, 1384–1667*, edited by Maurice Bond, Windsor 1945.
34 Guide to *St George's Chapel, Windsor Castle*, Jarrolds Publishing 1993.
35 Quoted in Brayley, see note 32.
36 See Tatlock (Chapter III, note 20).
37 See Barber and Pykitt (Chapter IV, note 12).
38 See Morris (note 14).
39 According to Skene (Chapter IV, note 9), Aneurin wrote 'popular poetry recording the resistance to the Picts and Scots under a native guledig in an area which had been the most sensitive outpost of empire.' The Manau Gododdin was a Cymric kingdom south of the Firth of Forth, in what is now the Lothian district.
40 A verse in the *Scots Musical Museum* 1797. Quoted in Charles Kightly, *Folk Heroes of Britain*, London 1982.
41 Local tradition is preserved in the placename of Coylton, near Ayr. The story is first cited by Hector Boece in his *History of the Scots from the Origins of the Race*, written in the 1520s. See also Westwood (note 16).
42 The word *cymru* first appeared in the history of Cumbria, and was gradually adopted by Welsh writers as a substitute for Brython, the original term for the ancient Britons. In later Welsh law, a *cymro* was a free man. John E Lloyd, *History of Wales*, London 1911.

Chapter VI: Trier

1 *Catholic Encyclopaedia*, see Chapter II, note 2.
2 See David Jones, 'Magnus Maximus at Trier' *History Today* 18.
3 Sulpicius Severus, dialogue II,6, in *Select Library of the Nicene Fathers*, Vol XI, 1894.

4 Ambrose of Milan, letter no 24 to Valentinian, in *Select Library of the Nicene Fathers*, Vol X, 1896.

5 See Chapter II, note 18.

6 Gwyn Alf Williams (Chapter V, note 9) argues that the legend of Macsen was manufactured in the ninth century by royal genealogists in the service of Rhodri Mawr, grandson of Hywel Dda and his successor as High King of Wales. 'Wales is born in 383 with Macsen Wledig.'

7 See 'The Story of Constantine and Elene' in M I Ebbutt, *Myths and Legends of the British*, 1910.

8 See the invaluable recent biography by Michael Grant, *The Emperor Constantine*, London 1993. Also John Parry, 'Geoffrey of Monmouth and the paternity of Arthur', in *Speculum – a journal of Mediaeval Studies*, 1938.

9 Drivjers (Chapter II, note 23) concluded that Helena was born in 248, and was working at an inn somewhere in Bithynia when she met Chlorus in 270.

10 *Fronleichnam* is the festival of Corpus Christi, which celebrates the peculiarly Catholic belief in the real presence of the body of Jesus in the sacrament of the eucharist. It follows the great post-Easter festivals of Ascension Day, Pentecost (Whitsun) and Trinity, usually falling the Thursday after Trinity Sunday, and thus conveniently in early summer. The tradition was started in the 13th century and became very popular in the mediaeval period, being the occasion for processions, pageants and mystery plays. However, the feast was dropped by the Protestant churches when they rejected the doctrine of transubstantiation, that Christ's body and blood was literally manifest in the bread and wine of the communion ceremony. The descriptions in this chapter first appeared in a travel article, 'Saintly Place with a Head in the Crypt', in *The Daily Telegraph*, 17th January 1998.

11 See the guides to the Porta Nigra, Barbara Baths, Amphitheatre and Imperial Baths published by the Verwaltung der Staatlichen Schlösse Rheinland-Pfalz (Administration of the Castles of the State of Rhineland-Palatinate), Mainz 1995.

12 *Reheinisches Landesmuseum Trier: introduction to the collections*. Trier 1994.

13 Constantine was a prolific builder but, apart from what can be seen at Trier, all his churches have either fallen down through shoddy workmanship or been swamped by the efforts of later emperors. See Grant (note 8). The palace at Trier was begun around 306 and mentioned by a panegyrist in 310; the surviving throne-room (or Aula Palatina) is known locally as the Basilika. However, this secular building is not to be confused with the remains of the double-basilica which was Constantine's church, on the site of the current cathedral, whose construction is dated locally to 326. *A Tour through Trier*, Verkehrsamt der Stadt Trier, 1990.

14 John 19.23.

15 Exodus 20.4.

16 Chadwick, see Chapter II, note 15. The story comes from Eusebius' funeral oration, *In Praise of Constantine*. Constantia, the emperor's half-sister, was wife of his arch-enemy Licinius; although her marriage failed to end the rivalry, she was credited with negotiating a temporary reprieve for her husband after his military defeat in 324. See Grant (note 8).

17 *Catholic Encyclopaedia* (Chapter II, note 1), entry on cross.
18 *Constantinian ceiling paintings from a Roman palace under the Cathedral at Trier*, Bischöfliches Dom und Diözesanmuseum Trier (museumsführer Nr 2), 1986.
19 *Das Münzkabinett im Rheinischen Landesmuseum Trier*, 1996.
20 Quoted by Grant, see note 8.
21 Zosimus, *New History*, trans Ronald Ripley, Canberra 1982.
22 Drivjers (Chapter II, note 23) suggests that the younger Helena came from Trier.

Chapter VII: Rome

1 Master Gregorius, *Mirabilia Urbis Romae – The Marvels of Rome*, 1375, trans Francis Nichols, London 1889.
2 Eusebius, *Life*, I. 30.
3 Quoted in Diana Bowder, *The Age of Constantine and Julian*, London 1978.
4 Another version claims she converted to Christanity around the age of 60, after the battle of Milvian Bridge: see Alison Jones, *The Wordsworth Dictionary of Saints*, 1994. There was also a healthy tradition that Helena was Jewish – a tale put about by the fifth-century *Acts of Sylvester*. This tells how the pagan Constantine was afflicted with leprosy for persecuting Christians but was cured by converting; Helena wrote to congratulate him on his recovery but express disappointment he had not embraced Judaism. Accordingly Constantine organised an intra-faith debate which Pope Sylvester won, prompting Helena to convert too. Drivjers (Chapter II, note 23) speculates that the idea Helena was Jewish might reflect her Eastern origins.
5 Eusebius, *History*, VIII. 13.
6 Lanctantius Firminus, 'On the Deaths of the Persecutors', in *The Ante-Nicene Fathers*, ed Alexander Roberts and James Donaldson, Buffalo, USA 1886.
7 Eusebius, *Life*, III. 47.
8 Alistair Kee, *Constantine versus Christ*, SCM 1982.
9 Eusebius, *Life*, I. 31.
10 Grant (Chapter VI, note 8) dismisses this story as fictitious, invented by the panegyrist in the hope that a temple in his own town would receive aid from the emperor. However, he goes on to acknowledge that since the story was believed, the association with the sun-god didn't do Constantine any harm.
11 See Grant (Chapter VI, note 8).
12 See Grant (Chapter VI, note 8).
13 See *Catholic Encyclopaedia* (Chapter II, note 1), entry on altars. Christians face towards the East, not towards Jerusalem, unlike the Muslim convention that the faithful should pray towards Mecca. The bishop speaking *ex cathedra* literally means 'from the easy chair' – see *Dictionary of Christian Antiquities*, ed William Smith and Samuel Cheetham, London 1875; also *Dictionary of Christian Biography, Literature, Sects and Doctrines*, ed Henry Wace and William Smith, London 1880.
14 Michele Basso, *Guide to the Vatican Necropolis*, Rome 1986.

15 St Peter's originally held only three relics: Veronica's veil, St Andrew's skull, and the head of the lance that pierced Jesus' side on the cross. An eyewitness reported these items were being passed from hand to hand in the taverns after the sack of Rome in 1527. With order restored, a piece of the True Cross was subsequently transferred from the church of Santa Croce in Gerusalemme by Urban VIII in April 1629. The four pillars were adapted to house the four relics, with an altar at the base and a balcony so high above the congregation it would be difficult to discern the details of anything displayed from it. See Ian Wilson, *Holy Faces, Secret Places*, London 1991.

16 Dismas and Gestes were first named in the apocryphal third-century *Acts of Pilate*, also known as the *Gospel of Nicodemus* after the disciple who accompanied Joseph of Arimathea and helped embalm the body of Jesus.

17 Ambrose, see Chapter II, note 20.

18 G M Lee, 'The Inscriptions on the Cross', *Palestine Exploration Quarterly*, Jul–Dec 1968. Matthew 27.37; Mark 15.26; Luke 23.38; John 19.19–22.

19 Quoted in Thurston, see Chapter II, note 6. This view is echoed in William Cowper Prime, see Chapter I, note 1.

20 Carsten Peter Thiede and Matthew D'Ancona, *The Quest for the True Cross*, London 2000.

21 Wilkinson, *Egeria's Travels*, see Prologue, note 18.

22 Quoted by Thurston, see Chapter II, note 6.

23 P. Heinrich Drenkelfort, *The Basilica of the Holy Cross in Jerusalem*, Rome 1997. See also D Balduino Bedini, *Le Reliquie della Passione de Signore*, Rome 1987.

24 The notion that the True Cross was distinguished from the other two pieces of wood found on the site of the crucifixion by the expedient of laying a sick woman on all three, and seeing which one caused her to recover, was first put forward in a fifth-century Syrian manuscript now in the British Museum. The discovery was attributed to Protonice, a wife of the first-century Emperor Claudius, though no such historical person existed and indeed the Greek *proto nike* means 'first victory' and is thus obviously a made-up name. Voraigne's version of the story has Helena threatening the Jewish elders with torture unless they hand over a scholar called Judas who knew the location of the crucifixion: after seven days down a well he agreed to show her the site. He found three crosses and held them over the body of a young man from a passing funeral cortege, at which the corpse promptly came to life. The *Legenda Aurea* also recounts how Constantine challenged Helena to bring back to Rome the leading men of the Jews 'whom he would confront with the Christian doctors so as to bring out the true faith by mutual discussion.'

25 See Lancelot Sheppard, *The Saints Who Never Were*, USA 1969.

26 The Rev W H Withrow, *Catacombs of Rome*, London 1888. The dedication of the fourth-century basilica of Saints Peter and Marcellinus was one of the first acknowledgements in the city of the conversion to Christianity. See also Augustus Hare, *Walks in Rome*, 1897.

27 Fabrizio Mancinelli, *The Catacombs of Rome and the Origins of Christianity*, Florence 1981.

28 Even the official guidebook admitted that the Helena link was a mediaeval

tradition 'not as yet adequately documented.' The Scala Sancta is first mentioned in the *Liber Pontificalis* of the ninth-century Pope Sergius, about a hundred years after earlier versions of the papal books first record either the Sancta Sanctorum or the Acheropite image. See *The Holy Staircase – its history and devotion*, Rome 1994.

29 Eusebius, *Life*, III. 46.

30 Socrates Scholasticus, in his fifth-century *Sacred History*, said Helena's remains were 'conveyed to new Rome, the capital, and deposited in the imperial sepulchres.' *Select Library of the Nicene Fathers*, Vol II, 1891.

31 The identification was based on the likeness to Helena's coinage, which shows a combination of sleek-combed hair, a knot in the middle of the head, a diadem and visible ears. Drivjers (Chapter II, note 23) says there is another bust in the Palazza del Governatoro inside the Vatican.

Chapter VIII: Constantinople

1 Emperor Alexius I Comnenus, letter to Robert, Count of Flanders, 1095; quoted in Laurence Kelly, *Istanbul: a travellers' companion*, London 1987.

2 *Sant'Elena – un'Isola, un Monastero, una Comunita*, Provincia de Venezia 2003.

3 See John Freely, *Blue Guide Istanbul*, London 1997.

4 See John Freely, *Istanbul – the Imperial City*, London 1996.

5 See John Julius Norwich, *Byzantium – the Early Centuries*, London 1998.

6 *Epitome of the Ecclesiastical History of Philostorgius*, compiled by Photius, Patriarch of Constantinople, trans Edward Walford, Bohn's Ecclesiastical Library, London 1855.

7 Eusebius, *Life*, IV. 60.

8 *Stavros* means cross.

9 Paul's shipwreck is described in Acts 27.

10 Eusebius, *Life*, III. 44.

11 Constantine was actually baptised (naked as was the custom) by Eusebius of Nicomedia. Since the bishop was heavily involved in the Arian controversy, the church subsequently invented a story about the baptism being conducted by Pope Sylvester, who unfortunately had been dead for several years. See Grant (Chapter VI, note 8).

12 Eusebius, *Life*, IV. 61.

13 Procopius of Caesarea, *The Buildings*, trans H B Dewing, Loeb Classical Library, London 1940.

14 Photius, see note 6.

15 The other Eusebius, bishop of Nicomedia,was a pupil of Lucian, and himself influential with the imperial family, particularly Constantine's stepsister Constantia. See Chapter IX, note 13.

16 There are still natural hot springs to be found today at the spa resort of Termal, in the hills west of the Yalova ferry dock.

17 William Leake, *Journal of a Tour in Asia Minor*, London 1824.

Chapter IX: The Pilgrims' Road

1 Theodoretus, *Church History*, in *Select Library of the Nicene Fathers*, Vol III, 1892.
2 Quoted in Norwich, see Chapter VIII, note 5.
3 John 1.1.
4 According to Norwich, see Chapter VIII, note 5.
5 Quoted in Grant, see Chapter VI, note 8.
6 See Chadwick (Chapter II, note 15).
7 Eusebius, *Life*, III. 25.
8 Eusebius, *Life*, III. 41. The conventional reading of this passage is that it signals Helena was responsible for the discoveries. Eusebius' biography has traditionally been regarded with scepticism by scholars because it is so obviously a work of flattery, and therefore not to be taken literally. In it, Constantine does everything himself – from demanding a church be built on the site of the resurrection, to discovering the sites of the nativity and ascension. According to the *Life*, Helena simply turned up later to dedicate churches on these latter sites. Now, we know Constantine couldn't do all this personally because he wasn't there; while we are also told that Helena definitely did go there. Nevertheless, it is also possible that Constantine did the ordering and someone else put his instructions into effect, with Helena turning up later. On a strict reading of this particular passage, it is possible that all Eusebius meant was that Helena was responsible because she was Constantine's mother and the instrument for bringing him into the world. In other words, the valuable benefit she conferred on mankind was giving birth to the subject of this eulogy.
9 Quoted in Hunt, see Prologue, note 4.
10 Eusebius, *Life*, III. 42.
11 The Bordeaux pilgrim's route is described in *Itinerarium Burdigalense*, trans Aubrey Stewart, Palestinian Pilgrims Text Society, London 1896.
12 William Ramsay, *Historical Geography of Asia Minor*. London 1890.
13 Chadwick, see Chapter II, note 15. Eustatius, or Eustace, was the victim of a plot by the pro-Arian bishop Eusebius of Nicomedia, who intervened in an animated doctrinal dispute that Eustatius was having with his namesake, Eusebius of Caesarea. The charge he levelled of slandering Helena's reputation became caught up with the legend that Helena was devoted to the memory of Lucian the martyr – possibly because Eusebius of Nicomedia was the pupil of Lucian.
14 This Oriental tradition is noted by Prime (Chapter I, note 1). According to the eighth-century nun Hugebure, who wrote a life of Willibald, an English monk who travelled in the East, Helena built a church at Emesa, near Tartus, on the road to Damascus. Quoted in Wilkinson, *Egeria's Travels* (Prologue, note 18).
15 Eusebius, *History*, IV. 7.
16 Christopher de Hamel, *The Book: A History of the Bible*, Phaidon 2001.
17 See Bruce Metzger, *The Canon of the New Testament*, Oxford 1987.
18 Quoted in Elaine Pagels, *The Gnostic Gospels*, USA 1979.
19 Surah IV:157 in *The Koran*, trans N J Dawood, Penguin Classics 1956. Jesus is regarded by Muslims as a great prophet, second in importance to Muhammad.

He is mentioned 25 times in the Koran, and although credited as a miracle-worker of virgin birth, is not seen as divine. *The Wordsworth Dictionary of Beliefs and Religions*, 1995.

20 Metzger, see note 17.

21 Acts 8.9–24.

22 Eusebius, *History*, II. 13. Eusebius here relies heavily on the denunciations of Simon Magus in works by earlier church fathers, particularly Justin Martyr (*Apologies*) and Irenaeus (*Against Heresies*).

23 Eusebius, *History*, III. 26 on Menander; IV. 7 on Basilides.

24 Quoted in Eusebius, *History*, IV. 22.

25 Epiphanius, *Against Heresies*, trans Frank Williams, 1987.

26 In portraying Helena as a role model for Christian piety, Drivjers sees the discovery of the cross in conventional terms as a symbol of victory over pagans and/or the Jews. He argues that the defeat of paganism in the fourth century created a need for a greater differentiation between Christianity and Judaism in the fifth century.

27 Mark 15.40; Luke 24.4; Matthew 28.9; John 20.1–18.

28 Susan Haskins, *Mary Magdalen*, London 1993.

29 Quoted in Pagels, see note 18.

30 The fascinating hypothesis that Jesus was married to Mary and had a child, the existence of whom became secret knowledge transmitted down the centuries, has become a popular sub-culture of its own since Michael Baigent, Richard Leigh and Henry Lincoln first published *The Holy Blood and the Holy Grail* in 1982. One recent version traces the hidden lineage of Jesus to the surviving members of the dethroned royal house of Stewart; see Laurence Gardner, *Bloodline of the Holy Grail*, London 1996.

31 Corinthians 14.34–35. Paul's target in his letters to both the Corinthians and the Colossians are the adherents of early gnostic heresies. See Chadwick (Chapter II, note 15).

32 When Paula finally reached Jerusalem she let go all inhibitions: 'Before the cross she threw herself down in adoration, as though she beheld the Lord hanging upon it, and when she entered the tomb which was the scene of the resurrection she kissed the stone which the angel had rolled away from the door of the sepulchre. Indeed, so ardent was her faith that she even licked with her mouth the very spot on which the Lord's body had lain, like one athirst for the river which he has longed for. What tears she shed there, what groans she uttered, and what grief she poured forth all Jerusalen knew.' Jerome, *Letters*, in *Select Library of the Nicene Fathers*, Vol VI, 1893.

33 Deborah F Sawyer, *Women and Religion in the First Christian Centuries*, London 1996.

34 I Timothy 2.9–12. 'Also that the women should dress themselves modestly and decently in suitable clothing, not with their hair braided, or with gold, pearls or expensive clothes, but with good works, as is proper for women who profess reverence for God. Let a woman learn in silence with full submission. I permit no woman to teach or have authority over a man: she is to keep silent.'

35 Quoted by Pagels, see note 18.

Chapter X: Palestine

1 Colin Brewer, 'Cross Purposes', article in *New Humanist* magazine no 94, Summer 1978.
2 See A N Wilson, *Jesus*, London 1993, and the same author's *Paul – the Mind of the Apostle*, London 1998.
3 John 20.31.
4 See Lane Fox (Prologue, note 5).
5 John 21.24.
6 Acts 2.44–46.
7 Cited in Morton Smith, *Jesus the Magician*, London 1978.
8 Acts 18.18.
9 Matthew 2.23.
10 Mark 14.67 and 16.6.
11 Epiphanius, writing the *Panarion* as late as 375, identified the Nazoreans as one of the gnostic groups who falsely called themselves Christian, alongside the Ebionites and the Essenes. He said the sect of the Nazoreans started when all the disciples were living in Pella, across the Jordan, after the fall of Jerusalem. 'Now at that time all Christians alike were called Nazoreans, although for a short time they were also called Jessaeans before the disciples were called Christians at Antioch.'
12 Acts 24.5. Paul conducts a spirited defence of his version of Christianity against the protagonists of The Way, but the author of Acts describes Felix as 'having more exact knowledge concerning the way' and the governor keeps Paul in custody.
13 See A N Wilson, *Jesus* (note 2).
14 Matthew 27.37: 'And they set over his head his accusation written, THIS IS THE KING OF THE JEWS'. See Colin Cross, *Who was Jesus?* 1970.
15 John 20.25.
16 Luke 24.39.
17 Psalm 22 starts with the cry 'My God, my God, why has thou forsaken me?' and goes on to paint a pitiable picture of human helplessness, some of whose imagery (but not all) is taken up in the crucifixion story:

> The assembly of evil doers have enclosed me;
> They pierced my hands and my feet;
> I may tell all my bones;
> They look and stare at me;
> They part my garments among them;
> And upon my vesture do they cast losts.

18 Colossians 2.14.
19 Acts 13.28: 'And when they had fulfilled all things that were written of him, they took him down from the tree, and laid him in a tomb.'
20 William D Edwards, Wesley Gabel and Floyd Hosmer, 'On the Physical Death of Jesus Christ', *Journal of the American Medical Association*, March 1986.
21 Frederick T Zugibe, *A Medical Examiner Investigates the Crucifixion*, New York 1982.

22 N Haas, 'Anthropological observations on the skeletal remains from Giv'at Ha-Mivtar', *Israel Exploration Journal* 20, 1970. Reviewed by Zias and Sekeles, *Israel Exploration Journal*, 1985.
23 John 19.33–34. Longinus means spear-carrier. The name first appears in the apochryphal *Acts of Pilate*, thought to be a third-century Christian response to a pagan forgery, the *Memoranda* of Pilate. Eusebius mentions the *Acts* in his *History* (IX. 5) as being recently published in order to blacken the name of the Saviour.
24 John 19.36–37, referring to Zechariah 12.10 and Exodus 12.46.
25 Mark 15.44. 'And Pilate marvelled that he was already dead.'
26 Matthew 27.45; Mark 15.33; Luke 23.44. John 19.14 says it was 'about the sixth hour' when Pilate's verdict was delivered. Josef Blinzler, *The Trial of Jesus*, Westminster 1959, reconstructs the chronology of the day from Peter's denial at cockcrow in order to suggest that Jesus was crucified at noon (the sixth hour after dawn), died around 3 pm (the ninth hour), and was buried before sunset (6 pm) in accordance with Jewish tradition. There is an alternative tradition that Jesus died on 7th April AD 30.
27 John 19.29 and Luke 23.36. Matthew 27.34 records the offer of wine mingled with gall (which Jesus tasted but did not drink) separate from the later offer of vinegar on a sponge (27.48), as does Mark (15.23 and 15.36) though for him the wine was mingled with myrrh.
28 Matthew 27.46 and Mark 15.34: see note 17. Luke 23.46 and John 19.30. For the psalm references, see J K Elliott, 'The Trials and Death of Jesus', *History Today* 30, April 1980.
29 Hugh Sconfield, *The Passover Plot*, London 1965, noted that in Mark 15.43–45, Joseph of Arimathea asked for the body of Jesus (*soma*) while Pilate referred to his corpse (*ptoma*). Schonfield argued that Jesus believed he was the Messiah, and orchestrated the events of his last days to fulfill the scriptures. 'His whole ministry was purposeful, masterful and practical. He plotted and schemed with the utmost skill and resourcefulness, sometimes making secret arrangements, taking advantage of every circumstance conducive to the attainment of his objectives. It is difficult to credit that he had neglected to do anything about the extreme crisis of his career, when it was imperative that he should outwit the forces arrayed against him and wrest victory from the very jaws of death.'
30 Matthew 28.11–15.
31 I Corinthians 15.14.
32 Morton Smith (note 7) argued that Jesus was a professional miracle worker whose 'act' paid for the travelling company. He was mobbed by the multitude as a healer of the sick, but feared by the authorities for his hold over the mob. The Christian faith was the product of 'the pyschological inability of Jesus' followers to accept his death, their subconscious resistance to it, and the hallucinations this resistance provoked in them.'
33 John 20.17 and Luke 24.39.
34 Acts 1.15–22. 'And the lot fell on Matthias, and he was numbered among the eleven apostles.'
35 For example, that Jesus was a mortal Essene priest who married and was

divorced (Barbara Thiering, *Jesus the Man*, 1992); an Egyptian sorcerer-priest teaching esoteric secrets (Lynn Pickett and Clive Prince, *The Templar Revelation*, 1997); or an imaginary pagan mystery God who had no earthly existence (Timothy Freke and Peter Gandy, *The Jesus Mysteries*, 1999).

36 II Peter 1.16.

37 I Corinthians 15.8.

Epilogue: Jerusalem

1 William Cowper Prime, see Chapter I, note 1.

2 The descriptions in this chapter first apppeared in a travel article, 'Pilgrims and Playboys', in *The Daily Telegraph*, 3rd April 1999. The visit it referred to took place the previous Easter.

3 'Of the whole of the Church of the Holy Sepulchre as it is today, this is by far the most impressive part. Away from the flood of tourists, dimly lit, nothing else in this heterogenous church is more conducive to meditation.' André Parrot, *Golgotha and the Church of the Holy Sepulchre*, Studies in Biblical Archaeology 6, SCM Press 1957.

4 See Murphy-O'Connor (Prologue, note 9).

5 Luke 23.27–28. 'Jesus turning unto them said, Daughters of Jerusalem, weep not for me, but weep for yourselves, and for your children.'

6 The Veronica legend was a staple of the mediaeval mystery plays but it had a complicated history of its own. Tradition held that the woman 'with an issue of blood' whom Jesus healed during his Galilee ministry (Mark 5.25–34, Matthew 9.20–22, Luke 8.43–48) was called Berenice, or in its Latinised form, Veronica. In his *History*, Eusebius recalled seeing a bronze statue of the woman (and indeed of Jesus himself in the act of healing) in the town of Caesarea Philippi, whence she was thought to hail. She was first named in the third-century forgery known as the *Acts of Pilate*. 'And a certain woman named Veronica said: I was afflicted with an issue of blood twelve years, and I touched the hem of his garments, and presently the issue of my blood stopped.' Over subsequent centuries the legend developed, first that Veronica had a portrait of Jesus which could heal the sick, and then that her cloth was an actual imprint of Jesus' features. See Ian Wilson (Chapter VII, note 15).

7 André Parrot, *The Temple of Jerusalem*, Studies in Biblical Archaeology 5, SCM Press 1957.

8 John 19.17.

9 Stewart, see Chapter IX, note 11.

10 Gibbon, see Chapter III, note 16.

11 The ultra-rationalist Drivjers concludes: 'Although the founding of churches by Helena in Palestine is a recurring theme in historically-unreliable late-antique and mediaeval legendry, it seems that no churches were in fact built on Helena's initiative.' (see Chapter II, note 23).

12 Quoted in Wilkinson, *Egeria's Travels* (Prologue, note 18). See Epilogue note 19 for an alternative translation.

13 See Martin Biddle, *The Tomb of Christ*, Stroud 1999.
14 Quoted in Wilkinson, *Egeria's Travels* (Prologue, note 18).
15 Eusebius, *Life*, III. 31–39.
16 H A Drake, 'Eusebius on the True Cross', *Journal of Ecclesiastical History* 36, 1985.
17 Eusebius, *In Praise of Constantine*, trans H A Drake, Berkeley 1976.
18 P W L Walker, *Holy City, Holy Places – Christian Attitudes to Jerusalem and the Holy Land in the 4th Century*, Oxford 1990.
19 Eusebius, *Life*, III. 25.
20 Quoted in Walker (note 18). Egeria carried a Latin translation of the *Onomasticon* when she travelled to Palestine in 384. However, this gazeteer of Biblical place-names was written before 324 because there is no mention of Constantine's buildings in the Holy Land. Some scholars believe it was even written before the *History*, which was first compiled in 316, after the defeat of Maximian and the promulgation of the edict of toleration.
21 Eusebius, *Life*, III. 28.
22 Joan Taylor, 'Helena and the Finding of the Cross', *Bulletin of the Anglo-Israel Archaelogical Society* 12, 1992/3.
23 Eusebius, *Life*, III. 30.
24 Private correspondence with Fr Michele Piccirillo of the Studium Biblicum Franciscanum, Jerusalem.
25 Quoted in Wilkinson, *Egeria's Travels*, see Prologue, note 18.
26 Luke 24.51 and Acts 1.9.
27 Parrot, *Golgotha*, see note 3.
28 *The Garden Tomb and Resurrection Garden*, published by The Garden Tomb (Jerusalem) Association, 1996. The smaller and more home-spun guidebook available on my earlier visit, six years previously, reproduced half a dozen Victorian photos of the site.

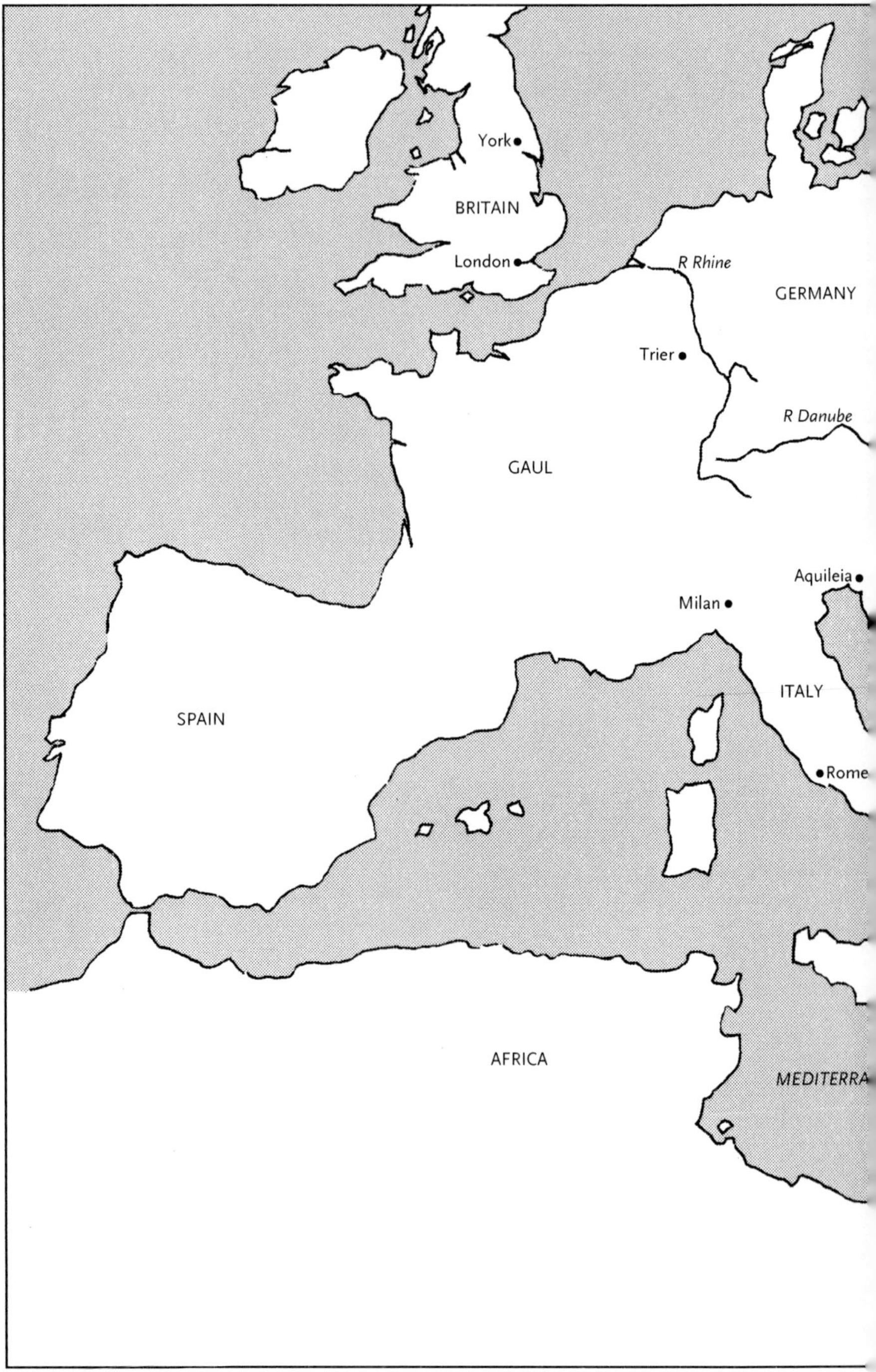
York
BRITAIN
London
R Rhine
GERMANY
Trier
R Danube
GAUL
Aquileia
Milan
ITALY
SPAIN
Rome
AFRICA
MEDITERRA